GREAT ADVENTURES IN FOOD

GREAT ADVENTURES IN FOOD

FRESH WAYS TO CELEBRATE EVERY MEAL

ELLEN HAAS

Original Recipes and Recipe Development by Bonnie Moore

St. Martin's Press
New York

Design by Jennifer Muller and Amy Goldfarb/Red Herring Design

ISBN 1-58238-037-6

First Edition: December 1999

10 9 8 7 6 5 4 3 2 1

To Lisa and Jason, whose laughter and love I cherish

CONTENTS

AcKNOWLEDGmENTS

Writing this book has been an amazing—and truly different—experience for me. Having spent my career representing consumers in very vocal ways, it was a tremendous change to finally sit down and write about all these things that I believe in. Though I had often dreamed of writing this book, I never really thought it would happen. It did happen because so many wonderful people gave me so much of their time, knowledge, and experience throughout this process. The enthusiasm and encouragement that I received from family, friends, and colleagues kept me going right to the end.

Special thanks go to many talented, generous individuals who provided invaluable contributions to this challenging undertaking:

First, my mother inspired me to enjoy all the wonders of food and family. She shows me how important nurturing and nourishment are to a healthy life. Not only does she provide an incredible role model, but she shared many wonderful ideas, delicious food commentary, and even editorial advice. I deeply appreciate all the insights she provided for this book—and how much she always gives to me personally.

Bonnie Moore tirelessly and magically worked with me throughout the project, continuously adding her spectacular culinary talents and knowledge. As both a chef (she has been the sous-chef at the Inn at Little Washington in Washington, Virginia) and chef instructor (at L'Academie de Cuisine in Gaithersburg, Maryland) and now Executive Chef and Culinary Director of Foodfit.com, she combined her exquisite taste and heartfelt commitment to this effort with a sensitivity to the health considerations that are essential to this book. Bonnie cheerfully spent endless hours with me working on the book and developed these delicious recipes and menus. I cannot thank her enough for her incredible contribution—and friendship.

Linda Smith, a uniquely talented nutritionist, graciously shared her fresh perspective on how to convey nutrition information. Linda took complex ideas about food, cooking, nutrition, health, and culture and blended them in ways I've never seen before. Her insights enhance the book immensely. Barbara Blessi skillfully provided nutritional analysis for the recipes, and she enthusiastically contributed additional information on nutrition.

When I started to write, I reached out to chefs across the country to gather their ideas about how families could enjoy healthy food that also tasted great. These conversations were invaluable to me and provided the foundation for the book. These talented individuals spent hours sharing their passionate ideas and practical tips for making this total food experience come alive. My gratitude goes to Rick Bayless, Todd English, Susan Feniger, Michael Foley, Joyce Goldstein, Bob Kinkead, Michael Lomonaco, Mark Miller, Mary Sue Milliken, Patrick O'Connell, Nora

Pouillon, Eric Ripert, Michael Romano, Anne Rosenzweig, Nancy Silverton, Annie Somerville, Gordon Sinclair, Susan Spicer, Allen Susser, Charlie Trotter, and Alice Waters.

Other people also contributed in special ways. My dear friend, the noted author Susan Richards Shreve, was always there to share her writing experiences and to provide steady encouragement to me as a new writer. Her thoughtful guidance and helpful insights were invaluable. Best of all, her friendship made it a fulfilling experience. Ellen Jacob brought her tremendous creative energy to the early conceptual discussions about the book; Christy Zink provided intelligent editorial assistance, especially in those early days when her skillful response and encouragement mattered so much; Marion Nestle, a respected nutrition leader and nutrition chair at New York University, reviewed the manuscript for nutritional accuracy with her critical eye; Joyce Goldstein, nationally recognized chef, cookbook author, and consultant, graciously reviewed the introductory cooking narrative and gave her experienced perspective; Patty Morris, nutritionist and children's nutrition educator, reviewed the manuscript with a special focus on family fun and nutrition, and her engaging ideas were tremendously helpful throughout the process; and Terri Lehman brought her experience as a produce buyer and vegetable grower to her careful review of the seasonal guides.

Thanks to the many others who shared their thoughts and offered many useful suggestions, in particular Catherine Brandel, Odonna Matthews, Janet Tenney, Greg Drescher, Jason Haas, Lisa Haas, Chris Hitt, Patricia Kelly, John Burns, Sue Borra, Rick Frank, Dr. Ann-Marie Gebhart, Dr. Sol Katz, Michael Jacobson, Naomi Kulakow, Marissa Rothkopf, Maris Siegal-Goodis, Will Weaver, Bob Weinberger, and Dr. Catherine Wotecki. And thanks to Earl Wood, who provided critical computer assistance.

I am most grateful to the many friends and colleagues who tasted and tested all these recipes and offered their suggestions and critiques. It was great fun to share delicious food with so many wonderful people at tasting dinners at my home and theirs. To the Foodfit.com team, who expressed such delight at the marvelous dinners Bonnie Moore prepared: Thanks for your support and understanding about how much time and effort it took to produce the book.

Thanks to my talented and supportive editor Cassie Jones. I truly appreciate her intelligence, patience, and warmth. I could not have completed this book without her incredibly positive energy, invaluable editorial suggestions, and encouragement. Her delight in this project from the outset meant a lot to me. Also, I am very grateful for the marvelous encouragement and intelligent perspective of my wonderful editor at St. Martin's, Marian Lizzi.

A special thanks to Marissa Rothkopf and Bonnie Moore for the special care and incredible attention they gave to the final edits of the manuscript.

And thanks to my agent and wonderful friend Timothy Seldes, who for years believed that I could write this book and with his charm and wit convinced me to do it. I am truly thankful for his never-ending support and wise guidance.

INTRODUCTION

Food can connect us to so many important things in life: health, taste, family, nature. *Great Adventures in Food* takes you to the two places where this connection is made—at the market, where there is an exciting array of delicious, healthy foods to add to your basket, and at home, where family and friends can share the pleasure of the meal and have fun together.

For more than twenty years my life has focused on promoting healthy food and nutrition. When I began my activism in the 1970s, I simply wanted the best for my children, Lisa and Jason. In 1973 I invited a few neighbors to start a local consumer group, the Maryland Citizens Consumer Council. Ten of us met in my basement family room to discuss the skyrocketing prices of food and the declining nutritional value of many advertised foods. We also wanted to organize to improve the quality of the school lunches that were served to our children. This experience in community action laid the foundation of my life's work. I went on to fight for new laws that required nutrition labels on all food products, improved seafood safety, and reformed the national school lunch program in my role as head of Public Voice for Food and Health Policy.

My biggest chance to make a difference came in 1993 when President Bill Clinton appointed me to head the nutrition programs at the United States Department of Agriculture, a government agency that was until then known more for caring about cows than children. For the first time in the fifty-year history of the school lunch program, the nutritional standards were updated and improved. I am proud that now schoolchildren eat healthier lunches that meet the United States Dietary Guidelines. Plus, hundreds of chefs contributed their talents so that these healthier lunches taste better, too.

In 1995, First Lady Hillary Rodham Clinton joined us at the Department of Agriculture to launch a new program, Team Nutrition, which provided nutrition education to children and training for school food service staff. This successful campaign promotes healthy food choices and, in so doing, changed the role of government.

I realized that I wanted to do even more to bring these ideas to a wide audience, and after four fulfilling years at the USDA, I decided to leave government service so that I could share my enthusiasm for healthy, seasonal food and active living. That is what this book is all about.

It is well known that our dietary choices strongly affect our health and longevity. In fact, three of the four leading causes of death are diet-related. Children's eating patterns are formed by the time they are twelve, and as they grow older, these patterns become harder and harder to change. Research shows that the younger children are, the more likely they will respond to nutritional messages.

But we shouldn't approach eating as if it were homework; food is also the most basic expression of nurturing. My mother, Ethel Weinberger, always cooked from her heart. When I was growing up in Forest Hills, New York, my father, my brother Michael, and I felt her love every day through the meals she served. I have tried to recreate that special feeling through the foods I've prepared for my own family.

When I first got married and moved to Oklahoma City, my mother thought I was going a world away. She worried about how I would survive in the kitchen, so she gave me a special present. It was a little three-ring notebook that she had titled *Home Cooking*. It was filled with recipes for all kinds of foods that she said would make us happy. There was her way of making chicken soup (which is found on page 163), roasted chicken, and spaghetti with meatballs. But what I will never forget is the opening sentence of the book: "Always remember, the first thing you do when you go into the kitchen...*wash your hands*." That is still good advice today.

The many warm, happy moments shared at the table when Lisa and Jason were growing up made each day special. The understanding of how much these personal food experiences mean to each of us contributed to my movement beyond school lunches and government programs to sharing the delight of cooking and serving great, healthy food at home. It is my hope that *Great Adventures in Food* gives you what you need to get started on your own great adventure.

Part I: Fresh Choices at the Market is filled with the tools and nutrition information you need to select a wide variety of foods that promote both good health and good taste. Easy-to-use charts and tips help you select the freshest, best-tasting fruits and vegetables through the seasons and explore how different kinds of grains and beans add variety and nutrition to your family meals.

Part II: Cooking Adventures at Home shares simple secrets to cook family meals that everyone will love, with more than one hundred recipes, menus, tips, and techniques to inspire you. Bonnie Moore, a gifted chef and culinary teacher, worked closely with me to develop the recipes and made suggestions for easily preparing fantastic, healthy meals at home. The recipes feature lots of fruits, vegetables, and grains along with other healthy ingredients to achieve the variety and balance that is so important. Nutritional analysis for each recipe is provided.

Twenty award-winning chefs also share their personal insights about food and cooking at home, as well as some great recipes. I have known and worked with most of these chefs and deeply respect their passion about food, family, and community.

Use the sidebars throughout the book to find helpful tips, quick ideas, and useful information on how to grow herb gardens, find new varieties of vegetables at the farmer's market, or enjoy a family hike and picnic lunch. Here is a key to the kind of information you'll find:

Nutrition Power Points

Foods that carry a nutritional punch to help everyone perform at his or her best.

Healthy Time-Savers

Shortcuts and surprising techniques that highlight flavor and good health.

Tips and Trivia

Facts and fables about where food comes from, and tips for making it easy to prepare and delicious.

For Safekeeping

Reminders for practicing food safety and avoiding foodborne illness.

Family Fun

Food and fitness ideas for active families.

Finally, it is at the table that families come together and make memories that will last a lifetime. Alice Waters, the chef and owner of Chez Panisse in Berkeley, California, underscored the importance of eating together in a letter to President Bill Clinton on December 9, 1995: "I am convinced that food can again be, as it once was, the everyday vehicle for learning mutual responsibility. Families who eat together pass on values such as courtesy, kindness, generosity, thrift, respect, and reverence for the goodness of nature."

I hope that this book will inspire you to renew this important tradition. Enjoy your adventure of celebrating food in all its dimensions; there is so much we can do today to ensure a healthy future for our families. Treasure these good times and great food!

PART 1

FRESH

CHOICES AT THE

MARKET

CHAPTER 1

FOOD SHOPPING FOR HEALTH

Family food shopping takes a new turn when you link it with healthy living. Shopping can become an adventure as you discover an abundance of new foods and taste experiences. Bringing all kinds of different delicious foods to your kitchen not only introduces your family to new flavors, but also provides a variety of foods to help everyone get the necessary nutrients for good health.

Walking down a supermarket aisle in search of healthy food choices is not always an easy task. Too often the grocery shelves are more confusing than accessible. And the messages on the boxes, packages, and jars seem to add to the confusion. What has been lost is the simple understanding of how to shop for food in a way that promotes the health of those we care most about.

As all parents know, finding the way to balance priorities among family, friends, and work is quite a challenge. After all, doing the family food shopping is really a balancing act because several factors must be considered:

- health concerns
- cost
- convenience
- ease of preparation
- flavor

Balancing these five factors does not have to be mission impossible. Before starting to aisle-hop for health, it is worthwhile to step back and look at what is important and why.

Linking Food and Health

What is a healthy diet? There seems to be so much conflicting information in the news, and you probably wonder who and what to believe. The *Dietary Guidelines for Americans,* updated in 1995, is the best place to begin. It is information you can count on.

After twenty-five years of careful scientific research, the *Dietary Guidelines for Americans* was first drafted in 1980 by the United States Departments of Agriculture and Health and Human Services. These seven guidelines provide the most up-to-date advice from nutrition experts and form the basis of federal nutrition policy.

Looking for healthy, good food may seem like difficult detective work. It need not be. You will be prepared for the task when you use the Three Rules for Healthy Eating and the Food Guide Pyramid and the Nutrition Facts Label, which take the guesswork

NUTRITION POWER POINTS
Dietary Guidelines for Americans

- Eat a variety of foods.
- Balance the food you eat with physical activity—maintain or improve your weight.
- Choose a diet with plenty of grain products, vegetables, and fruits.
- Choose a diet low in fat, saturated fat, and cholesterol.
- Choose a diet moderate in sugars.
- Choose a diet moderate in salt and sodium.
- If you drink alcoholic beverages, do so in moderation.

U.S. Department of Agriculture and U.S. Department of Health and Human Services, 4th Ed., 1995.

out of making healthy food choices. With these as your guides, planning healthy, delicious family menus becomes much easier. Remember, you are in control, and your choices mean a lot to your family.

Three Rules for Healthy Eating
1. Expand the variety of foods in your diet.

The old saying "variety is the spice of life" still rings true today. It sparks our interest and heightens our enjoyment. By eating many different foods, we

What Are We Eating?

Are Americans adventurous eaters? According to USDA studies, not very. Consider this:

- **Five foods—canned tomatoes, fresh and frozen potatoes (excluding potato chips), head lettuce (excluding leafy lettuce), and onions—accounted for about one-half of the total vegetable consumption in 1994.**

- **Six foods—orange juice, bananas, grapes, fresh apples, apple juice, and watermelon—accounted for one-half of the fruit consumption in 1994.**

increase the chances of getting the forty-plus nutrients we need to be healthy. The carbohydrates, protein, vitamins, minerals and fiber you need for good health are most available when they come from a variety of foods. No single food can supply them all.

Food shopping becomes a new experience when you are open to the myriad foods in the modern market. Steer your cart in the right direction by varying your fruit and vegetable choices and get the benefits from different nutrients. For example, oranges, grapefruits, and salad greens offer vitamins A and C and provide needed folic acid, but in different amounts. So try mixing and matching when shopping

and start combining foods in new and tasty ways.

Eating is a sensory experience, and its pleasures increase with the amount of variety in our diets. Let everyone in the family use his or her tastebuds and help build the family food repertoire. At the table, talk about new foods in the market and get suggestions from everyone about things they might want to try. Get new ideas from friends, books, magazines, and the Internet.

Here are some easy ways to give variety and zip to your meals:

- Turn everyday salads into something special. Add quick-cooking grains such as quinoa and couscous. Throw in a few grilled shrimp or chunks of chicken. Add color by shredding purple cabbage on top. Feta and goat cheese also make wonderful salad toppings.

- Explore different ethnic vegetables such as bok choy, bean sprouts, and snow peas; or enjoy Indian seasonings such as coriander, cardamom, and curries. (For more on World-Class Flavors, see page 118).

- Breakfast becomes brighter when you combine ingredients in unexpected ways. Serve fruit juice blends such as orange and tangerine (see page 64) or grapefruit and cranberry. My daughter, Lisa, says her breakfast of cottage cheese, sliced pineapple, and slivered almonds puts her in a cheery mood before she goes off to work.

- Combine chicken with dried apricots, or pork chops with apples, for sweet taste treats. When you add a legume such as white beans or lentils to these dishes, you also add powerful nutrients.

2. Add more fruits, vegetables, and grains to the foods you already eat.

Most of us know that eating plenty of fruits, vegetables, and grains is good for us. But the plain fact is that we are just not doing it. Consider these facts from USDA studies:

- 35 percent of elementary school children and 60 percent of teenagers eat no fruit on an average day.
- 25 percent of school-age children eat no vegetables on an average day.
- Fewer than 20 percent of Americans eat the recommended number of daily total grain servings.
- The average vegetable servings for Americans are about 80 percent of the Food Guide Pyramid recommendations (see page 11), but include little variety.
- Americans eat only about half of the recommended daily total fruit intake.

But there are some promising signs on the horizon: American families are starting to get the message, and eating patterns are changing. For example, the USDA reports that Americans now eat nearly one and a half times more grain products and a fifth more fruits and vegetables than they did in 1970. Keeping the trend going in this direction will reap real health rewards.

The health advantages of eating more fruits, vegetables, and grains are many. A prime benefit is the fiber you get in a diet that is high in complex carbohydrates. Fiber helps digestion and may protect against certain types of cancer and heart disease. Both forms of fiber, soluble (in water) and insoluble, are important for overall health. Carrots, kidney

---

NUTRITION POWER POINTS
Family Energy Boosters

Carbohydrates, found in grains, fruits, and vegetables, are the key nutrients for providing energy. Your body transforms these power foods into glucose, which is necessary for thinking and moving any body part. Carbohydrates come in two basic forms—sugars and starches—that balance energy demands. There is a bonus when these foods are minimally processed: They contain more fiber, which is essential for digestion.

---

beans, and oat bran are great examples of foods rich in soluble fiber. Also, you'll feel more satisfied eating a fiber-rich diet, and you will consume fewer calories. If you eat more whole grains, fruits, and vegetables, it becomes easier to reach the recommended level of 25 grams of fiber per day.

Here are a few easy ways to start making fruits, vegetables, and grains the foundation of your family meals:

- Add cut-up fresh vegetables to packaged soup. In the winter, when not all vegetables are available fresh, add canned or frozen vegetables to give even more energy to basic chicken soup. My mother mixed cooked broccoli and spinach in the blender with chicken stock and seasoning for a delicious soup.
- Stock up on simple snack foods such as apples,

pears, and raw broccoli, carrots, and celery, cut into small pieces. Whole-grain cereals are great to munch on whether at home or on a walk. Reusable plastic bags can be used to take healthy snacks wherever the family goes.

- Family favorites get a healthy twist when you add peas to mashed potatoes, or zucchini and eggplant to lasagna or whole-wheat pizza. Be creative and try different whole-wheat pastas with tomato sauce, then throw different cooked veggies, such as peas or broccoli, into the sauce at the last minute.

- Take home hearty, whole-grain breads from the neighborhood bakery. Be sure to linger a bit with the children to take in the aromas of baking bread.

3. Select more lower-fat food choices.

The overconsumption of fat in the American diet has been a public health focus for the past thirty years.

VEGGIE CITY DIP

A Food Guide Pyramid package of delicious veggies loaded with vitamins and great taste.

Makes: 3 cups
Preparation time: 15 minutes
Cooking time: 25 minutes

1 tablespoon olive oil
1 cup finely chopped onions
1 cup finely chopped green or red peppers
1 cup finely chopped zucchini
1 cup finely chopped celery
1 cup peeled and finely chopped eggplant
1 cup chopped tomatoes
1 tablespoon chopped fresh oregano or basil,
   or 1/2 teaspoon dried
Salt to taste
Freshly ground black pepper to taste
1 tablespoon red wine vinegar
1 teaspoon sugar

1. Heat the oil in a skillet over medium heat. Add the onions and peppers. Cook for 2 minutes.
2. Add the zucchini, celery, and eggplant. Cook 2 minutes more.
3. Add the tomatoes, oregano or basil, salt, and pepper. Simmer about 20 minutes, uncovered. Let cool.
4. Add the vinegar and sugar. Adjust the salt and pepper to taste.
5. Serve cold as a dip with pita bread, crackers, or tortilla chips.

PER SERVING: 63 CALORIES, 22 CALORIES FROM FAT, 2 GRAMS PROTEIN, 10 GRAMS CARBOHYDRATES, 2 GRAMS TOTAL FAT, 3 GRAMS FIBER, 217 MILLIGRAMS SODIUM

Over time we went from not getting enough nutrients to getting too much fat and saturated fat. Today's scientific studies link too much fat in the diet with increased risk of heart disease, diabetes, and some cancers, leading to recommendations that we limit the fat in our diet and balance energy intake with physical activity.

The statistics on increasing obesity are reason to be concerned. *The Journal of Obesity* (1998) reports that one-third of all Americans are overweight. American children are growing fatter; according to *Pediatrics* (1998), one-fourth of our children and adolescents today are either overweight or at risk for being overweight.

The majority of American diets do not meet the Dietary Guidelines for total fat and saturated fatty acids. Medical experts agree that effective strategies are needed to lower fat in the diet and to reduce the weight of American consumers in order to promote health and lower the risk of serious chronic diseases.

Although too much fat clearly increases our health risks, remember that it is also an essential nutrient. Fat is a valuable energy source, and it carries fat-soluble vitamins that we all need for our health. It also contributes to the taste and texture of foods that we enjoy. That's why the Dietary Guidelines' message is to moderate, not eliminate, the intake of fat and balance your fat intake with physical activity.

The Dietary Guidelines recommend limiting the amount of calories from fat to 30 percent of our daily totals. This means that other major nutrients such as

---

NUTRITION POWER POINTS
Not All Fats Are Created Equal

Saturated fats: The main sources are meat, dairy products, and some vegetables. They can also be found in bakery products such as cakes and cookies. They can raise blood cholesterol levels and increase the risk of heart disease. Dietary Guidelines recommend limiting saturated fat to 10 percent or less of total fat.

Monounsaturated fats: These are found mainly in olive, peanut, and canola oils. They reduce blood cholesterol when used to replace saturated fats in the diet.

Polyunsaturated fats: The main sources are safflower, corn, soybean, sunflower, and cottonseed oils, as well as fish. They are effective in lowering total blood cholesterol.

Trans-fatty acids: The main source is partially hydrogenated vegetable oil such as that found in many margarines and shortenings. This form of fat may raise blood cholesterol levels.

---

carbohydrates and protein should represent the remaining 70 percent of your calories. How many grams of fat you need depends on the calories you need and use. "The real issue is calories and whether you use them," says Marion Nestle, nutrition chair at New York University. Fat is a concentrated source of calories; each gram of fat contains 9 calories, twice the amount in protein or carbohydrates. Cutting back on fat will also mean cutting down on calories.

To achieve the recommended levels, it is best to watch what goes in the shopping cart and on the table. Dr. Nestle emphasizes that "a recommendation to eat less fat is another way of saying eat less meat, dairy, and processed food products." Checking the food labels for fat can put balance in your cart.

The food product explosion that began in the 1950s brought large numbers of fat-laden processed foods to the market. Not surprisingly, consumption of fat and saturated fat soared. In recent years, as public health recommendations and the availability of low-fat and fat-free products have grown, total fat consumption has begun declining, but the amount of calories consumed is going up. Special attention is still needed to watch dietary fat intake and calories. Remember that calories still count.

Today's marketplace includes many low-fat options. *The Wall Street Journal* reports that twenty-two hundred new low-fat products came onto grocery shelves between 1995 and 1997. In 1995, sales reached $29 billion; it is expected that sales of reduced-fat products will reach $40 billion by the year 2000.

Many of these lower-fat products are interchangeable with the traditional ones, such as low-fat salad dressing. Look for these fat-modified foods and check the label to see how much fat is reduced. Also check for calories, especially cookies and cakes, because the calorie level might still be high.

If dinner tonight is lasagna with meat and cheese, you can limit the fat you get from other meals. Try a mixed vegetable salad for lunch. Keep in mind that not every food has to hit the target and give 30 percent of its calories from fat. Walking through the supermarket with a calculator or testing every food for its fat content is just not necessary.

Here are some easy ways to lower the fat on family menus:

- Add new flavors by replacing cooking fat with stock, salsas, reductions, and herbs (see recipes in chapters 5 through 8).
- Buy low-fat and fat-free dairy products such as skim milk, nonfat yogurt, and low-fat cheeses. Ice milk, frozen yogurt, and sorbet make great desserts; serve them topped with cut-up fresh fruit. Try low-fat sauces for pasta, rice, and potatoes, and fat-free salad dressings and spreads.
- Buy poultry, fish, and lean cuts of meat such as loin and round. Remove the skin from poultry before you cook it, or buy it skinless.
- Buy low-fat snacks such as popcorn, pretzels, rice cakes, and fat-free or low-fat crackers.

Staying Active: The Healthy Link

The amount of calories in the foods you eat and drink should be balanced with the amount of calories your body uses. Physical activity is an important way to use food energy and maintain or improve your weight. The more active you can be, the more calories you will burn.

Moving and Grooving

Healthy living means both healthy eating and regular physical activity. The 1995 *Dietary Guidelines for Americans* includes the recommendation of thirty minutes or more of moderate-intensity physical activity on all or most days. The 1997 Surgeon General's Report on Physical Activity and Health says that regular physical activity improves health in many ways, including:

- reducing the risk of heart disease, diabetes, and some cancers
- reducing feelings of depression and anxiety
- reducing the risk of dying prematurely
- helping to control weight
- helping to build and maintain healthy bones, muscles, and joints

Active children are more likely to become active adults and start building patterns that include regular physical activity. There are all kinds of ways to make fitness an everyday happening. In every chapter you will find ideas for family fun that are active and get everybody moving.

The Food Guide Pyramid: The Tool for Making Choices

The Food Guide Pyramid is a simple tool to help you make dietary choices in today's confusing marketplace. Use it to help balance or moderate your family's diet.

The pyramid is built around a range of servings for your total diet. Each food group component includes a recommended serving amount. Serving sizes for children depend on their ages.

Here's how to use the pyramid. Find out how your diet rates!

1. Start at the base with the grains, breads, and cereals—the biggest group. How many slices of whole-grain bread and servings of various grains, cereals, pasta, or rice will you eat today? Can you count six or more? Research suggests that you consume from six to eleven servings, depending on your energy needs and exercise level.

2. Skip up the chart to the fruits and vegetables. Think variety! Will you eat a total of five or more from these fine groups?

3. Protein-rich foods are next. They include meat, poultry, fish, beans, eggs, and nuts, plus milk, yogurt, and cheese. Amounts are important here. It is easy to eat more than you need for health and weight control. Do you know how many ounces of meat, poultry, fish, or cheese you are eating today? Aim for two to three small servings of 2 to 3 ounces each.

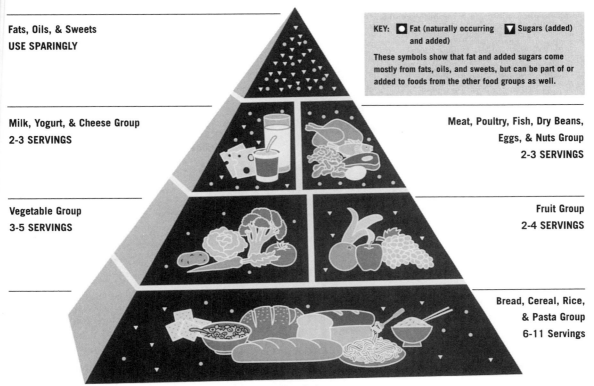

Fats, Oils, & Sweets
USE SPARINGLY

KEY: ○ Fat (naturally occurring ▽ Sugars (added)
and added)
These symbols show that fat and added sugars come
mostly from fats, oils, and sweets, but can be part of or
added to foods from the other food groups as well.

Milk, Yogurt, & Cheese Group
2-3 SERVINGS

Meat, Poultry, Fish, Dry Beans,
Eggs, & Nuts Group
2-3 SERVINGS

Vegetable Group
3-5 SERVINGS

Fruit Group
2-4 SERVINGS

Bread, Cereal, Rice,
& Pasta Group
6-11 Servings

SOURCE: U.S. Department of Agriculture/U.S. Department of Health and Human Services

4. The tip of the pyramid is for the smallest group— the fats, oils, and sugars. It is recommended that most people eat these foods only sparingly because they contribute a lot of calories and few vitamins and minerals. But these ingredients are added to many prepared and processed foods such as salad dressings, soft drinks, candies, and sweet desserts. Do you know if fat, oil, or sugars have been added to the foods you are eating?

The Nutrition Facts Label: A Working Partner

The Food Guide Pyramid works best when it is used with the Nutrition Facts Label. Since the foods within the pyramid food groups have different nutritional values, it is important to be able to make quick comparisons when selecting food in the store. The label makes it easy to find the differences in nutrient content that might be present between brands and between foods.

This wasn't always so. The food market I shopped in when my children were young was so confusing

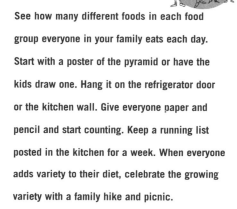
that it was difficult to compare the nutritional value of different products. Nutrition labels were voluntary then and appeared on fewer than 50 percent of the food packages. The labels also had little or no information about fat content. As a consumer advocate I worked hard to do something about that. It took twelve years of persistence and patience, and the large coalition of organizations we put together made a big difference. When the Nutrition Labeling and Education Act was signed into law in 1990, all processed food packages were required to have the new label.

Today the Nutrition Facts Label is really popular with shoppers. FDA research shows that 75 to 80 percent of consumers regularly read labels when they make a new food purchase. And 48 percent reported that they had changed their minds about buying a food product after reading the food label. A lot of information is packed on the label. At right are five steps to make it work for you.

Smart Shopping Simplified

Smart shopping may take a little extra time because you need to plan ahead, but you will save time and money in the long run. Make good use of the Food Guide Pyramid and the Nutrition Facts Label, and follow these keys to smart shopping.

Use a shopping list and newspaper ads for planning.

Keep a grocery list handy in the kitchen and add to it all through the week. It's fun to have the kids add their favorite vegetables or fruits, too. For simpler shopping, organize the list in the same order that you shop or in the order that the food is presented in the grocery store. For example, start with produce and build your menus around that section. A few minutes of list-making can save you from running back to the store for forgotten items. Keep the list flexible so that seasonal surprises that look good and fresh can be added to the basket, and take note of specials that are advertised in the newspaper.

Connect to your community marketing options.

Support your community by finding sources of foods grown close to home. Take a trip to the local farmer's market as a weekend family outing and savor the freshness and different tastes or enjoy the wonderful aroma of fresh bread made by your neighborhood baker. Supermarkets offer an abundance of choices and often have competitive prices, but talking with local farmers and food merchants is a

Five Steps for Using the Nutrition Facts Label

Step 1. Look at claims like "reduced," "low," or "light" on the front of food packages. They must tell the truth and be consistent for all foods. You can also check the % Daily Values to compare claims like "low-fat." If the word "light" is on a label, it generally means that it contains 50 percent fewer calories from fat than a comparable product. Also read the fine print next to the claim for important information such as how many calories the food really has.

Step 2. Check the serving size. It is based on what people really eat. The serving size, found at the top of the label, shows the number of servings in the package and how much is in one serving. Match this with what your family normally eats. The numbers for calories and nutrients are based on the serving size. If you eat two servings, remember to double the calories, fats, and other nutrients.

Step 3. Focus on the nutrient information that is most important to your family. The list of nutrients offers vital health facts that help fit the food into your overall diet. Check to see how much total fat, saturated fat, cholesterol, fiber, and other nutrients are contained in each serving.

Step 4. Use the % Daily Value to find out if the food is high or low in a nutrient. Compare foods easily by learning how a food serving meets the recommended amount in a diet of 2,000 calories a day. This amount is about right for moderately active women and children, and less active men. To limit fat and sodium, look for low numbers. Servings with 5 percent or less are considered low. To increase nutrients such as protein or calcium, look for high numbers. You can use these numbers to gauge your daily diet and figure out what nutrients you may be missing.

Step 5. Find out all the different ingredients in the products. There need be no secrets when you want to know the ingredients in a product. Just about all food packages, even those of standardized products like ketchup and bread, must list all the ingredients in descending order by weight, including artificial colors and additives. This is especially important for family members who have allergies and need to avoid certain foods.

Nutrition Facts

Serving Size 1 cup (228g)
Servings Per Container 2

Amount Per Serving

Calories 260   Calories from Fat 120

	% Daily Value*
Total Fat 13g	20%
Saturated Fat 5g	25%
Cholesterol 30mg	10%
Sodium 660mg	28%
Total Carbohydrate 31g	10%
Dietary Fiber 0g	0%
Sugars 5g	
Protein 5g	

Vitamin A 4%	•	Vitamin C 2%
Calcium 15%	•	Iron 4%

* Percent Daily Values are based on a 2,000 calorie diet. Your daily values may be higher or lower depending on your calorie needs:

	Calories:	2,000	2,500
Total Fat	Less than	65g	80g
Sat Fat	Less than	20g	25g
Cholesterol	Less than	300mg	300mg
Sodium	Less than	2,400mg	2,400mg
Total Carbohydrate		300g	375g
Dietary Fiber		25g	30g

Calories per gram:
Fat 9 • Carbohydrate 4 • Protein 4

special social experience not to be missed.

Shop by season for savings, freshness, and super tastes.

Seasonal shopping brings foods to your family table when they are freshest and taste best. In season, fruits and vegetables are plentiful, so the price is

lower. Menu planning around the seasons adds to the variety and comfort of feeding your family (see the seasonal menu ideas in chapter 9). At the same time, it connects everyone to nature in wonderful ways.

Use the consumer information tools for better buys.

With so many choices of sizes and packages, finding the best price can be confusing unless you use the unit pricing. Most supermarkets provide this information. Check the value per unit (that is, pound) on the label found on many grocery shelves. To ensure freshness, especially of dairy products, fresh meats, and chicken, check the "use by" date on the product.

Be flexible and make healthy substitutions.

Look for low-fat options as you shop; you can use these to modify recipes and make them healthier. Check to see if these low-fat products are also lower in calories. Throughout the book there are tips for making low-fat substitutions, and in Part Two, ingredient substitutions are suggested along with recipes. Be flexible when you buy vegetables, fruits, and grains; you can usually interchange recipe ingredients and still have a delicious meal. Be adventurous: Try something new each time you shop. Your family meals will be more fun.

Use convenience to your benefit.

The aisles are loaded with all kinds of convenience items, so be alert and open to taking advantage of what is out there. Remember, though, that convenience often comes at a cost. When you need just a small amount of celery or grated carrots for a salad or soup, it's a good idea to shop at the supermarket salad bar. It avoids waste, too. When you are in a hurry, add fresh vegetables to a prepared pasta salad to get a great treat.

Resist the temptations at the checkout.

The checkout area of the supermarket is designed for impulse buyers and munchers. Too often that is where the candy bars and other snacks are displayed. Resist the urge and keep the kids busy by chatting with them about the colorful packages in the cart or buying a piece of fruit that they can eat at checkout time.

Aisle-Hopping for Good Health

Let's take a quick trip through the aisles to see what opportunities are out there. The average supermarket layout encourages you to spend your time and money. Remember, the outside rim of the store is where you will find all the basics—produce, dairy, meat, poultry, and seafood. The inside aisles are loaded with items that can add fat, sugar, and salt to your diet, and not a lot of nutrients.

This discussion does not include specific product brand names because new ones are always coming on the market, and some brands are only available in some parts of the country. It is meant to capture the highlights to help steer you in the right direction. In today's ever-changing marketplace here is *what to look for* and *where to watch out*.

Produce

Start shopping here to begin building healthy menus. Be spontaneous and let the seasonal displays spark new tasty picks. Organic fruits and vegetables are becoming more widely available, and consumers often prefer their taste (see Organic Options, page 33). Organic farming has been a way of life for many small farmers for the past forty years, and there has been a fortyfold growth in the market since 1986. Sales total $3.5 billion yearly, and they are sure to grow even more.

What to Look For. Favorites such as bananas, carrots, and broccoli are good in any season, but most fruits and vegetables are both cheaper and better tasting when bought in season (see chapter 2 for advice on what to buy when). Also notice the many

---

HEALTHY TIMESAVERS
Salad Bump-ups

Charlie Trotter, noted chef and cookbook author, suggests that the next time you are out of time and looking for a convenient idea, stop by the supermarket salad bar and get the rice salad. Then bump it up a little by adding sautéed mushrooms, diced red peppers, and a little cooked chicken, and sprinkle on some hot sauce. Put it all over a bed of greens. What a delight!

---

convenient packaging choices. Prewashed, precut salads in a bag save time, and so do the handy precut vegetables such as carrots, celery, and broccoli. They make snacks, soups, and salads into healthy fast food. Convenience costs more, so you decide whether it is worth it. Precut, prepackaged produce does lose some nutrients with extra processing, so use it quickly to avoid more loss.

Fruits such as watermelon and cantaloupe make easy summertime desserts. Buying them precut may double the unit price, but if you have a small family, there will not be any waste. In the fall you can try the many varieties of apples and pears.

Where to Watch Out. Amid the bounty of fruits and vegetables lurk some hidden marketing tricks. The creamy dips next to the cut-up veggies add more fat than nutrients. To avoid unneeded fat in the mix, check the labels of packaged salads. Salad dressing packaged with the salad can be loaded with fat, and so can the croutons and salad dressings on the shelves.

Carefully check the packages of premixed greens if any family members are sensitive to preservatives such as sulfites. They must be listed. Think about storage and spoilage when you decide how much produce to buy at a time. Experience has taught me that if you ask, most produce clerks will be happy to split a large package for you.

Dairy

Today you can get the calcium and other valuable nutrients you need without getting a lot of fat as well. The availability of fat-free and low-fat choices is terrific. For information on ice cream and frozen yogurt see page 236.

What to Look For. Just about every dairy product has a fat-free and a low-fat version. Checking the label is key to making healthy choices. Try different flavors of nonfat and low-fat yogurt for breakfast, lunch, and snacks. Fat-free plain yogurt is great for making smoothies (see chapter 5 for recipes) or added to soups and sauces. The colorful kid packs of fruity low-fat yogurt make a fun snack.

Check out the skim, 1 percent, or 2 percent milk. It is a key calcium contributor and provides all-around good nutrition with less fat than whole milk.

Get to know the many domestic and international varieties of cheese and do taste tests with your family to find everyone's favorite, keeping an eye on the fat content. Pick up packaged sticks of string

---

FAMILY FUN
Udder Delight

A visit to a dairy farm is a fantastic way for kids to learn where their food comes from. It's an awesome experience to milk a cow for the first time and to see firsthand where milk, cheese, and ice cream begin. Here is a chance to touch the udder and learn which teats to pull to get the milk to drop into the bucket.

During my days of fighting for fair consumer prices, I was invited to stay on a dairy farm near LaCrosse, Wisconsin, to see how much hard work went into producing a gallon of milk. They were really surprised when I was up and in the barn by 5:30 A.M. to help milk the cows. The local paper ran a headline: "City consumer leader moo-ved by farm life."

Family and school visits are welcomed by many local farmers. Also the National Park Service runs historic farms. Check with your county cooperative extension service or weekend newspaper listings for a fascinating family trip.

---

cheese, a healthy snack that delivers 25 percent of your calcium Daily Value.

Where to Watch Out. Dairy products that are high in fat can be avoided when you check the food label for the Daily Value of fat in the product. Many cheeses

Making the Egg Grade

The grade and the freshness of eggs are tied together. Grading is performed just after the eggs are laid. Check the grade and expiration date:

Grade AA: **The eggs were ten days old or less when graded.**

Grade A: **The eggs may have been three weeks old or more when graded.**

Grade B: **The oldest eggs. For best results, avoid buying these.**

and other dairy products contain fat, but because taste and texture are still important, experiment to find family favorites. Not all low-fat cheeses retain their flavor when their fat content is reduced, and many will not stand up to cooking.

Pasta

The popularity of pasta is well deserved. Many sizes, shapes, colors, and textures are available. Pasta can be found on the grocery store shelf, in the refrigerated case, and in the frozen foods case.

What to Look For: Have fun with the tremendous variety in shapes and sizes. I counted more than twenty different kinds at my local supermarket. My kids loved fusilli. When they were young, they called it squiggly because of its shape. Try pasta made from whole wheat if you can find it.

Flavored pasta, such as chili pepper penne or spinach linguini, brings color to the table. The nutritional value is about the same. The lowest-fat pasta sauces are the tomato basil, marinara, and mushroom varieties.

Where to Watch Out. Noodles made with egg yolks add cholesterol. Fresh pasta is more likely to be made this way. Creamy alfredo sauces are high in fat. Parmesan cheese adds good taste and texture but also adds a bit of fat. If you buy it grated, it is less than 5 grams per serving. A little goes a long way.

Cereal

Sometimes it seems as if the cold and hot cereal options are endless. I counted over one hundred different choices at my supermarket. Think about serving cereal beyond breakfast. Kids will tell you it makes a great snack. To save money, check out the house brands. The savings might be as much as 40 percent.

What to Look For. Some cereals have as little as 1 gram of fat per serving. Make whole-grain cereals a shopping priority. There are all kinds of healthy choices, such as rolled oats and whole wheat. And with packages of instant hot cereal, breakfast can be ready in a flash. For granola fans there are fat-free options and granola made from whole grains. Check the label for products that contain 3 grams of fiber or more per serving.

Where to Watch Out. Cereals that contain brown sugar, corn syrup, honey, or high fructose corn syrup are more like candy than anything else. Make sure that these sugars are not listed among the first few ingredients. Less than 5 grams of sugar (about 1 teaspoon per serving) in the cereal is considered okay. Check the ingredients to avoid added fats such as partially hydrogenated oils. Remember that most granolas are high in fat and sugar, so check the label. Breakfast toaster pastries have little nutrition and are high in calories and fat.

Grains

There has been an explosion of new, easy-to-use grain products on the market. The simple cooking instructions on the packages sometimes suggest stir-in ideas. Add poultry, pork, beef, or vegetables to make a meal.

What to Look For. Enriched brown rice has only 40 calories per cup and plenty of fiber. Buy grains like bulgur or quinoa in bulk to save money. International dinners are easy to fix with rice packages with Italian, Spanish, or Middle Eastern flavors. Couscous is a quick fix and comes in many different varieties. Try basmati rice and experience its aroma and nutty flavor.

Where to Watch Out. Some seasoned or flavored rice dishes are high in sodium and contain sulfites or monosodium glutamate (MSG). Be alert if anyone in your family is sensitive. Some risotto mixes provide 58 percent of your Daily Value of sodium. Others are made with one-third less salt.

Beans

Healthy shopping is simple when you pick up beans. Naturally low in calories and almost fat-free, beans are a terrific source of protein and fiber. Dried beans deliver more taste but usually have to be soaked overnight before cooking. When you are in a hurry, use the many different kinds of canned beans.

What to Look For. Stock up on a variety of beans and add them to almost anything. Baked beans, the great American favorite, now come in low-fat versions. Packaged rice dishes with beans are a meal put together for you that provides a complete protein—especially good for vegetarians.

Where to Watch Out. Combinations like beans with franks or chili con carne with beans often deliver a lot of fat.

Juices

An assortment of delicious fruit flavors such as apple, grape, grapefruit, and peach are available in juices. Many juices also come fortified with calcium and vitamin C.

What to Look For. 100 percent fruit juice with no sugar added is the best choice. The drink's total percent of fruit or vegetable juice must appear on the top of the package's information panel. The cartons of juice in the refrigerated cases are fresh and tasty choices; many are good sources of vitamin C.

Where to Watch Out. Punches, cocktails, and juice drinks contain less than 100 percent juice. Check the label to avoid the ones that are little more than sugared water mixed with chemicals. Vegetable juices may be high in sodium. Unpasteurized cider and juice can contain bacteria such as *E coli* that can make some people sick, especially children. Processing eliminates bacteria. If the juice is fresh, check to see if the label is dated because the package might not say it is unpasteurized. Bacteria have a chance to grow in juice that is more than a few days old.

Soups

There are many healthy quick-fix options and packaging choices to try. Whether you choose soup in a can, jar, or cup, most are low in calories, averaging only 130 per serving. The fat-free soups are even lower in calories.

What to Look For. The claims on the front label of the soups signal their healthful features. Look for the 98 percent and 99 percent fat-free choices that are also low in cholesterol and calories. Try lentil and bean soups, and get both fiber and good taste. Fat-free vegetable and chicken broth or bouillon cubes are good to keep on hand in your pantry and can be used in preparing many recipes found in the book. Pick up some cup-of-soup mixes to take to work or school. Try low-sodium soups at home and season with fresh herbs.

Where to Watch Out. The sodium level in some soups is very high, so check the label. Some soups contain 30 to 40 percent of the Daily Value of sodium in one serving. Cream soup varieties may be high in fat and cholesterol. Ramen noodle soups are popular with many families, but sometimes the noodles are fried. Check for low-fat options.

Breads

Supermarkets stock many different varieties of bread that go far beyond the traditional sliced white bread. Stop by the bakery counter and see the different whole wheat breads that are baked fresh each day. Smell the aroma.

What to Look For. Products with whole grain and no added fat are best. Fat-free sourdough bread is a tasty option. Multigrain breads are a good source of fiber, but check the label because some do not have as much fiber as simple whole wheat bread. Bagels, in every flavor imaginable, are often fat-free or 98 percent fat-free. French baguettes and Italian loaves are crunchy and tasty while low in fat and high in fiber and nutrient content.

Around the World with Bread

Go globetrotting and enjoy some worldly experiences the next time you buy bread. Try pita bread from the Middle East, lavash from Armenia and Lebanon, chapatis from India and East Africa, rye bread from Sweden, bread sticks from Italy, and baguettes from France. Tack up a map and mark the countries whose bread your family has tasted.

Where to Watch Out. Bread made from white flour has fewer nutrients and less fiber than bread made from whole wheat flour. Some breads are made with fat to make them softer and last longer. Some are also high in sugar. Even bagels are sometimes made with fat, so check the label. In bagel shops this information is sometimes posted on display bins. Not all bread products are labeled because of a loophole in the law. If there is no nutrition label, check the ingredients and take note if butter is high on the list; if so, it is high in fat.

Canned Vegetables and Fruits

These can be a convenient, inexpensive source of needed nutrients and can help fill in the gaps in the quest to reach the Food Guide Pyramid's goal of five fruits and vegetables per day. Some vitamins and minerals are lost due to the heat in the canning process, but they are still a healthy choice.

What to Look For. Canned tomatoes are a must for every pantry. Whether chopped, crushed, stewed, whole, or in a sauce, they provide fiber and vitamin C. Applesauce is great to serve with a main dish or as a tasty snack with no fat, a little fiber, and few calories (see page 142 for an easy recipe for applesauce).

Canned fruits make a good dessert or snack when fresh fruits are out of season. Look for the light ones packed in real fruit juices from concentrate and water, not syrup. The difference in packing can add unwanted calories, sodium, or sugar. Pick up canned fruit snack packs to stuff in bag lunches.

Where to Watch Out. Although canned vegetables deliver the nutrients you want, they might be high in sodium that was added during processing. Check the label and explore the "no-salt-added" options. Also, cinnamon applesauce is higher in calories than regular applesauce because it has high fructose corn syrup as a sweetener.

Cookies and Crackers

With the current move toward low-fat options, our supermarkets are glutted with new products intended to reduce the guilt factor. Just about every cookie and cracker favorite now comes in reduced fat and fat-free versions. But most of these new products are still made from refined flour and plenty of sugar. A positive change has been the replacement of vegetable oil for lard or coconut oil.

What to Look For. Buy the fat-free flat breads with only 40 calories each and the whole-grain crispbreads that contain just 30 calories. There are all kinds of fruity flavored cookies that are fat-free and only 100 calories per serving. Check the labels and see the big difference in fat and calories when you buy the reduced-fat choices.

Where to Watch Out. This aisle still can be a big fat and calorie contributor if you don't check labels. Some cookies can provide more than 15 percent of your Daily Value for fat. Look closely at the serving size. If the cookies are bite-size, you'll consume more fat and calories than you think by the time you finish nibbling. Be wary—store merchandisers sometimes place pasteurized cheese spreads that are high in saturated and total fat next to reduced-fat crackers.

Chips, Pretzels, and Other Snacks

Seek and you will find healthy snacks—but it takes a careful eye. There are all kinds of chips and just as many claims about reduced fat or low-fat. Check the label for the Daily Value of fat.

What to Look For. Popcorn is a popular snack to enjoy at home as well as at the movies. Popcorn that is labeled "light" is required by the FDA to be lower in fat and delivers good dietary fiber. The benefits of this low-fat snack are lost when butter is added, so check the labels. Try popcorn cakes and rice cakes; they are available in fat-free and low-fat varieties and are low in calories. Another good snack is pretzels, which come in low-fat and fat-free varieties as well as salted, unsalted, and low-sodium.

Where to Watch Out. Conventional potato and corn chips pack in too much fat. But mixing low-fat chips with high-fat dips doesn't help, either. Canny mar-keters place high-fat dips such as ranch and French onion next to low-fat chips. Go for the salsa instead. It has no fat, but watch the sodium. Multigrain chips sound healthy, but they can still have too much fat.

Condiments and Oils

Use vinegar to add zesty flavor to salads, vegetables, and other dishes without adding fat. Balsamic vinegar is terrific on almost anything. Fat-free and reduced-fat salad dressings are almost limitless in variety. Buying cooking oil can be tricky, though. Remember that it is 100 percent fat.

What to Look For. The low-fat and fat-free varieties of mayonnaise are considerably lower in fat than the real stuff and still taste good. A serving of regular mayonnaise contains 17 percent of the Daily Value for fat, while the low-fat option (salad dressing) has only 1 percent and the fat-free has none. Mustard is a tasty, nonfat substitute for mayonnaise to spread on sandwiches. It now comes in many different flavors. And don't forget ketchup for adding a spark to your meals; it is now available with no salt added.

There is really a salad dressing for every mood. The selection of fat-free and reduced-fat salad dressings can be overwhelming. Do family taste tests and choose a healthy favorite. The best choices for cooking oil are olive oil and canola oil. Both contain more monounsaturated (good) fat than others do. Canola oil is the lowest in saturated fat.

Where to Watch Out. Conventional salad dressings such as French, Thousand Island, caesar, and ranch pack an awful lot of fat into the bottle. Some contain almost 20 percent of the Daily Value for fat per two tablespoons or one serving. Check the label to be sure. The many varieties of vegetable cooking oils can be confusing because the labels claim different nutrient attributes. For example, safflower oil is high in the antioxidant vitamin E.

Frozen Foods

Take advantage of the time-saving choices that fill today's freezer cases. Frozen fruits and vegetables have a nutritional value comparable to fresh. This is the place to stock up for quick meals, but check the label first for hidden fat and calories.

What to Look For. Keep a supply of your family's favorite vegetables, such as beans, corn, peas, and spinach. They're ready for quick cooking, pureeing, or adding to a dip. Choose fruits with no sugar added, packed in their natural juices, for desserts and yogurt toppings.

French fries are popular with everyone, and if you bake frozen fries, they can be rather low in fat.

Look for low-fat ethnic meals, and for a change try low-fat options such as vegetarian enchiladas and veggie patties. Check out the lighter versions of breakfast foods such as pancakes that have 50 percent less fat and whole wheat and multigrain toaster waffles.

Search out nonfat and low-fat frozen desserts. Try fat-free sorbets in all kinds of fruit flavors. Fat-free and low-fat frozen yogurt is a nutritious, calcium-rich treat. Fat-free ice creams are now on the market that taste good but might be high in calories, so look closely.

Where to Watch Out. Scattered among the packages of plain frozen vegetables are combination dishes in rich cheese and cream sauces that add fat and calories. Although many frozen dinners are lighter these days, they may still be high in sodium. Check the label to find low-sodium choices.

From deep-dish to thin-crust pizzas, the frozen cases seem to be filled with every kind of pizza imaginable, but it's hard to find many low-fat options. Even most packaged veggie pizzas deliver a lot of fat and saturated fat. The frozen kids' dinners are a cute idea, but the choices are limited and too often are loaded with fat.

Fresh Meat and Poultry

Healthy choices can be found if you look carefully. The Nutrifacts Update sign over the meat counter may give the nutritional breakdown for many cuts but not all. Ground beef is a popular purchase. The range of fat content varies quite a bit—as low as 7 percent and as high as 28 percent. **What to Look For.** Focus on the leaner cuts of beef, pork, and poultry. For the leanest beef, try flank steak and top round. Stick with the "Select" grade for lower fat and lower prices than the "Choice" grade. Pork tenderloin is tasty and low in fat. Light-meat poultry is leaner than dark. Keep boneless, skinless chicken breasts on hand in the freezer. Oven-roasted breast of turkey is fat-free and makes a great sandwich. Find bacon that has less fat and less sodium, or choose turkey bacon, which has 65 percent less fat than pork bacon. Lower-fat chicken and turkey sausage adds flavor to pasta and cooks quickly; also try lower-fat chicken and turkey breakfast sausages. **Where to Watch Out.** Because of a loophole, there is no nutrition labeling on fresh meats and poultry, and this makes smart shopping harder. The convenient preseasoned meat and poultry with sauces and pasta found in a supermarket's refrigerated cases can be hefty in price. Another costly convenience is prepackaged roasted chicken. The deli section usually has more economical, healthier, and tastier choices.

Seafood

As word has spread about the health benefits of fish, its popularity has grown. It's an excellent source of protein and has less cholesterol than lean red meats. Today's fish and shellfish come to American markets from all around the world. Ask the person behind the counter for more information about its source and freshness, and for cooking tips.

What to Look For. There is no mandatory inspection program for seafood, so be sure to purchase fish and shellfish from dealers you trust. Also be especially careful in the way you handle seafood at home (see Healthy Chills, page 23). When buying fresh cuts, look for moist fish with no fishy odor, bruises, or odd-colored spots. Choose leaner types of fish such as flounder, perch, and grouper. They not only have less fat but are less likely to have pesticide residues stored in the fatty portions of the fish (see page 215 for information about fat content). Oysters, clams, and mussels are very sensitive to bacterial contamination, so make sure they are purchased live. But that does not guarantee contaminant-free fish. The shrimp in the refrigerated case may be fresh or previously frozen. Ask at the fish counter. It is usually fresher if it is still in its shell.

Where to Watch Out. Be aware of fish from waters near major industrial sites because they may be contaminated. Buy only what you need, because fish deteriorates quickly when it contains harmful bacteria. The frozen packages of already cooked breaded fish are full of calories and fat. Be alert to the packages that call for frying the fish; it is just as easy to broil it. ■

Healthy Chills

The refrigerator and freezer keep food safe and fresh while stopping the growth of most, but not all, harmful bacteria. Keep the refrigerator temperature no higher than 40 degrees Fahrenheit and the freezer no higher than 0 degrees Fahrenheit. The length of time you keep food stored also affects its freshness and safety. Food that has been stored too long will start to smell or look bad. When that happens, toss it. For safekeeping in your refrigerator and freezer:

- Store food in plastic wrap, aluminum foil, or self-sealing plastic bags or containers. Leave meat and poultry products in the store wrapping to avoid handling that might spread bacteria.

- Be careful not to overload the refrigerator. For all foods to be cooled evenly, the air needs to circulate freely. Make a regular check and toss out spoiled food.

- Meat, poultry, and seafood must be placed in the coldest part of the refrigerator; there is usually a special shelf available.

- Frozen foods in their store wrappings can keep for a month or two. To store longer, overwrap the package with airtight heavy-duty foil, freezer wrap, or a plastic bag. Mark the date, too.

- The taste and quality will be better if you quickly freeze foods that you do not intend to use in the next day or so.

- Defrost frozen food safely in the refrigerator or in the microwave, never out on the counter where bacteria can quickly grow.

CHAPTER 2

SHOPPING THROUGH THE SEASONS: FANFARE FOR FRUITS AND VEGETABLES

I love to see the changes of season when the new colors in the market are first peeking through. It still amazes me to see the kaleidoscope of colors that nature presents. Spring comes to market with the light green color of new, sweet asparagus, artichokes, leeks, and peas. Baby vegetables capture the beginning of a growing season in many parts of the country. Soon the colors become more vivid as summer fruits and vegetables ripen. The bright yellows and reds of juicy tomatoes contrast with the rich colors of ripe peaches, plums, and other delicious fruit. As the seemingly endless summer closes, you can see it in the colors of fall vegetables. Burgundy eggplants and golden squash blend with the deep greens of broccoli. The colors of fall leaves are reflected in a rich variety of apples and pears. As winter turns, white vegetables such as parsnips and mushrooms mix with the dark greens of kale and collards.

Shopping starts off right with fruits and vegetables. It is fun to share the experience with your children and find a rainbow of colors among the hundreds of varieties. Supermarket produce aisles are loaded with more than 400 produce items today, up from 250 in the late 1980s. A growing percentage of our produce is imported. Farmer's markets and local growers sell heirloom vegetables whose seeds have been used for generations. With so many different varieties to choose from, shopping can become a new venture filled with all kinds of possibilities.

> *Vegetables are much more exciting than other foods because they are so versatile. They can be eaten raw, pureed in soups and stocks, braised, grilled, roasted, steamed, stir-fried, or stewed.*
>
> —CHARLIE TROTTER, CHEF AND OWNER, CHARLIE TROTTER'S, CHICAGO, ILLINOIS

Finding New Directions

Find something new that your family has not tried and bring it home to share with everyone. Nancy Silverton of Campanile Restaurant in Los Angeles has done the produce shopping with her children ever since they were little. They talked together about their choices, laughing at Ugli fruit until the children actually tasted it and found out how delicious it was. Trying new foods can be a family game that everyone enjoys. Cut up new vegetables or fruit into little pieces and let everyone discover the palette of flavors that are available.

Get to know the different parts of the plants that we eat. A fun way to learn is to fill a basket with a variety of plants and then have a tasting party around the kitchen table one rainy afternoon. Here are some examples:

Roots: The part we eat grows underground. Try

TIPS AND TRIVIA
Family Favorites

As of 1996, here are our favorite fruits and vegetables, according to the USDA:

Fruits: **oranges, apples, grapes, bananas, grapefruit**

Vegetables: **potatoes, tomatoes, lettuce, sweet corn, onions**

FAMILY FUN
Reinventing Roots

Carrots, turnips, and beets can grow new roots if you help them along, and children love to watch it happening. Just cut off the top 1 inch of the root vegetable. Put the top in a small saucer, cut side down. Add a little bit of water so that the bottom of the vegetable top is wet. Place in a sunny window and water every day so that the bottom of the vegetable stays wet. Put it in a pot, surround it with soil, and look for new leaves sprouting and growing.

carrots, potatoes, turnips, beets, and parsnips.

Stems: The long stalks are great to eat. Try celery, asparagus, rhubarb, and bamboo shoots.

Seeds: The small kernels are sweet. Try corn, butter beans, and peas.

Leaves: The leaves of lettuce in all its varieties, along with spinach, kale, and cabbage, taste delicious. Parsley and other herbs are also leaves.

Flowers: Broccoli and cauliflower are little florets, and their taste is lovely as well.

Fruits: Vegetables that contain seeds are truly fruits. Tomatoes, cucumbers, peppers, and squash are all fruits. Other fruits, such as apples, oranges, plums, pears, and mangoes, contain either seeds or pits.

A Link to Health

Eating vegetables and fruits makes it easy to get a variety of needed nutrients every day, including vitamins, minerals, and fiber. Vegetables also contain starchy forms of carbohydrates, and fruits contain

---

NUTRITION POWER POINTS
Color-Coded Veggies

A vegetable's color can be a clue to the vitamins and minerals found inside. Use this chart to help prepare meals with great visual variety and terrific nutritional value:

Vegetable Color	Key Nutrients
White (potatoes, cauliflower, onions)	Fiber, potassium, and other minerals
Dark Green (spinach, kale, collards, broccoli, bell peppers)	Vitamins A and C, folic acid (a B vitamin), fiber, and some minerals
Green (asparagus, beans, zucchini, peas)	Fiber, potassium, vitamin A, and some B vitamins
Orange (carrots, sweet potatoes, winter squash)	Vitamin A, fiber, potassium, and trace minerals such as iron and zinc
Red (tomatoes, beets, red cabbage, red peppers, chilies)	Fiber, minerals, and vitamins A and C

simple forms of energy (fruit sugars), along with water. Both are naturally low in fat.

The Food Guide Pyramid suggests three to five servings of vegetables and two to four servings of fruits a day. Although fruit and vegetable consumption increased 15 percent between 1980 and 1995, it is still far below the recommended levels of the pyramid. There is wide agreement in the medical and nutrition community that we need to eat more fruits and vegetables.

Vegetables and fruits offer unique health protection. The fiber found in these plant foods helps maintain a healthy digestive tract and may lower the risk for heart disease and some cancers. The National Cancer Institute reports that about one-third of all cancer deaths may be related to what we eat.

Vegetables and fruits also contain the antioxidant vitamins A, C, E, and beta-carotene, which protect sensitive body tissue. Vitamin C and B vitamins travel through your blood to spark the transfer of energy and strengthen the tissue that forms all body parts. Fruits also give your body fructose, a fast-absorbing sugar that combats fatigue. The little-known mineral boron, which is found in apples, pears, pineapple, and grapes, helps maintain mental alertness.

A Market Basket of Nutrition Stars

Vegetables and fruits provide a star-studded array of vitamins and some minerals. Vitamins help meet the demands of active lives by making energy available, protecting against chemicals in our environment, and strengthening body tissues. The mineral

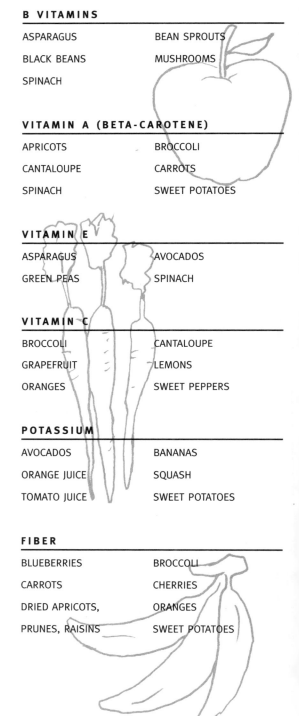

B VITAMINS

ASPARAGUS	BEAN SPROUTS
BLACK BEANS	MUSHROOMS
SPINACH	

VITAMIN A (BETA-CAROTENE)

APRICOTS	BROCCOLI
CANTALOUPE	CARROTS
SPINACH	SWEET POTATOES

VITAMIN E

ASPARAGUS	AVOCADOS
GREEN PEAS	SPINACH

VITAMIN C

BROCCOLI	CANTALOUPE
GRAPEFRUIT	LEMONS
ORANGES	SWEET PEPPERS

POTASSIUM

AVOCADOS	BANANAS
ORANGE JUICE	SQUASH
TOMATO JUICE	SWEET POTATOES

FIBER

BLUEBERRIES	BROCCOLI
CARROTS	CHERRIES
DRIED APRICOTS,	ORANGES
PRUNES, RAISINS	SWEET POTATOES

potassium assists in maintaining the proper fluid balance in our body and is also important in transmitting messages through our nerves. These nutrition stars have been selected because they are tops in providing essential vitamins, fiber, and potassium.

Farmer's Market Finds

Farmer's markets come in all sizes, but they all have something wonderful in common: Local farmers are there to sell their fresh farm products directly to consumers. You can usually count on the produce to be freshly picked and reasonably priced. These markets differ from regular food stores in several ways. They usually take place only once or twice a week during the summer and fall. They can pop up in all kinds of unexpected places, such as parking lots, streets, parks, and plazas. Most often the farmers sell their products right from their trucks.

The shopping hours vary, too. Check out your local farmer's market to see if it is open all day or just in the morning or afternoon. Going just as the market opens and shopping early in the day is the best approach. Farmers leave when they sell out, and you don't want to be disappointed. The produce will also last longer if it is not exposed to high temperatures for long periods of time.

Be sure to take the kids with you. Farmer's markets are fantastic places to see food in its most basic state and learn where it comes from. My kids grew up in the city and never knew that carrots had tops or that zucchini had blossoms until they visited an outdoor market. Try the many different kinds of tomatoes and apples. The tasting experiences are a

---

HEALTHY TIMESAVERS
Fast Fruit

Nora Pouillon of Restaurant Nora in Washington, D.C., suggests keeping a tempting bowl of washed fruit on the kitchen counter or on a table near the TV; it's the best kind of fast food. Load the family fruit bowl with the season's best. Oranges, apples, pears, and bananas are great in the fall and winter, and for spring and summer, add grapes, peaches, plums, and cherries. This show is always a big hit!

---

wonderful way to awaken everyone's senses. If the kids get to select their favorite fruit or vegetable, they are certainly more likely to eat it.

A family outing to the farmer's market is a wonderful way to connect to your community. It's a great place to meet old friends. It seems that every time I go to the farmer's market in Dupont Circle or Takoma Park in Washington or the one on Martha's Vineyard, I run into friends. The atmosphere is so lively and friendly, and everyone's enthusiasm shows at the sight of the first strawberries or corn of the season.

Here are some hints to have the most fun and get the best prices and best quality products:

- Forget about a firm shopping list. Be flexible and open to the terrific treasures you find at the market. It's better to plan menus after you have seen what looks good. That way you won't have to pass up brilliant green beans or perfect sweet peppers because they were not on your list.

- Take a walk through the market first before you buy anything. Compare prices and find the best-looking fruits and vegetables. Then let everyone in the family pick out his or her favorite peaches, melons, or tomatoes.

- Farmer's markets are a great place to learn about food. Farmers know their produce better than anyone, and it is often easy to get cooking advice along with your purchase. If you have never cooked Swiss chard or leeks, just ask the grower how to prepare them. Farmers will be delighted to show you how to pick a ripe melon or choose fresh spinach.

- Try to go home directly after shopping at the farmer's market. The heat of a closed car can do terrible damage to your delicious berries, sweet corn, and other goodies. If you are not going right home, put the fragile fruits and vegetables in a cooler.

- Buy only as much as your family can use. Everything looks so tempting, but if you let fresh produce sit in your refrigerator too long, you lose lots of the nutritional value and good taste. Include longer-lasting produce like potatoes, eggplants, and squash in your purchases.

Perfect Picks Made Easy

With the wide abundance of produce available, a careful eye can easily pick the best value, taste, and nutrition for your family. Use the seasonal guides (see pages 35 to 65) for helpful information on specific fruits and vegetables. Here are four steps to the best pickings:

1. Buy vegetables and fruits in season. They will be plentiful, cheaper, and better tasting.

2. Choose ripe fruits and vegetables. They will look and taste better and make the cook's job easier.

3. Pick smaller and younger vegetables for these benefits:

- The flavor is sweet because the natural sugars have not turned to starch.

- The tender skin on young vegetables may not need to be peeled.

- The interior flesh is best at this stage of development. It has not become woody or hollow.

- They look pretty and are easy to present at the table.

4. If you have trouble picking the best, ask the produce clerk or farmer for guidance.

TIPS AND TRIVIA
Refrigerator Refreshers

Have a corner in the refrigerator reserved for easy-to-reach nibbles. If healthy snacks are there every day, everyone will count on it and dip in regularly. Cut up some washed carrots, celery, radishes, peppers, and shelled peas, and place them in airtight see-through containers or plastic bags. Watch them disappear.

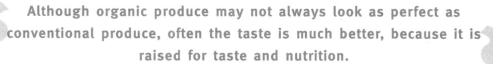

> *Although organic produce may not always look as perfect as conventional produce, often the taste is much better, because it is raised for taste and nutrition.*
>
> ALICE WATERS, OWNER AND CHEF, CHEZ PANISSE, BERKELEY, CALIFORNIA

Organic Options

How our food is grown means a great deal to the future of the land and the future of American families. Because many farming practices of the past have raised environmental and health concerns, interest has risen in sustainable agriculture and organic growing. Sustainable farming means keeping the land in existence for future generations and supplying nourishment to the land and to our food. The growing methods used prevent soil erosion and water pollution while lessening the use of toxic pesticides and chemical fertilizers.

From a very tiny, even minuscule part of the landscape, organic products now command a solid place on the map of food options. Look on the label or package to see if it is certified organic or is grown without pesticides. Organic products can often be more expensive. As the supply is growing, however, the prices are coming down. You might want to consider mixing purchases of organic and conventional produce. The choice is yours, but here are some good reasons to go organic:

- Organic produce tastes better, with more flavor and freshness.
- It protects the environment by preventing soil erosion and by safeguarding water quality and energy resources.
- It protects family health by reducing the exposure of children and adults to chemical pesticides, some of which have been found to cause cancer.
- It supports small farms and local farmers, and protects farmworkers by lessening their exposure to chemicals.

A Word About Canned and Frozen Vegetables and Fruits

Fruits and vegetables in all their forms—fresh, canned, and frozen—are part of a healthy diet. Canned and frozen produce is convenient, economical, and still quite nutritious.

Heat used in canning vegetables and fruits changes sensitive vitamins and antioxidants. Canned vegetables are comparable nutritionally to cooked vegetables because some of their valuable nutrients are leached into the cooking liquid. Canned fruit is nutritionally more like fresh because the natural acid in fruit may protect the vitamins. Water- and juice-packed fruits are best, and the tasty liquid contains nutrients. Check the different quality grades; for better appearance and taste, choose Fancy or U.S. Grade A. In the winter, packaged or canned tomatoes are a good bet since there is no frozen alternative and fresh winter tomatoes are tasteless.

Frozen produce comes straight from the fields and compares nutritionally with fresh. Make sure the package is clean and firm and that the contents aren't frozen into a block. Avoid packages you suspect have been defrosted; thawing and refreezing affects the taste, texture, color, and nutritional benefits. For maximum nutritional benefit choose whole, unseasoned vegetables rather than sliced or diced.

FoUr SeAsONs Of vEGeTaBleS aNd FrUiTS

Almost all vegetables and fruits are at their best in a particular season. To simplify your shopping, use the following handy charts to take you through the seasons. The most popular vegetables and fruits in today's market are listed. You'll discover what to look for, storage and preparation ideas, and the best uses for each vegetable. The fruits and vegetables whose quality is most consistent year-round are marked with an asterisk (*). Also, after each season you'll find an easy recipe that captures its best tastes and flavors. Many more delicious vegetable and fruit recipes can also be found throughout the book.

SpRiNG VeGeTaBLe GUiDe

Vegetable * (Available Year Round)	What to Look For	Safekeeping and Preparing	Best Uses
Artichokes Globe	Heavy for size and firm when squeezed. Tightly closed bud.	Recut the stem and place the end in water as you would a flower. Keeps in the refrigerator for a few days. When ready to cook: Trim the stem end and the first few bottom leaves. Cut off the top inch of the head to remove the thorny tips of the uppermost leaves. After each cut, rub with lemon to prevent discoloration.	Steam the artichoke above water for 30 to 45 minutes. Check for doneness by piercing the bottom of the artichoke with a sharp knife; the knife should slide in easily. Serve hot immediately with olive oil and lemon wedges. To serve cold: Plunge into ice water to chill thoroughly, drain upside down, and serve with Basic Vinaigrette (see page 175).
Asparagus Green or white	Thin or fat shoots with tight buds at the top. Firm, smooth stalks with no wrinkles.	Recut the stem and place the end in water as you would a flower. Keeps in the refrigerator for a few days. Store in the refrigerator for no more than a few days. When ready to cook: Cut off the woody end of the stalks.	Steam above water for 3 to 5 minutes. Serve hot, drizzled with olive oil, lemon juice, salt and pepper. To serve cold: Plunge into ice water to chill thoroughly and serve with Basic Vinaigrette (see page 175).

SPRING VEGETABLE GUIDE CONTINUED

Vegetable * (Available Year Round)	What to Look For	Safekeeping and Preparing	Best Uses
Greens, Salad* Head lettuce (Bibb, iceberg), leaf (red and green leaf, arugula), and romaine	Bright, crisp, tender leaves with no sign of discoloration, blemishes, or wilting. Avoid overgrown heads; the leaves are tough and tasteless.	Store in the refrigerator in a plastic bag to prevent drying. Do not store for more than a few days.	Best raw with homemade Basic Vinaigrette (see page 175). Add other veggies to the salad such as mushrooms, cucumbers, and shredded carrots. See page 172 for more on greens.
Peas English	Bright green pods with few wrinkles. Pods should be filled with peas but not bulging. If the peas are too large, they are old and starchy.	Keep in the refrigerator and use within a day or two. Rinse peas. Remove the peas from the inedible pod.	Cook in boiling salted water for 3 to 5 minutes. Carrots, pearl onions, and mushrooms go well with peas. Fresh dill and mint add lively zip.
Radishes Black, red or white	Firm, smooth skin without splits; round or elongated. Attached green tops should have no signs of wilting or discoloration.	Keep very well in the refrigerator, although the tops should be used within a day or two. Scrub well and cut off the ends.	Use in salads or as garnishes. Young green tops also add zest to salads.

ROASTED ASPARAGUS SALAD

This salad just sings spring. The roasted flavor adds a woodsy touch.

Serves: 6

Preparation time: 5 minutes

Cooking time: 10 minutes

1 1/2 pounds fresh asparagus

1 tablespoon olive oil

Salt to taste

Freshly ground black pepper to taste

3 tablespoons Basic Vinaigrette (see page 175)

1. Preheat the oven to 350°F.

2. Prepare the asparagus by cutting off the last inch or so of the woody stalk.

3. Place the asparagus stalks on a baking sheet. Sprinkle them with the olive oil, salt, and pepper.

4. Roast in the oven for 5 to 10 minutes, until the stalks begin to get tender on the outside. (Thin asparagus spears will take less time than thick spears.)

5. Transfer the asparagus to a cold platter and cool in the refrigerator.

6. Toss with the vinaigrette and serve.

PER SERVING: 90 CALORIES, 63 CALORIES FROM FAT, 3 GRAMS PROTEIN, 5 GRAMS CARBOHYDRATES, 7 GRAMS TOTAL FAT, 2 GRAMS FIBER, 134 MILLIGRAMS SODIUM

HEALTHY TIMESAVERS
Zappy Vegetables

Microwaving vegetables makes it fast and easy to prepare a meal or snack. For best results follow these tips:

- Cut the vegetables into same-size pieces for even cooking.
- Pierce whole, unpeeled vegetables such as potatoes with a fork so they do not burst when cooking.
- Use only microwaveable containers and rotate a half turn midway through cooking.
- Loosely cover the container with waxed paper, microwaveable wrap, or the container lid so that steam can escape.
- Take the vegetables out of the microwave when they are just tender. Let stand for three to five minutes to finish cooking.
- Watch out for hot steam!

SuMmER vEGeTaBLe GuiDe

Vegetable * (Available Year Round)	What to Look For	Safekeeping and Preparing	Best Uses
Beans, Snap Green, string, wax, romano, round, flat	Young, small beans with a velvety feel. Plump seeds should be formed but not bulging. Avoid beans that are even slightly soft; they should snap easily when bent. Green beans should be bright green in color; wax beans should be pale yellow.	Store in the refrigerator for no more than 5 days. Snap off the stem end.	Cook in boiling salted water for 8 to 15 minutes, to desired doneness. Serve hot or plunge into ice water, drain, and store for later use. Beans may be served cold or reheated with olive oil in a pan or in the microwave. Slivered almonds and chopped red peppers make colorful, tasty additions to beans.
Beets * Red, yellow, white, candy stripe	Firm, smooth roots without splits. Small- to medium-size beets taste best. If possible, buy beets with greens still attached. They are usually freshest. The greens are also edible when young.	Remove the tops and refrigerate in plastic bags. The tops will stay fresh for a day or two and can be used as salad greens or sautéed. They keep a week or more in the refrigerator. Prepare by scrubbing well. Do not peel.	Put beets in a saucepan and cover with cold water. Bring to a boil and cook for 30 to 45 minutes. Beets are done when a knife slides in easily. Drain and cool. Slip the skin off. Reheat to serve or use cold in salads. Flavors such as orange, caraway seed, mustard seed, and dill go well with beets.

SUMMER VEGETABLE GUIDE CONTINUED

Vegetable * (Available Year Round)	What to Look For	Safekeeping and Preparing	Best Uses
Celery*	Young, tightly formed celery hearts with tight stalk formation are less bitter. Leaves should not be wilted. Prepackaged cellophane wrapping promotes rot; avoid when possible.	Keeps 5 days or more if refrigerated. Scrub thoroughly to remove sand. Cut to desired size.	Use raw in crudités. Kids love eating it with peanut butter. Braise hearts in well-seasoned chicken stock until fully cooked, 25 to 30 minutes.
Chili Peppers Anaheim, cayenne, jalapeño, poblano, serrano	Glossy, deep color. Well-shaped, firm, thick walls with no soft spots.	Will keep 3 days or more if refrigerated.	Use sparingly at first to determine how hot the chili is. (For more tips see chapter 4.) Try in stir-fries, chili, and couscous for an international flavor.
Corn Yellow, white, bicolored	Freshly picked, moist, green husk and silks; plump, glossy kernels without spaces between them.	Best eaten within a few hours of purchase. Will keep for a day or two if refrigerated in husks. Remove husk and silks only when ready to cook.	Cook, covered in simmering, salted water, for 3 to 5 minutes. Cut the kernels from the cob and sauté for 3 to 5 minutes. Or peel back the husk, remove the silks, soak in water, sprinkle with lime juice and salt, and put the husk back in place. Grill for 6 to 8 minutes.

SuMmER vEGETaBLe GUiDe coNTInUEd

Vegetable *(Available Year Round)	What to Look For	Safekeeping and Preparing	Best Uses
Cucumbers* Common or seedless; pickling, kirby, lemon	Slender cucumbers are younger and have tender skins. The skin should be dark green; avoid cucumbers that are dull and yellow. Cucumbers should be firm.	Will keep 5 days or more if refrigerated. Rinse; peel if waxed.	Best used raw in salads, sandwiches, soups, and dips. Goes well with chives, dill, mint, red onion, salt, and vinegar.
Eggplant* Common (purple), white (egg-shaped), oriental (long and thin)	Smooth, taut skin with fresh-looking green cap at the stem end. Heavy for its size. Avoid overgrown eggplants that are more than 5 inches in diameter.	Store at a cool room temperature or in the refrigerator. After a few days, eggplants become unpleasantly bitter. The skins are edible and a good source of nutrition, but they may be peeled with a common vegetable peeler if preferred.	It's important to cook eggplant thoroughly for good taste and texture. Grilling a 1/2-inch slice takes about 2 minutes, while baking 2 halves takes about 30 minutes. Season with basil, oregano, tomatoes, olives, peppers, and lemon juice.
Mushrooms* Common (white), cremini, oyster, Shiitake, Portobello	Small to medium size; minimum dirt; uniform color. Tight caps with gills (located under the cap) intact and not slimy. Avoid mushrooms that appear to be darkening.	Will last 5 days or more if refrigerated. Clean with a damp towel or a mushroom brush. Avoid soaking in water.	Cook in a small amount of oil over low heat for 4 to 6 minutes. Parsley, pepper, rosemary, and thyme make good partners for mushrooms.

SuMmER VeGeTaBLe GuiDe coNTInUEd

Vegetable *(Available Year Round)	What to Look For	Safekeeping and Preparing	Best Uses
Okra Green, red	Pods have a velvety feel. No bruises or discoloration. Pods should be less than 3 inches long.	Will keep up to 4 days if refrigerated. Rinse and remove stem end.	Add to Creole- or Cajun-style soups, stews, and sauces to thicken and add flavor. Needs to simmer for 10 minutes to thicken effectively. Complements tomatoes, corn, and peppers.
Onions * Bermuda, red, pearl, Spanish, yellow, Vidalia, Walla Walla; shallot	Clean, firm, well-shaped bulbs with no sign of mold. Dry, papery skins.	Can be stored in cool, dry place with ventilation for 1 month or longer. Or store in the refrigerator for up to 5 days. Peel the papery skin and cut or slice.	Use sweet onions (Bermuda, red, Vidalia, Walla Walla, and shallot) raw. All others may taste better cooked. Cook cut onions in a small amount of olive oil. Boil whole, peeled pearl onions in salted water for 6 to 10 minutes.
Onions, Green * Scallions, leeks	A firm white root end. Crisp, straight, bright green stems.	Keep in the refrigerator for 5 days or more. Both the white bulb end and the green stems are edible. Remove the roots. Wash and remove any loose skin.	Scallions are best used raw for flavor and garnish. Leeks must be fully cooked.

SuMmER vEGETaBLe GUIDe coNTINUEd

Vegetable ✻ (Available Year Round)	What to Look For	Safekeeping and Preparing	Best Uses
Peas, Snow Snap	Bright green edible pods that are filled with peas but not bulging. If the peas are too large, they are old and starchy.	Buy as soon after harvest as possible and plan to use them within a day or two. Rinse and snap off the stem ends.	Cook in boiling salted water for 5 to 10 minutes. Stir-fry in olive oil with salt and pepper for 2 to 4 minutes. Carrots, pearl onions, and mushrooms complement peas well. Dill and mint go well with peas.
Peppers* Sweet bell (green, red, yellow, orange)	Uniform, glossy, deep color. Well-shaped, firm, thick walls with no soft spots.	Will keep refrigerated for 3 days or more. Rinse and cut into desired shapes.	Use raw or cooked. Especially tasty when grilled, roasted, or in a stir-fry.
Potatoes* Baking, Idaho, russet New: red bliss, fingerling, purple, Yukon Gold, creamer	Very firm, without sprouted eyes. No greenish tint to the skin. New: Look for small potatoes with thin skins.	Store in a cool, dark place; do not store in the refrigerator. Will keep up to 2 months. Use before they sprout or get soft. New: Store in a cool, dark place for up to 2 weeks. Scrub under running water. Avoid peeling whenever possible; the skins are very nutritious.	Prick the skin several times and bake at 350° F for 45 to 60 minutes, or microwave for 10 to 15 minutes. New: Start covered with cold water and boil 20 to 30 minutes, until tender when pierced.

Vegetable * (Available Year Round)	What to Look For	Safekeeping and Preparing	Best Uses
Squash, Summer Yellow, pattypan, zucchini	Small squash with thin, glossy skins. Yellow squash and zucchini should be less than 8 inches long. Pattypan should be less than 3 inches in diameter.	Will keep for 3 days or more if refrigerated. Rinse and remove stem and blossom end. Cut into pieces of desired size.	Bake whole or halved, drizzled with olive oil and salt and pepper, at 350° F. for 20 to 35 minutes. Or wilt in a very small amount of water with salt, pepper, and olive oil for 6 to 8 minutes. Fresh basil makes a good accompaniment.
Tomatoes Red, yellow, Roma, cherry, and hundreds of heirloom varieties	plump and heavy for its size. Color should be uniform and blemish-free. Color and shape vary according to variety.	Will keep at room temperature for a few days. Avoid refrigerating if possible; it stops the ripening process. Wash and remove stem.	Very ripe tomatoes are best raw. Roma tomatoes make the best sauce. Canned tomatoes should be simmered for 30 minutes or more. Delicious with basil, olive oil, salt, and pepper.

GRILLED SUMMER VEGETABLES

A simply marvelous way to mix and match the season's finest. The fresh, ripe vegetables soar with good flavor.

Serves 4

Preparation time: 15 minutes

Cooking time: 5 minutes

For the marinade:

1/4 cup olive oil

1 clove garlic, crushed

1 teaspoon chopped fresh basil

Salt to taste

Freshly ground black pepper to taste

For the vegetables:

1 eggplant, sliced 1/3-inch thick

1 summer squash, sliced 1/3-inch thick

1 pepper, quartered and seeded

1 onion, sliced 1/3-inch thick

4 large mushrooms, whole

1. Combine all the ingredients for the marinade and let stand 15 minutes or longer. (This can be done ahead and kept in the refrigerator up to 1 week.)

2. Preheat the grill.

3. Brush the vegetables with the marinade on all sides.

4. Grill on a hot grill for 2 minutes on each side. To keep the onions together, slide a spatula completely underneath to pick up all the rings. Turn carefully. Serve hot or at room temperature.

PER SERVING: ABOUT 168 CALORIES, 135 CALORIES FROM FAT, 2 GRAMS PROTEIN, 10 GRAMS CARBOHYDRATES, 15 GRAMS FAT, 4 GRAMS FIBER, 154 MILLIGRAMS SODIUM

Great Growing Gardens

Help your children discover how foods grow: Start a family garden. Gardens reconnect everyone to the fundamentals of food. You can grow a great garden even if you don't have a lot of space. Windowsills, decks, and porches make wonderful growing places if you don't have a backyard. The size and type of garden is up to you. Here are some different ways you can go—and grow.

Starter Garden. Start small with a container garden using seeds whose labels indicate that they grow well in containers, such as tomatoes, peppers, cucumbers, and herbs. You can find a wide assortment of containers at your local garden center or hardware store. Be sure to place your container in a sunny location and keep the seedbed watered well.

Pizza Garden. Grow all kinds of different veggies to put on your pizza. Include tomatoes, peppers, spinach, onions, and anything else the whole family loves. (See page 184 for a homemade pizza recipe.)

Herb Garden. Herbs grow great in sunny southern windows, indoors or outdoors, in a container or in the garden. Snip the mature leaves, and you will have new plants springing up often.

Outdoor Vegetable Garden. Begin by planning what vegetables to grow and where. Do a planting calendar. Start the seedlings indoors, develop the soil, and then transplant the seedlings carefully. Have children make and put markers in the soil to identify different crops.

School Gardens. Many local schools have started Team Nutrition gardens. Ask the principal of your children's school if your community can get growing. Involve the students in all stages of the planting and harvesting.

Community Gardens. This is a great way to meet neighbors and produce great results on your own plot of land. Many cities have urban gardens that grow all kinds of vegetables and flowers. Find out where the nearby gardens are by calling the local cooperative extension service office.

Taste Treasures of Summer

Tomato lovers know that there is nothing better than the taste of a locally grown tomato that has just been plucked off the vine and is still warm from the sun. It is something I anticipate all through the cold winter months. There are thousands of varieties, shapes, and colors of tomatoes with wonderful names like Green Zebra, Golden Jubilee, and Yellow Pear.

Tomatoes provide fiber, minerals, including potassium, and vitamins, especially beta-carotene, vitamin C, and folic acid. They also provide lycopene, a stable antioxidant that tolerates cooking heat and offers important health benefits such as helping to build our immune systems and lowering the risk of cancer and heart disease.

Recently there has been a growing interest in heirloom tomatoes whose seeds go back more than one hundred years. They are fragile and do not ship well, but they have a marvelous flavor and tenderness. The seeds of these tomatoes have been passed down from generation to generation. When you visit the farmer's market, ask the farmers what heirloom tomatoes they might be growing and taste the difference.

Culturally, tomatoes are a vegetable, but botanically, they are a fruit. The tomato is said to have been cultivated first by the Aztecs, who gave it its name and considered it a symbol of good luck from the gods.

You'll enjoy these at their peak, as no-cook treats that have top nutrition and taste:

Simple Salsa: Chop a tomato and toss it with minced jalapeño chilies, fresh cilantro leaves, salt, and a little garlic (see page 113 for Fiesta Salsa recipe).

Tomato and Mozzarella Salad: On a plate, alternate slices of tomato and fresh mozzarella. Top with snipped basil and drizzle with olive oil, salt, and pepper.

Tomato Sandwich: Place thick tomato slices on crusty sourdough bread. Salt and pepper the tomato slices.

Uncooked Summer Pasta Sauce: Toss together a few chopped tomatoes, a couple of crushed garlic cloves, and a cup of fresh basil leaves. Add olive oil and toss again. Add hot cooked pasta and toss with a little Parmesan cheese.

FALL VEGETABLE GUIDE

Vegetable * (Available Year Round)	What to Look For	Safekeeping and Preparing	Best Uses
Brussels Sprouts*	Small sprouts with tight-fitting leaves and no browning or yellowing. Best when purchased on the stalk. Prepackaged cellophane wrapping promotes rot; avoid when possible.	Will last 4 days or more if refrigerated. Trim stem end and use a paring knife to mark an X in the stem to aid in cooking the stem.	Steam over boiling salted water for 8 to 12 minutes. Finish by sautéing in olive oil and seasoning with salt and pepper. Complementary flavors include mustard, mustard seed, vinegar, and bacon.
Carrots*	Young, firm, small carrots with the tops still on will be sweet and fresh. Avoid soft or shriveled carrots or those that have splits. Prepackaged cellophane wrapping promotes rot; avoid when possible.	Will keep in the refrigerator for 1 week or more. Remove the tops and discard.	Cook in boiling salted water or over steam for 8 to 12 minutes. Cook baby carrots for about 5 minutes. Or glaze by cooking, uncovered, in a small amount of stock until the stock has evaporated and the sugars left behind coat the carrots. Flavor with dill or mint.

FaLL VeGeTaBLe GuIDe coNTInUEd

Vegetable ✳ (Available Year Round)	What to Look For	Safekeeping and Preparing	Best Uses
Cauliflower✳ White, green, purple	Firm white or cream-colored head with tight florets and bright green leaves. No spots or bruises.	Will keep for 3 days or more if refrigerated. Remove leaves and core. Divide florets into even-sized pieces.	Boil in salted water for 6 to 10 minutes. Serve with cheese, bread crumbs, caraway seeds, paprika, or parsley.
Fennel	Pale, firm bulbs with green stalks and feathery fronds. The condition of the fronds (if still attached) is the best way to tell freshness.	Keeps 3 days or more if refrigerated. Cut the stalks from the bulb.	The bulb can be used raw in salads or cooked for a wonderful accompaniment to fish. Chop the fronds and use as an herb to add an anise/licorice flavor. Use the stalks in stocks and soups.
Greens, Cooking Collards, broccoli rabe, kale, Swiss chard	Crisp, tender leaves that are not overgrown. Bright color. Available year round, but tend to be tough and woody in hot summers.	Keep refrigerated in plastic bags to maintain moisture. Rinse as many times as necessary to remove sand. Remove thick, tough leaves.	Use raw in salads when small and tender. Cook in skillet with small amount of olive oil until just wilted, or steam using the moisture that clings to greens after washing.

FALL VEGETABLE GUIDE CONTINUED

Vegetable * (Available Year Round)	What to Look For	Safekeeping and Preparing	Best Uses
Rutabagas	Smooth, thick, yellow to tan skin. Heavy for its size.	Will keep in cool, dry place for 1 month or longer. Rinse and peel the skin with a paring knife. Cut according to use.	Boil in salted water for 10 to 15 minutes. May be mashed and served by itself or added to mashed potatoes for a richer, turniplike flavor. Serve as an accompaniment to strong meats and game. Great side dish for holiday meals.
Salsify (Oyster plant)	Firm, tapered roots with black or white skin.	Will keep for 2 weeks or more if refrigerated. Remove the tops and thin skin.	Cook in boiling salted water for 10 to 15 minutes. Mash plain or use in stews. Serve with chives, parsley, and pepper.
Spinach*	Firm, fresh, crisp, deep green leaves. No blemishes, insect damage, or wilting.	Will keep for 1 or 2 days if refrigerated. Remove the central ribs if they are large and tough. Wash well in several changes of water to remove sand.	Use small spinach leaves in salads with mushrooms, red onion, and a sprinkle of chopped egg. Steam briefly with only the water that clings to the leaves after washing. Season with shallots, nutmeg, salt, and pepper.
Sweet Potatoes*	Firm, medium-sized with tapered ends. Avoid blemishes, sprouts, or any sign of decay.	Store in a cool, dark, dry place. Avoid refrigeration. Will keep for several weeks. Scrub well when ready to use.	Bake unpeeled at 350° F. for 30 to 45 minutes. Or, microwave for 10 to 15 minutes. Alternatively, peel, cut in half, place in a pot with cold water, and bring to boil. Boil 20 to 30 minutes (depending on size), drain, and mash.

All-Star Vegetable Cooking

For freshest taste and most nutrients:

- Wash vegetables under the faucet or put in a bowl with several changes of water. Avoid soaking them because you will likely lose the watersoluble nutrients. Don't wash the vegetables until you are ready to use them; otherwise, rot might develop.

- Steam for the shortest time possible in a small amount of liquid in a covered pot or microwave. For best results, cook the veggies last.

- Taste the vegetables often as you cook them.

To find the texture your family likes best, experiment by cooking vegetables for different lengths of time. Ask everyone to taste and decide.

- Cook vegetables with the skin on, because most nutrients are found just under the skin and are absorbed during cooking. You can always peel them after they are cooked.

- Use the water from blanching or boiling vegetables as a base for soups or use the liquid to cook rice or couscous because it is loaded with minerals and the water-soluble vitamins such as C and B.

ROASTED ROOT VEGETABLES

This roasted medley with jewel-like colors is rich in vitamins A and C. It takes little preparation but bursts with divine warmth and taste.

Serves 4

Preparation time: 15 minutes

Cooking time: 15 to 20 minutes

1 1/2 pounds assorted root vegetables such as parsnips, carrots, rutabagas, potatoes, sweet potatoes, and beets

2 tablespoons olive oil

Salt to taste

Freshly ground black pepper to taste

1. Preheat oven to 350° F.

2. Peel and cut vegetables into 1/2-inch cubes. Toss in olive oil and season with salt and pepper.

3. Place on a baking sheet and roast in the oven for 15 to 20 minutes. The vegetables are cooked when they do not resist being pierced by a fork.

PER SERVING: ABOUT 147 CALORIES, 63 CALORIES FROM FAT, 2 GRAMS PROTEIN, 21 GRAMS CARBOHYDRATES, 7 GRAMS FAT, 6 GRAMS FIBER, 182 MILLIGRAMS SODIUM

MAGICAL GrEENS

Fresh greens are delicious but wilt quickly in the refrigerator. Magic happens when they are steamed for a minute or two. Enjoy this power food that is a great source for vitamins A and C, folic acid, and calcium. Serve as a side dish or stir into pasta.

Serves 6

Preparation time: 5 minutes

Cooking time: 5 minutes

3 cups greens such as spinach, kale, chard, or arugula, or a combination

1/4 cup chicken stock (see page 162 for Basic Chicken Stock recipe)

1 tablespoon finely chopped shallots

Salt to taste

Freshly ground black pepper to taste

1. Wash the greens, remove any tough stalks, and cut into 2-inch lengths.

2. Bring the stock and shallots to a simmer in a skillet over medium-high heat. Cook for 1 minute.

3. Add the greens, salt, and pepper. Toss quickly until the greens are barely wilted.

4. Transfer to a serving plate.

PER SERVING: 7 CALORIES, 0 CALORIES FROM FAT, 1 GRAM PROTEIN, 1 GRAM CARBOHYDRATES, 0 GRAMS TOTAL FAT, 0 GRAMS FIBER, 305 MILLIGRAMS SODIUM

WiNtER VeGETaBLE GUIDE

Vegetable *(Available Year Round)	What to Look For	Safekeeping and Preparing	Best Uses
Avocados Hass, Fuerte	Yield when pressed gently. Uniform color without blemishes or bruises.	Store at room temperature. Will ripen at room temperature. Cut lengthwise around the large stone in the center. Gently twist the 2 sides apart. Rub the cut surfaces with lemon to prevent discoloration. Use a spoon to scoop out the flesh.	Do not cook. Serve in a salad with olive oil, lemon juice, salt, and pepper. Great mashed with salsa for a quick homemade guacamole.
Broccoli*	Firm stems with dark green-purple color and closed buds. No yellowing.	Will keep for 3 days or more if refrigerated. Rinse. Remove outer leaves and tough stems. Cut tender stems and florets into even-sized pieces.	Steam in boiling salted water for 8 to 12 minutes or use raw. Lemon juice, cheese, parsley, and dill partner well.
Cabbage, Winter Red, white, Savoy, napa, bok choy	Tight, firm, heavy heads with no broken or bruised leaves.	Will keep 1 week or more if refrigerated. Keep the outer leaves attached to protect and help retain moisture during storage. Wash, quarter, and core when ready to use.	Use raw in coleslaw or salads. To cook: Boil, uncovered, in salted water for 5 to 7 minutes. Good with a touch of butter, parsley, and pepper.

WINTER VEGETABLE GUIDE CONTINUED

Vegetable * (Available Year Round)	What to Look For	Safekeeping and Preparing	Best Uses
Celery Root	Heavy for its size. Watch for bruises or spade marks. Avoid roots larger than a softball because they are overgrown and will be woody on the inside.	Will keep for 1 week or more in a cool, dry place. Wash and peel when ready to use.	Delicious raw in coleslaw. Use in stews, with roasts, or boil and add to mashed potatoes for a great new flavor.
Parsnips	Well-shaped, small, firm roots. Large, older parsnips require more peeling and have a woody core.	Will keep for 1 week or more if refrigerated.	Use in soups or stews. Add boiled and mashed parsnips to mashed potatoes for a new taste.
Squash, Winter Acorn, butternut, Hubbard, spaghetti	Heavy for its size. Thick, hard skin without blemishes.	Will keep for 1 month or more in a cool, dry place.	Halve, remove seeds, sprinkle with salt, pepper, and olive oil, and roast at 350° F. for 30 to 45 minutes, until the flesh is tender. Great in soups and risottos.
Turnips	Smooth white and purple skin. Small- to medium-sized, 2 to 3 inches in diameter. Heavy for its size.	Will keep for 1 week or more if refrigerated. Cut off the root and greens, and peel.	Cook in boiling salted water for 15 to 25 minutes. Serve mashed, glazed, or in stews. Complements stronger meats and game. Good with caraway seeds, chives, parsley, and pepper.

PUREE OF WINTER VEGETABLES

A wonderfully smooth comfort food with a distinctive flavor combination that is a perfect accompaniment to hearty roasts and stews.

Serves 4

Preparation time: 5 minutes

Cooking time: 45 minutes

2 pounds mixed winter vegetables such as celery root, parsnips, and potatoes

1/2 cup milk

2 tablespoons butter

Salt to taste

Freshly ground black pepper to taste

1. Peel and cut the vegetables into 2-inch cubes. Place in cold salted water. Bring to a boil and cook for 25 to 40 minutes, until a knife can be inserted without resistance. (Celery root takes a little longer to cook, so cut it a little smaller.)

2. Drain and mash well.

3. Return to the heat and add milk, butter, salt, and pepper. Serve hot.

PER SERVING: ABOUT 216 CALORIES, 63 CALORIES FROM FAT, 4 GRAMS PROTEIN, 36 GRAMS CARBOHYDRATES, 7 GRAMS TOTAL FAT, 5 GRAMS FIBER, 393 MILLIGRAMS SODIUM

Sense-ational Family Tastings

Learning to use your five senses is a fun way to explore new food flavors, colors, textures, and smells. Have a family tasting party to introduce new foods to everyone and expand the variety of foods your family will eat. Gather everyone around the table and

- see it. Is it wrinkled or smooth?
- touch it. Is it soft or hard?
- smell it. Is it spicy or mild?
- taste it. Is it sweet or sour—or something else?
- hear it when you chew it. Is it crunchy or mushy?

Mark Miller, the chef at Coyote Café in Santa Fe, New Mexico, still remembers tasting McIntosh apples when he was a young boy in Massachusetts. He recalls how cinnamony they smelled. He suggests a family game to experience the different delicious tastes of apples. First, buy six different kinds of apples at the market. Bring them home and cut them up into small pieces. Have the kids make a name card for each apple. Then have everyone choose a word to describe each apple. Have everyone pick his or her favorite.

Make up your own family game with tomatoes, cheeses, pastas, and vegetables. Watch the list of family favorites grow!

Making the Best for Baby

If you want the best and freshest food for your baby, try making your own baby food. It is so simple to puree cooked vegetables as the baby's first food. When you and your doctor have decided to feed your baby solid foods, start with mild-flavored vegetables such as carrots, peas, beets, sweet potatoes, and squash. When your baby is older and you have checked with your pediatrician, you can try the more strongly flavored vegetables such as broccoli and cauliflower.

Follow these simple steps to capture great nutrition:

- Rinse the vegetables thoroughly under cold water and peel them if necessary.
- Steam, boil, or microwave the vegetables until tender.
- Puree the vegetables well in a food mill or blender or with a fork. Add a small amount of the cooking water to adjust the texture.

These basic steps can be followed to puree fresh fruits for your baby as well. Try delicious peaches, apricots, plums, or apples.

SpRiNG FrUiT GUiDe

Vegetable * (Available Year Round)	What to Look For	Easy Storage and Preparation	Best Uses
Cherries Sweet: Bing, Rainier Sour: Morello, Montmorency	Stems should be green and flexible. Avoid soft spots, bruises, and splits. Red cherries are ripe when deep red. White and yellow varieties are ripe when flushed with pink.	Will keep at room temperature for a few days, or longer in the refrigerator. Remove stems and pits before using.	Raw (sweet varieties only): out of hand, salads, smoothies, and sorbets. Cooked: compotes, cobblers, pies, and sauces for poultry.
Rhubarb	Long, thin, fully colored red stems.	Can be refrigerated for a few days. If stalks are thick, peel with a vegetable peeler to remove the fibrous strings. The leaves are poisonous.	Must be cooked. Use in fruit soups, compotes, crisps, jams, and pies. Good with rich meats such as lamb.
Strawberries	Fully colored red berries with fresh green tops.	Store at room temperature or refrigerate in a single layer. Use within a day or two. Wash before removing green tops and only when ready to use.	Best uncooked. Raw: fruit tarts, salads, smoothies, and sorbets. Cooked: jams and pies.

RHUBARB SaUCE

A tart, smooth sauce that dresses up sliced meats and poultry with its brilliant color.

Serves: 4

Preparation time: 5 minutes

Cooking time: 20 minutes

1 1/2 cups sliced rhubarb, cut 1/4-inch thick

1/2 cup sugar

1/4 cup water

Place all the ingredients in a pot. Cook, uncovered, over medium heat until the rhubarb is completely soft and falling apart. Serve warm with pork, duck, turkey, or Cornish hens.

PER SERVING: ABOUT 106 CALORIES, 0 CALORIES FROM FAT, 0 GRAMS PROTEIN, 27 GRAMS CARBOHYDRATES, 0 GRAMS FAT, 1 GRAM FIBER, 2 MILLIGRAMS SODIUM

SuMmER FrUiT GUiDe

Vegetable *(Available Year Round)	What to Look For	Easy Storage and Preparation	Best Uses
Apricots	Deep yellow with pink blush; no sign of green. Plump and firm with tender, velvety skin.	Store at room temperature or refrigerate. Use within a day or two. Poach underripe fruit in sugar and water to soften and bring out the flavor.	Raw (best at room temperature): salads, sorbets, and out of hand. Cooked: jams and tarts. Good with rich meats such as turkey.
Berries Blackberries, boysenberries, raspberries, blueberries, cranberries, currants	Firm, plump, fully colored berries.	Store at room temperature or refrigerate in a single layer. Use within a day or two. Wash before removing green top and only when ready to use.	Raw: fresh fruit desserts, salads, and smoothies. Cooked: cobblers, crisps, jams, muffins, and pies. Good with poultry such as duck and turkey.
Figs Black Mission, Kadota	Firm fruit that yields to slight pressure. Color varies according to variety from pale green/yellow to almost black. Sweet aroma.	Will keep at room temperature for a few days, or longer in the refrigerator. Skin, seeds, and flesh are edible.	Raw (best at room temperature): out of hand. Good with cheese, green salads, and ham. Cooked: tarts. Good with strong meats.

SuMmER FrUiT GuiDE coNTInUEd

Vegetable * (Available Year Round)	What to Look For	Easy Storage and Preparation	Best Uses
Lemons＊	Small fruit with a thin skin. Avoid hard, dry, or shriveled skins.	Will keep at room temperature for several days. Prepare by juicing the flesh or grating the zest (the colored part of the peel). If grating, avoid the white pith.	Spritz the juice on other foods to bring out their flavor. A great alternative to vinegar. Good in salad dressings.
Limes＊ **Key, Persian**	Bright green; heavy for size. Avoid hard, dry, or shriveled skins. Key limes have lighter-colored skin and sweeter juice.	Store at room temperature for several days. Prepare by juicing the flesh or grating the zest (the colored part of the peel). If grating, avoid the white pith.	Use in place of lemon juice for a new taste.
Mangoes	Yellow-red skin. Yields to light pressure. Sweet aroma. Smaller ones are best.	Keep at room temperature, where fruit will continue to ripen. Remove skin and pit. Work over a bowl to save the juice.	Raw: salads, salsas, smoothies, and sorbets. Cooked: chutneys and relishes.
Melons **Cantaloupe, honeydew, watermelon**	Yields to slight pressure at the stem end. Sweet scent. Avoid melons that are too soft.	Store at room temperature for 2 to 3 days. Refrigerate after cutting. Remove seeds and skins.	Best uncooked. Raw (best at room temperature): breakfast fruit, salads, salsas, smoothies, and sorbets. Good with salty ham.

SUMMER FRUIT GUIDE CONTINUED

Vegetable * (Available Year Round)	What to Look For	Easy Storage and Preparation	Best Uses
Nectarines	Plump fruit with a sweet aroma. Avoid hard or shriveled fruit.	Will keep at room temperature for a few days, or longer in the refrigerator. Remove pits.	Raw (best at room temperature): cereal topping, salads, salsas, smoothies, and sorbets. Cooked: jams and tarts. Good with poultry.
Papayas	Ripe: Yellow skin with deep orange flesh. Yields to slight pressure. Sweet aroma. Unripe: Green skin. Firm.	Store at room temperature. Remove skin. The peppery-tasting seeds are edible.	Ripe: Juice and out of hand; salads, salsas, sorbets, and as a meat tenderizer in marinades. Use underripe fruits mixed with lime juice and chilies for Asian salads.
Peaches Clingstone, freeston	Yields to slight pressure. Very fragrant. Avoid soft spots, bruises, or greenish color.	Will keep at room temperature for a few days, or longer in the refrigerator. Peaches bruise easily, so handle them carefully.	Raw (best at room temperature): cereal topping, salads, salsas, smoothies, sorbets, and out of hand. Cooked: crisps, jams, and pies.

SuMmER FrUiT GuiDe coNTInUEd

Vegetable * (Available Year Round)	What to Look For	Easy Storage and Preparation	Best Uses
Pineapple	Golden orange-brown skin. A leaf pulled gently comes away easily. Sweet aroma.	Will keep at room temperature for several days. Refrigerate after cutting. Remove leafy plume, skin, and core.	Raw: salads, salsas, smoothies, and sorbets. Cooked: with pork in Hawaiian and Chinese dishes. Good with ginger, curry, coconut, rum, or black pepper. Do not use with Jell-O.
Plums	Yields to slight pressure. Plump, heavy for size.	Will keep at room temperature for a few days, or longer in the refrigerator. Remove pits.	Raw (best at room temperature): salads and sorbets. Cooked: cobblers, crisps, jams, and tarts.

Fruity Ideas for a Change

Here are some easy ways to add marvelous fruits to your meals.

- Poultry and pork are delicious when cooked with oranges, lemons, limes, dried apricots, or prunes.
- Main-dish salads with meats or seafood get an extra spark when the greens are topped with pieces of orange or grapefruit.
- Tangerines are a great addition to chicken salads.
- Grilled or broiled seafood is even better topped with a citrus fruit salsa (see page 217 for a mango salsa recipe).

SUMMER FRUIT SALAD

Here is a lusciously sweet and simple way to enjoy summer and the delicious fruit of the season. This is a perfect ending for a picnic supper, and I love to keep it in the refrigerator for anytime snacks.

Serves: 4

Preparation time: 10 minutes

1 cup berries, whatever type looks best

1 mango, peeled, pitted, and cubed

1 nectarine, pitted and sliced

2 tablespoons orange juice

Mix the fruit in a bowl. Sprinkle with the orange juice. Serve for breakfast over yogurt, as a side dish, or for dessert over sorbet.

PER SERVING: ABOUT 66 CALORIES, 0 CALORIES FROM FAT, 1 GRAM PROTEIN, 16 GRAMS CARBOHYDRATES, 0 GRAMS FAT, 2 GRAMS FIBER, 1 MILLIGRAM SODIUM

FALL FRUIT GUIDE

Vegetable * (Available Year Round)	What to Look For	Easy Storage and Preparation	Best Uses
Apples* Red or Golden Delicious, Granny Smith, McIntosh, and many others	Very firm, with no bruises or broken flesh.	Store at room temperature or refrigerate. Remove core. Rub cut surface with lemon juice to prevent discoloration.	Raw: out of hand, salads, and sorbets. Cooked: cakes, pies, tarts, sauces with strong poultry, pork, and sausages.
Grapes*	Firm, plump. Color varies according to variety.	Wash thoroughly and store in the refrigerator for easy snacking.	Raw: salads and tarts. Good with cheese and nuts. Cooked: jelly.
Guava	Soft, pale yellow skins with pink flesh. Sweet aroma. Smaller ones are best.	Store at room temperature or refrigerate. Use within a day or two. Very delicate; handle carefully. Cut in half and remove flesh with a spoon. The seeds are edible.	Raw: dessert sauces, juice, sorbets. Good with a spritz of lime juice. Cooked: jam.
Kiwi*	Yields to slight pres- sure. No soft spots.	Store at room temperature or refrigerate. Skin, tiny black seeds, and green flesh are all edible.	Raw: Fresh fruit tarts, fruit salads, and out of hand. Good with ham. Do not use with Jell-O or gelatin because it will not get firm.

FALL FRUIT GUIDE CONTINUED

Vegetable *(Available Year Round)	What to Look For	Easy Storage and Preparation	Best Uses
Pears Bartlett, Bosc, D'Anjou, and others	Yields to very slight pressure. Color varies according to variety.	Store at room temperature to soften slightly, then refrigerate when ripe. Remove the core. Rub the cut surface with lemon juice to prevent discoloration.	Raw: salads, sorbets. Cooked: cakes and tarts. Good with cheese and game.
Persimmons	Soft, translucent, deep red-orange skin. Perfect when it looks swollen and overripe.	Store in the refrigerator. Slice off the top and scoop out the fruit pulp; discard the skin.	Raw: out of hand, fruit salads, green salads, cakes, and puddings.

SAUTÉED APPLES

The cinnamony softness of the apples creates a side dish that is both versatile and homey. Wonderful with turkey, pork, and pancakes.

Serves: 4

Preparation time: 5 minutes

Cooking time: 10 minutes

1 teaspoon butter

4 firm, tart apples (Golden Delicious, Granny Smith, Cortland), peeled, cored, and sliced

Pinch ground cinnamon (optional)

1. Melt the butter in a skillet over medium heat.
2. Add the sliced apples and cinnamon, if desired.
3. Sauté until the apples are soft.

PER SERVING: ABOUT 66 CALORIES, 0 CALORIES FROM FAT, 1 GRAM PROTEIN, 16 GRAMS CARBOHYDRATES, 0 GRAMS FAT, 2 GRAMS FIBER, 1 MILLIGRAM SODIUM

ALICE WATERS'S ORANGE JUICE

So simple, yet so sensational!

Serves: 1

Preparation time: 5 minutes

1 orange

1 tangerine

Juice the orange and tangerine, and combine.

PER SERVING: ABOUT 99 CALORIES, 0 CALORIES FROM FAT, 2 GRAMS PROTEIN, 25 GRAMS CARBOHYDRATES, 0 GRAMS FAT, 5 GRAMS FIBER, 1 MILLIGRAM SODIUM

WiNtER FrUiT GUiDE

Vegetable ✳ (Available Year Round)	What to Look For	Easy Storage and Preparation	Best Uses
Bananas✳	Ripe when skin is rich yellow color with a few brown specks.	Keep at room temperature so that fruit will continue to ripen. Spritz with lemon juice after slicing to prevent discoloration.	Raw: cereal topping and out of hand. Cooked: banana bread (the perfect use for overripe bananas).
Grapefruit✳ White, ruby red	Firm, thin-skinned. Heavy for size. Skin color varies from yellow to yellow flushed with pink and ruby red.	Will keep at room temperature for several days. Use the flesh for juice or sections. If grating the zest, avoid the white pith.	Raw: Sliced in half, juice, fruit salads, green salads, fruit salsas, and sorbets. Good with fish. Cooked: marmalade.
Kumquats	Thin-skinned, orange fruit about the size of an olive.	Store at room temperature for several days. Use whole.	Raw: out of hand (very refreshing after rich holiday meals). Cooked: sauce for dessert or poultry.
Oranges✳	Firm, thin-skinned.	Store at room temperature for up to several days. Use the flesh for juice or sections. If grating the zest, avoid the white pith.	Raw: juice, salads, and sorbets. Good with onions, olives, or cucumbers. Cooked: marmalade.

CHAPTER 3
THE GLORY OF GRAINS AND BEYOND

The route to discovering healthy new tastes lies in finding out more about the many different kinds of grains, pasta, rice, and legumes available today. Too few food shoppers venture into these exciting territories. So easy to cook, they are starting to get the glory they deserve. In many cultures, grains are the centerpiece of the plate, but in the United States most grains and legumes are hidden treasures awaiting discovery.

Exploring the tremendous diversity of grains and legumes is like discovering a new world. Introduce your family to new kinds of grains and learn the history and traditions of many cultures. There are thousands of varieties that make up this healthy group, such as polenta from Italy, kasha from Russia, couscous from North Africa, and basmati rice from India. There is good news for your pocketbook, too. Grains and beans are an economical source of protein. You get great value from these foods, and they can really stretch your budget.

To help you get started with your quest, this chapter includes charts filled with information to make shopping and cooking easy. After each chart is a simple recipe. Keep different varieties in the pantry, and your family will never get bored. As your horizons expand with each new taste, you may wonder why you never traveled this way before.

THE ROUTE TO GLORIOUS GRAINS

Grains are wonderful comfort foods to nourish and nurture your family. My mother talks of making barley soup to make us feel better in the winter. My daughter, Lisa, has adored down-home southern grits since she visited a friend in Georgia, where they had it for breakfast every day.

Loaded with nutrients, grains have been the foundation of the human diet for ages. What we commonly call grains are really the edible seeds or kernels of plants in the grass family. These are the four parts of a kernel of grain:

1. The *hull* or *outer husk* protects the seed with a hard covering that you cannot eat.

2. The *bran* is the next layer of protection. It is richest in vitamins, minerals, and fiber.

3. The *germ* is beneath the bran and is the embryo of the seed. It is rich in protein, enzymes, and oil, as well as some vitamins and minerals.

4. The *endosperm* is the starchy center of each grain. It is full of carbohydrates.

Whole grains contain the bran, germ, and endosperm, while refined grains such as white rice and pearl barley consist of the endosperm only and carry fewer nutrients.

Linking Grains and Health

Grains enjoy a place of distinction on the Food Guide Pyramid. Because of their wholesomeness as a high-fiber, low-fat food packed with many essential vitamins and minerals, they form the base of the pyramid and the largest section: the bread, cereal, rice, and pasta group. The pyramid recommends six to eleven servings daily from this food group.

Whole grains are an excellent source of B vita-

TIPS AND TRIVIA
What Are We Eating?

American families are eating more flour and cereal products. In fact, between 1975 and 1995 per capita use increased by 44 percent, according to the Department of Agriculture. But on average Americans are eating a serving or less a day of whole-grain foods, far below the minimum three per day recommended by the American Dietetic Association.

---

mins, vitamin E, potassium, trace minerals, and fiber. Grains also contain proteins that help our bodies repair themselves every day. As one of the best complex carbohydrates, grains promote endurance and protect brain power.

The fiber found in grains is important to the management of blood cholesterol and blood glucose. But be aware that not all grains have the same fiber content. The least processed grains, such as whole grains, contain more fiber and more vitamins as well as important trace minerals such as zinc and manganese.

Use It or Lose It

Grains give plenty of energy, so be smart and use it before you lose it. Getting moving also burns calories so that you stay healthy and don't gain weight. Being physically active is the flip side of healthy eating, and "just do it" is the best advice for everyone in the family.

Here are three fun ways to strengthen the heart and muscles, relieve stress, and lower the risk of heart disease, diabetes, and some cancers. All three do a good job of burning calories; how many depends on your weight and activity level.

To get everyone started, try at least thirty minutes of fun activity three times a week. Then, as it begins to feel Oeasier, gradually take it to the next level by increasing distance and speed and doing the activity more often.

Walk It! Every time you walk, you boost your metabolism. Walking is a workout that you can do almost anywhere and anytime. It has all kinds of benefits, such as burning calories and toning and strengthening calves, thighs, and ankles, and it is easy and inexpensive. Try all kinds of routes in your community and look for chances to walk up hills. Walk through the zoo or the park. Walk on the beach or to the library or the supermarket. Keep up a moderate pace that keeps your heart pumping vigorously. Then try "bursts" of even faster walking and feel the difference.

Bike It! Cycling is a family sport that gets everyone going. It is an energy booster, a power builder, and a calorie burner. Many communities have safe bike trails, and those are best to use when riding with children. Make sure everyone wears helmets and always bring along a water bottle. For a fun and charitable activity, ride with the whole family in a local bikeathon.

Dance It! Dancing is a lively way to exercise, and it's easy and enjoyable to do with your children. In fact, my kids always got a kick when I tried the newest dance steps. Ask them to teach you moves and then do them together. Any kind of dancing is good aerobic exercise and provides similar health benefits to walking and biking. For something different and entertaining, try country western line dancing or organize a dance contest with a group of neighborhood families.

The Short and Long Story of Whole Grains

Whole grains are better for you than refined grains. With more texture and flavor, whole grains also contain more fiber and micronutrients such as folic acid, magnesium, and vitamin E. Bran provides lots of fiber as well as the additional benefits of minerals and antioxidant enzymes. The fiber in whole grains helps maintain even blood sugar levels.

Whole grains may take a few minutes longer to cook, but they need no special attention. You can be doing all kinds of other cooking or even read a book while they are cooking. Pressure cookers and rice cookers get the job done even faster.

The milling process transforms nutritious whole grains into much less nutritious white flour. In fact, milled whole wheat loses 70 to 80 percent of its nutrients, including fiber, when made into white flour. Today thirty-five of fifty states require that white flour be fortified with four vitamins and one

NUTRITION POWER POINTS
Tale of Two Breads

The difference between whole wheat and white bread can make a difference to your health. Whole wheat bread contains four times as much fiber as does white bread (2 grams compared to .5 gram) because it is composed of the whole kernel—the bran, germ, and endosperm. White bread comes mainly from the endosperm.

Fiber is the nondigestible part of plants, and it offers many health benefits. Fiber-rich breads, for example, help reduce cholesterol levels, which lowers the risk of heart disease. Added benefits include its role in fighting colon cancer, diabetes, and obesity. Although both whole wheat and white breads are high in complex carbohydrates and low in fat, whole wheat bread contains many valuable minerals, such as selenium, copper, and manganese. Check the label ingredients to see that it really is a whole grain.

TIPS AND TRIVIA
Glory to Wheat

Wheat, the most cultivated plant in the world, is loudly praised for its hardiness and nutritive value. It had a part in what is known as "the quiet miracle": in the 1940s, wheat flour began to be enriched with iron and B vitamins. Along with their daily bread, Americans got protection against pellagra and beriberi, diseases linked to dietary deficiencies.

mineral. This "enriched" flour restores some of the vitamins but not all the fiber.

With all the positive features of whole grains it is surprising that we do not eat more of them. In fact, the American Medical Association recommends that half of your grain selections should be whole grains. Although scientific studies are ongoing, it has already been recommended that we eat more whole grains to prevent risks of heart disease and some cancers.

There are many ways you can add whole grains to your shopping basket. Try bringing home whole wheat flour, whole wheat pasta, and brown rice. Also check the cereal and bread labels for whole grains.

The chart that follows is based on what is generally available in most supermarkets. If grains are available in bulk, you have a chance to save even more money. For even more varieties of grains, try natural-food stores.

All-Star Grains

These grains make up an all-star team of foods rich in nutrients so important for good health.

FIBER

BROWN RICE	CORN, INCLUDING POPCORN
OATS	WHEAT BERRIES
WILD RICE	

B VITAMINS AND VITAMIN E

BARLEY	BUCKWHEAT
OATS	WHOLE WHEAT BERRIES
	AND GERM

MINERALS, ESPECIALLY POTASSIUM, MANGANESE, ZINC, AND SELENIUM

BARLEY	OATS
QUINOA	WHOLE WHEAT BERRIES
	AND GERM

Bringing Grains Home: Quick Hints for the Kitchen

- After opening, store grains in airtight containers in a cool, dry, semidark place. Glass jars with screw-top or vacuum-sealed lids work well. This inhibits bugs and prevents vitamin loss.
- Barley, bran, oats, couscous, and cracked wheat will last from six months to a year in the pantry.
- Whole grains such as buckwheat, bulgur, hominy grits, and wheat germ are stored best in the refrigerator in self-sealing plastic bags because they still contain the germ, which is oil-rich and goes bad over time. These grains will last in the refrigerator for four to six months.
- If surface grit is present, thoroughly rinse the grains before cooking. If there is no dirt, do not rinse them because it may wash away some of the B vitamins, which are water-soluble.
- Cook grains in a heavy pot; it will hold the heat best and prevent scorching.

THE GLORIOUS GRAINS GUIDE

Grain	What to Look For	Easy Cooking	Best Uses
Barley, Pearl	Polished white kernels.	Cook for 35 to 40 minutes in 3 cups boiling salted water to 1 cup barley.	Great in soups, with vegetables, or in salads.
Buckwheat and Groats (Kasha)	Whole or coarse roasted buckwheat kernels.	Simmer 1 part groats in 2 parts salted water for 15 minutes.	A terrific pilaf. Especially good with onions and mushrooms.
Corn and Cornmeal (Polenta)	White or yellow ground corn kernels; soft texture.	For cereal, simmer 1 part cornmeal in 4 parts salted water for 30 minutes.	Comforting uses include cereal, polenta, and baked goods. (See page 75 for polenta recipe.)
Hominy (Grits)	Ground coarse, medium, and fine. Similar texture to cornmeal, though a bit firmer.	Use 1 part grits to 4 parts salted water. Boil water, then lower heat and whisk grits into simmering water. Cook 10 minutes or more depending on coarseness, stirring occasionally.	Simple southern cereal or side dish.

THE GLORIOUS GRAINS GUIDE CONTINUED

Grain	What to Look For	Easy Cooking	Best Uses
Couscous (Semolina)	Little, round, yellow pellets of grains (semolina).	Stir in 1 cup couscous to 1½ cups boiling water. Let stand off the heat for 15 minutes, until all the liquid is absorbed.	Marvelous as a rice-type dish with vegetable, meat, or fish toppings.
Oats and Oatmeal (also Rolled Oats and Quick-Cooking Oatmeal)	Dried flakes of grain. Soft texture. The quick-cooking varieties are sliced more finely and are a bit precooked.	Mix 1 part rolled oats with 2 parts water. Cook on low for 5 minutes. Stir often until boiling. Remove from the heat, cover the pan and let rest 2 to 3 minutes more.	Outstanding as cereal, for baking, and as a gravy or soup thickener. (See page 143 for muesli recipe.)
Quinoa (pronounced *keen-wah*)	The whitest grains, about the size of mustard seeds. The grains will have a sweet flavor and a soft texture.	Rinse, then cook 1 part quinoa in 2 parts water or stock. Bring to a boil, then cook over medium-low heat for 12 to 15 minutes.	Unique ricelike side dishes, salads, and soups. Popular in Latin American dishes.

THE GLORIOUS GRAINS GUIDE CONTINUED

Grain	What to Look For	Easy Cooking	Best Uses
Wheat and Cracked Wheat	Small, crushed whole wheat kernels with a firm texture.	Simmer 1 part cracked wheat to 2 parts salted water for about 40 minutes.	Good as cereal or in casseroles, grain salads, and stuffing.
Bulgur	Steamed, dried, and hulled cracked wheat.	Cook 2 parts bulgur with 5 parts liquid over low heat for about 25 minutes. Remove from the heat and let stand, covered, 10 minutes more. Fluff with a fork.	Best served like rice or in salads and soups.
Bran	Outermost covering of the wheat seed.	Toast dry in a heavy skillet over low heat. Stir often to bring out the taste.	Delicious used in baking, especially muffins.
Wheat Germ	Tiny, crumblike, pale gold grains with nutty taste.	No cooking is necessary.	Great sprinkled over yogurt or cooked cereal.

PoLENTA

Warm, soft, and amazingly soothing. A homey partner to almost anything.

Serves: 6

Preparation time: 15 minutes

Cooking time: 10 minutes

1 teaspoon olive oil

1/2 teaspoon finely chopped garlic

2 1/4 cups milk

1 bay leaf

Cayenne pepper to taste

1/2 cup cornmeal

1/2 cup grated Parmesan cheese

Salt to taste

1. Heat the olive oil in a pot over low heat. Add the garlic and cook for 1 minute, keeping the heat low so as not to burn the garlic.

2. Add the milk, bay leaf, and cayenne pepper. Increase the heat and bring the milk to a boil.

3. Pour the cornmeal into the hot milk slowly, whisking constantly. After all the cornmeal has been added, cook 3 to 4 minutes more, stirring constantly.

4. Remove the pot from the heat and stir in the grated cheese.

5. Season with salt and pepper to taste.

This can be made ahead and refrigerated up to 2 days. Reheat, covered, in the microwave.

Twist: Use low-fat or skim milk to cut the fat.

PER SERVING: ABOUT 128 CALORIES, 54 CALORIES FROM FAT, 6 GRAMS PROTEIN, 12 GRAMS CARBOHYDRATES, 6 GRAMS FAT, 1 GRAM FIBER, 162 MILLIGRAMS SODIUM

THE RoUtE TO ROYaL RicE

Rice has been an important food source for humans since ancient times. It is said that rice was first cultivated in the Orient around 5000 B.C., although it was consumed long before that. In fact, no one knows for sure how old rice is. Its noble history includes a reference in the Koran to rice and barley as the "twin sons of heaven." It is amazing that over seven thousand varieties are grown around the world.

Rice is the grain that most of the world eats to survive. Because it is very filling, low in fat, and very cheap, it is an international staple. Here in the United States it has been a favorite for more than three hundred years. About nineteen billion pounds of rice are grown every year in just five states.

All rice is brown to begin with, until it is processed into polished whiteness. But it loses a lot of nutri-

TIPS AND TRIVIA
The Southern Way with Corn

Recipes for hominy grits, dodgers, spoon bread, and Hoppin' John are only some of the many uses southerners have found for corn. For almost three hundred years corn has been a staple of southern life in America, and not just for the meals it can provide. After they had used the grains for food, pioneer families in the South put the cobs to work as pipes, jug stoppers, hair curlers, and kindling. They wrote letters on corn husks, padded their pillows with shucks, and even brewed the silks for medicines. Such efficiency deserves a fitting toast, and what better way than by raising a glass of corn whiskey, a southern specialty.

tional fiber when it is stripped of its husk, bran, and germ. Brown rice has three times as much fiber as white rice and more vitamins and minerals because of the bran layer.

Like grains, rice is an important part of low-fat, high-fiber, low-calorie eating. It forms a complete protein, like meat, when eaten with beans. When eaten with smaller amounts of higher-fat meats, it creates a satisfying meal that is low in fat and calories.

Just about everyone likes rice, especially children. Its neutral taste and soothing appeal make it a wonderful comfort food. In her book *Cold Spaghetti at Midnight*, Maggie Waldron quotes the Asian wisdom that rice calms the nerves, banishes depression, and strengthens the internal organs. She believes it truly is a feel-good food.

Rice is universally popular because it goes with just about anything. From stir-fries, soups, and salads to casseroles and chicken dishes, there are many ways to use rice. Add to that the fact that some kinds of rice can be ready in a flash. So stock up on different kinds of rice and explore wonderful new tastes.

Bringing Rice Home: Quick Hints for the Kitchen

- Airtight, unopened packages have a long shelf life. Once opened, rice should be transferred to airtight jars. Glass or ceramic containers with screw-top or vacuum-seal lids work fine.
- Brown and wild rice keep best in the refrigerator. Transfer after opening to a self-sealing plastic bag to avoid mold and insects. Label and date the bag.
- Most rice should not be rinsed before cooking. This causes the starches to release too quickly, and the rice will not thicken. Wild rice, however, should be rinsed well.
- When cooking rice, use a heavy pot so that the rice does not scorch. Remember that rice triples in volume when cooked, so use a big enough pot.
- Use a tight-fitting lid on the pan, and no peeking

The Creation of Rice

Rice is an honored and ancient grain that even has its own creation myths. In Philippine lore it is said that the god Soro fell in love with the maiden Bright Jewel and wished to marry her. She tested him, hiding her love for him, and sent him on a quest to bring food back to her that was better than any ever tasted. When Soro did not return, Bright Jewel was so overcome with sadness that she died. The first rice is said to have grown from her grave.

Getting More for Your Money

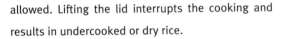

Your money goes a long way when you cook these good foods.

- Rice triples as it cooks (1 cup dry = 3 cups cooked).
- Barley quadruples as it cooks (1 cup dry = 4 cups cooked).
- Most varieties of dried beans triple as they cook (1 cup dry = 3 cups cooked).

allowed. Lifting the lid interrupts the cooking and results in undercooked or dry rice.

- To keep grains separate, add a tablespoon of butter or oil to the cooking water.
- If rice is too watery after simmering, fluff it with a fork over low heat until the water evaporates.
- Make an extra batch for when you are short on time. Cooked rice keeps in the refrigerator for up to five days or in the freezer for up to two months. Then add a little stock or water and reheat it in the microwave.

THE ROYAL RICE GUIDE

Rice	What to Look For	Easy Cooking	Best Uses
Basmati (aromatic long-grain rice from India)	Long, slender, fragrant grains.	Wash the rice in cold water to remove dirt and prevent stickiness. Simmer 1 part rice in 1 1/2 parts salted water for 15 to 20 minutes.	Delicious as a side dish, especially in Indian and Middle Eastern meals.
Italian Arborio (short grain)	Small, polished kernels that develop a creamy consistency.	Do not rinse.	Risotto: See the risotto recipe on page 189.
Long-Grain (brown)	Golden, whole, unpolished grain with bran intact. Firm texture with a nutty flavor.	Bring 1 part rice and 2 1/2 parts salted liquid to a boil. Simmer, covered, for 45 minutes. Soaking the rice overnight cuts the cooking time in half.	Delicious with curried vegetables or as a stuffing for pork chops. Makes an excellent pilaf, side dish, or salad.
Long-Grain (white)	Long, polished kernels. Bland and somewhat firm in texture.	Bring 1 part rice and 2 parts salted liquid to a boil; lower the heat. Cook, covered, for 15 minutes.	Flexible favorite. Great in soup, salads, side dishes. Perfect for pilaf (see recipe on page 81).

THE ROYAL RICE GUIDE CONTINUED

Rice	What to Look For	Easy Cooking	Best Uses
Medium-Grain (brown)	Short, plump kernel but less dense than arborio. Moist, tender texture.	See long-grain (brown).	An all-purpose rice used in soups, side dishes, and salads.
Medium-Grain (white)	Polished kernels with features similar to medium-grain (brown).	Bring 1 part rice and 1 1/2 parts liquid to a boil; lower the heat. Cook, covered, for 15 minutes.	An all-purpose rice.
Parboiled (converted)	Resembles long-grain white rice, but it's steamed and cooked before milling. Firm texture and bland taste.	Bring 1 part rice and 2 parts salted liquid to a boil; lower the heat. Cook, covered for 15 minutes.	An all-purpose rice.

THE RoYaL RiCE GUiDe coNTInUEd

Rice	What to Look For	Easy Cooking	Best Uses
Texmati and other aromatics	Milder in flavor than basmati. Grown in the United States, it is also cheaper and easier to prepare.	Bring 1 part rice and 1 3/4 parts salted liquid to a boil; lower the heat. Cook, covered for 15 minutes	Versatile. Use like basmati.
Wild Rice	Really a seed, not a rice. Long, unpolished kernels with a strong nutty flavor. Chewy texture.	Rinse well under cold water. Bring 1 part wild rice and 3 parts salted water to a boil. Simmer, covered, for about 50 minutes.	An elegant though expensive way to make a special salad, side dish, or stuffing.

RICE PILAF

A classic all-purpose side dish that adds style and flavor to the meal.

Serves: 6

Preparation time: 10 minutes

Cooking time: 20 minutes

1 teaspoon butter

1/2 cup finely chopped onion

1 sprig fresh thyme (optional)

1 cup converted rice

1 1/2 cups Basic Chicken Stock (see page 162)
   or water

Salt to taste

Freshly ground black pepper to taste

---

1. Preheat the oven to 350° F.

2. In a small ovenproof pot, melt the butter over medium heat. Add the onion and thyme, and cook for 3 to 4 minutes, until the onions become translucent but not brown.

3. Add the rice and stir to coat evenly with butter. Cook for 3 to 4 minutes.

4. Add the stock and bring to a boil over high heat.

5. As soon as the stock comes to a boil, cover the pot and place in the oven for 18 minutes.

6. Remove the sprig of thyme. Add the salt and pepper, and fluff with a fork.

PER SERVING: ABOUT 124 CALORIES, 9 CALORIES FROM FAT, 2 GRAMS PROTEIN, 26 GRAMS CARBOHYDRATES, 1 GRAM FAT, 1 GRAM FIBER, 99 MILLIGRAMS SODIUM

THE ROUTE TO PHENOMENAL PASTA

It is no wonder that pasta has become a great favorite. With so many shapes, sizes, and colors to choose from, it is the ultimate family-friendly food. Pasta's food roots are truly international—almost every culture has its own form. But from Italian fettuccine and ravioli to Japanese soba noodles, there is a common characteristic to pasta: It is simply delicious.

The powers of pasta are many. Fat-free and high in complex carbohydrates, it packs the kind of readily available energy that everyone needs. Quick and easy to cook, it is a great bargain, especially dried pasta. It is versatile, providing a backdrop for an unlimited variety of flavors. Finally, contrary to popular perception, pasta is not fattening. An average serving (2 cups cooked) has only 200 calories.

Pasta is available both dried *(pasta secca)* and fresh *(pasta fresca)*. Although dried pasta consists of just flour and water, the type of flour used is key. The best dried pastas contain durum semolina, which provides more proteins and vitamins than regular flour, and its high gluten content prevents the starches and nutrients from cooking away in the water.

Look for durum semolina on the label of dried pasta packages. Fresh pasta is lighter in texture and is traditional in northern Italy. Its richness comes from eggs, which are added to all-purpose flour.

The seemingly endless varieties of pasta shapes and sizes lend fun to the plate. Keep several kinds in the pantry and let the children choose their favorites. The various shapes were developed to hold heat differently and to work with the many kinds of sauces and liquids. The charts that follow provide quick shopping and cooking tips as well as ideas for pasta toppers.

Bringing Pasta Home: Quick Hints in the Kitchen

● Dried pasta will last at least two years in a cool, dry place. Fresh pasta needs to be refrigerated, so check the expiration date on the label.

● Leftover pasta tastes great when reheated. Cover the pasta and microwave it for a minute to keep in good flavor and moisture. Or place in a 350° F. oven until hot, about 20 minutes.

THE PHENOMENAL PASTA GUIDE

Pasta	What to Look For	Easy Cooking	Saucy Ideas
RIBBONS			
Fettuccine	Flat ribbons, usually egg noodles	6 to 8 minutes	Light vegetable and cream sauces, tomato and meat sauces
Lasagne	Long, wide, strips. Edges can be straight or curly.	10 to 12 minutes	Hearty vegetable or meat sauces
Linguini	Long, thin ribbons	7 to 9 minutes	Light, fresh tomato, seafood, or broth-based sauces
Pappardelle	Wide, flat noodles	6 to 8 minutes	Hearty vegetable or meat sauces
Tagliatelle	Wide egg noodles	6 to 8 minutes	Hearty vegetable or meat sauces

THE PhEnOMEnAL PaSTA GUiDe CoNtINueD

Pasta	What to Look For	Easy Cooking	Saucy Ideas
STRANDs			
Cappelli d'angelo (Angel Hair)	The thinnest pasta strand	2 to 3 minutes	Light tomato or broth-based sauces; light vegetable sauces
Cappellini	Thinner than spaghetti	3 to 4 minutes	Light tomato or broth-based sauces; light vegetable sauces
Spaghetti	Long, thin, round strands	10 to 12 minutes	Basic tomato and meat or seafood sauces and cream sauces
Spaghettini	Very thin spaghetti	8 to 10 minutes	Light tomato, seafood, or broth-based sauces; light vegetable sauces
Vermicelli	Thin strands, thicker than cappellini and thinner than spaghetti	4 to 6 minutes	Light sauces; good broken into soups

THE PHENOMENAL PASTA GUIDE CONTINUED

Pasta	What to Look For	Easy Cooking	Saucy Ideas
TUBES			
Bucatini	Thick, hollow spaghetti	12 to 14 minutes	Hearty vegetable or chunky meat sauces
Canneloni	Large tubes	7 to 9 minutes	Usually cooked, stuffed, and baked. Hearty vegetable or chunky meat sauces
Macaroni	Thick-walled "small pipes" and elbows	8 to 10 minutes	Light, fresh tomato, seafood, or broth-based sauces
Manicotti	Large tubes	7 to 9 minutes	Usually cooked, stuffed, and baked. Hearty vegetable or chunky meat sauces
Penne	Diagonal-cut tubes, like "quills." Smooth or ridged	10 to 12 minutes	Hearty vegetable or meat sauces
Rigatoni	Slightly curved tubes	10 to 12 minutes	Hearty vegetable or meat sauces
Ziti	Narrower, slightly curved tubes called "bridegrooms"	10 to 12 minutes	Hearty vegetable or meat sauces

THE PHENOMENAL PASTA GUIDE CONTINUED

Pasta	What to Look For	Easy Cooking	Saucy Ideas
STUFFED			
Agnolotti	Stuffed pasta shaped like half-moons	7 to 9 minutes	Light vegetable or cream sauces; light cheese or butter sauces
Cappelletti	Stuffed pasta shaped like little hats	8 to 10 minutes	Light vegetable or cream sauces; light cheese or butter sauces
Ravioli	Stuffed square or round pasta with straight or pinked edges	7 to 10 minutes, depending on size	Robust tomato sauces for meat- and cheese-stuffed ravioli; light vegetable sauces with vegetable fillings
Tortellini	Small, stuffed hatlike shapes	10 to 12 minutes	Robust tomato sauces for meat- and cheese-stuffed tortellini; light vegetable sauces for vegetable fillings
Tortelloni	Large, stuffed hatlike shapes	12 to 14 minutes	Robust tomato sauces for meat- and cheese-stuffed tortelloni; light vegetable sauces for vegetable fillings

THE PHENOMENAL PASTA GUIDE CONTINUED

Pasta	What to Look For	Easy Cooking	Saucy Ideas
SPECIAL SHAPES			
Cavatelli	Small, shell-like pasta with a ruffled edge	8 to 10 minutes	Light vegetable, cream, cheese, or butter sauces
Conchiglie	Shells in various sizes	10 to 12 minutes	Chunky vegetable or tomato sauces: small (soups), medium (salads), and jumbo (stuffed)
Farfalle	Bow tie or butterfly shaped	8 to 10 minutes	Chunky vegetable or tomato sauces
Fusilli	Corkscrew-shaped strands	10 to 12 minutes	Light vegetable, tomato, or cream sauces. Use with a vinaigrette in salads.
Orecchiette	Small, fat disks like "little ears"	7 to 9 minutes	Light tomato, vegetable, or cream sauces. Use with a vinaigrette in salads.
Orzo	Rice-shaped pasta	8 to 10 minutes	Use like rice with light sauces or with a vinaigrette in salads. See page 89 for a recipe.

THE PHENOMENAL PASTA GUIDE CONTINUED

Pasta	What to Look For	Easy Cooking	Saucy Ideas
Rotelle	Small wheel-shaped pasta	8 to 10 minutes	Light vegetable, tomato, or cream sauces. Use with a vinaigrette in salads.
Rotini	Short corkscrews	8 to 10 minutes	Light vegetable, tomato, or cream sauces. Use with a vinaigrette in salads.
Ruote	Large wheel-shaped pasta	8 to 10 minutes	Tomato or chunky vegetable sauces

ORZO SALAD

Discover a light way to enjoy this lovely little pasta, a colorful and flavorful accompaniment to grilled foods or roasted chicken. This salad tastes best at room temperature.

Serves: 10

Preparation time: 10 minutes

Cooking time: 10 minutes

8 ounces orzo

1 cup seeded and chopped fresh tomatoes

1/2 cup pitted and halved black olives

2 tablespoons red wine vinegar

1/2 cup olive oil

2 tablespoons chopped fresh herbs (parsley, tarragon, chives, or a combination)

Salt to taste

Freshly ground black pepper to taste

1. Bring 1 gallon of well-salted water to a boil. Add the orzo and cook until *al dente,* about 7 minutes. Drain well and let cool.

2. Place the orzo in a large bowl. Add the tomatoes, olives, red wine vinegar, and olive oil. Mix well. Add the fresh herbs. Season with salt and pepper to taste.

PER SERVING: ABOUT 256 CALORIES, 108 CALORIES FROM FAT, 6 GRAMS PROTEIN, 32 GRAMS CARBOHYDRATES, 12 GRAMS TOTAL FAT, 1 GRAM FIBER, 1044 MILLIGRAMS SODIUM

NUTRITION POWER POINTS
A+ Pasta

Add extra fiber, B vitamins, and trace minerals to your diet when you choose pasta labeled "whole grain" or pasta made from a combination of grains, including buckwheat. A cup of pasta contains the same number of calories as a medium-size piece of fish or a few slices of lean turkey. A serving of plain pasta contains only 2 percent or less in fat calories.

THE RoUtE tO BRilLiaNT BEAnS

Great-tasting, healthy, inexpensive meals are easy when you stock up on beans. They're probably the biggest bargain in the food store, giving you the most protein for the dollar. Beans are part of the legume family, along with peas and lentils, and are seeds that have been dried over the winter months.

Beans come in amazing colors, from jet-black to pearly white, with all kinds of browns, deep reds, and tans in between. Getting to know the different kinds can be a fun activity for your kids. Just spread the beans on a counter or table and see who guesses the most right names. From adzukis to garbanzos, there are a lot to discover.

With all the many varieties and colors, beans add diversity to family meals. Mix and match the kinds of beans you buy to help build variety in taste and nutrition.

A Healthy Bargain

When you buy beans, your family's health and your pocketbook both benefit. Beans, peas, and lentils provide a low-cost bonus because they contain both carbohydrates and proteins. A small serving of beans has the same amount of protein as most meats. In fact, beans contain more protein than any vegetable, and unlike animal proteins, beans have no cholesterol and are low-fat, except soybeans. A 4-ounce serving of beans contains only 135 calories.

When beans are mixed with grains or vegetables, they complement each other to provide a set of nutritious proteins that are low in fat and high in fiber. Added to all this, beans are abundant in the B vitamins, iron, thiamin, and other valuable minerals.

Bulk purchases, available in some supermarkets and natural-food stores, offer good prices because

Double Hitters

Garbanzo beans are one of the most nutritious varieties. They're high in the B vitamins and vitamin C as well as iron, calcium, and potassium. The humble lentil is high in fiber, B vitamins, and minerals, especially molybedenum, a little-known mineral.

When There Is a Vegetarian in the House

Vegetarianism is a rising trend, especially among young people, and parents of vegetarians can help their children meet all their nutritional needs. To get the essential nutrients found in animal protein such as iron, vitamin B12, calcium, and zinc, the USDA recommends that vegetables, fruit, grains, and legumes make up most of your child's diet. Some of these foods can also add protein to the diet. Check labels to be sure children are getting what they need. Talk to your physician for other ideas and help in monitoring your child's growth. It is best to be positive and supportive of your child. No one wins food fights.

you do not pay for the packaging and branding. Dried beans bought in bulk are the best bargains. Find organic beans if you can because they often taste better. Canned beans are timesavers because they do not require long soaking, but they often contain sugar or additives, so it is wise to check their labels.

Brainy Bean Tricks: Quick Hints for the Kitchen

- Beans are easy to select. Look for a smooth surface and bright color. Watch out for cracked seams or a dull, wrinkled surface, clues that they are too dry.

- Use beans within a year, or they will be tough and take a long time to soften.

- Sort dry beans first to pick out withered beans and any stones that might be in the package. Rinse both dried and canned beans several times.

- It is necessary to soak most dried beans to ensure even cooking and to help digestion. Small legumes such as lentils and split peas do not need soaking.

- To soak, cover beans in a bowl with 2 or 3 inches of cold water. Let soak at least 12 hours or overnight in the refrigerator. For a quicker soak, cover the beans in a saucepan with 2 or 3 inches of cold water,

THE BRILLIANT BEAN GUIDE

Bean	What to Look For	Easy Cooking	Best Uses
Adzuki (or Aduki)	Small, deep red bean. Somewhat sweet, with a delicate texture.	Bring to a boil, then simmer for 1 1/2 hours.	Delicious with rice or barley and Asian flavors such as soy sauce.
Black Turtle	Small, oval, black bean. Earthy flavor with a soft texture.	Bring to a boil, then simmer for 1 1/2 hours.	Great in Latin American–style soups, stews, and sauces. Terrific in chopped vegetable salads.
Black-eyed Peas	Oval, creamy white bean with a black "eye." Soft texture.	Bring to a boil, then simmer for 1 hour.	It's a southern tradition to cook them with rice and greens. Toss with vinaigrette and chopped tomatoes.
Fava (or Broad)	Oval-shaped light brown beans. Earthy flavor and creamy texture.	Remove tough skin before cooking. Bring to a boil, then simmer for 40 minutes.	Lovely in soups and salads. Puree for tasty dips.
Garbanzo (Chickpeas)	Large, round, cream-colored bean. Nutty flavor and crunchy texture.	Bring to a boil, then simmer for 2 1/2 hours.	Features in Middle Eastern and Mediterranean dishes. Add to salads and soups.

THE BRILLIANT BEAN GUIDE CONTINUED

Bean	What to Look For	Easy Cooking	Best Uses
Great Northern	Medium-size, oval white bean. Delicate taste with a firm texture.	Bring to a boil, then simmer for 1 1/2 to 2 hours.	A nice addition to stews and salads.
Kidney, Red or White (or Cannellini)	Large, kidney-shaped, deep reddish brown or white bean. Bland taste with a soft texture.	Bring to a boil, then simmer for 1 1/2 hours.	A hit in southwestern chilies, soups, and salads. White cannellini beans star in Italian stews and minestrone soups.
Lentils	Small green, brown, or red legumes with a round, flat shape. Flavorful, with a firm texture.	No need to presoak. Bring to a boil, then simmer for 30 to 40 minutes.	Tasty in soups and stews; a terrific addition to salads. (See page 166 for recipe.)
Lima	Flat, oval, creamy white bean. The smallest dried ones have the mildest taste. Mushy texture.	Bring to a boil, then simmer for 1 1/2 hours.	Good for soups and stews.

THE BRILLIANT BEAN GUIDE CONTINUED

Bean	What to Look For	Easy Cooking	Best Uses
Pinto	Medium-size beige-and-brown-speckled bean. Earthy flavor and mealy texture.	Bring to a boil, then simmer for 2 hours.	Use in southwestern bean dishes and stews. Refried beans, or *frijoles refritos*, are great in corn tortillas.
Soy	Medium-size oval, yellowish bean. Very bland flavor and firm texture.	Bring to a boil, then simmer for at least 3 hours.	Best mixed with other flavorful ingredients in stews. Miso is used for soups. (See page 171 for a recipe.)
Split Peas	Small green or yellow halved peas. Earthy flavor with a creamy texture.	No presoaking necessary. Bring to a boil, then simmer for 50 minutes.	Makes a comforting soup.
White: Small White, Navy, or Pea	Small, oval white bean.	Bring to a boil, then simmer for 2 hours.	Use in soups, salads, stews, and dips.

*Unless otherwise indicated, all beans need to be soaked first. See the instructions on page 91.

HUMMUS

Serves: 6 to 8

Preparation time: 10 minutes

One 12-ounce can garbanzo beans (chickpeas)

1 tablespoon tahini

1 tablespoon lemon juice

1 teaspoon finely chopped garlic

About 3 tablespoons olive oil

Salt to taste

Freshly ground black pepper to taste

1. Drain and rinse the garbanzo beans.
2. Puree the garbanzo beans in a blender or food processor with the tahini, lemon juice, and garlic.
3. With the machine running, add the olive oil slowly, until the hummus becomes creamy and spreadable.
4. Add salt and pepper to taste.
5. Serve with pita bread.

PER SERVING: ABOUT 212 CALORIES, 18 CALORIES FROM FAT, 2 GRAMS PROTEIN, 7 GRAMS CARBOHYDRATES, 2 GRAMS TOTAL FAT, 2 GRAMS FIBER, 167 MILLIGRAMS SODIUM

NUTRITION POWER POINTS
The Joy of Soy

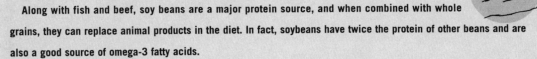

Along with fish and beef, soy beans are a major protein source, and when combined with whole grains, they can replace animal products in the diet. In fact, soybeans have twice the protein of other beans and are also a good source of omega-3 fatty acids.

Soy foods such as tofu, miso, and shoya (soy sauce) offer a healthy addition to everyday family meals.

bring to a boil for 2 minutes, remove from the heat, cover, and let stand for 1 to 2 hours. Drain and cook.

• For a microwave soak, put 2 cups of beans and 2 cups of water in a covered bowl. Microwave on high for 15 minutes and let stand for 5 minutes. Add 2 more cups of cold water, cover, and let stand for 1 hour. Drain and cook.

• Always throw away the soaking water and cover the beans with fresh water in a large covered pot—

3 parts water to 1 part beans. Most beans triple in volume when cooked.

• Give flavor to the beans while they cook by adding a few whole garlic cloves, some chopped onion, and a bay leaf. After cooking, add a final splash of flavor by adding olive oil, balsamic vinegar, lemon juice, or soy sauce.

• Wait until the beans are soft before adding acidic foods such as lemon, vinegar, or tomatoes. The acid slows down the softening process.

- Taste the beans and test for doneness. They should be tender but not mushy. If using beans in a salad, cool immediately under cold water.

- It's smart and time-saving to cook extra beans; they'll keep in the refrigerator for 3 or 4 days. Cooked beans freeze well, too. ■

CHAPTER 4

STOCKING A FLAVOR-FULL PANTRY

No food shopping experience is complete without including the ingredients that provide the spark to family meals. Modern cooking, with its focus on vegetables, fruits, and grains, moderates the use of fat. Herbs, spices, and seasonings step in to provide fresh, bright flavors without a lot of additional calories. Flavor combinations often signal the origin of the dish, such as the addition of lemon and oregano in Greek dishes or soy, ginger, and cilantro in Asian cooking. Use this chapter to learn about the many flavor options available and find out how a well-stocked pantry makes great meals easier to prepare.

Celebrating Herbs and Spices

The cook's appreciation of herbs and spices has a long history, going back at least five thousand years. In fact, Europeans discovered the New World while searching for new trade routes to Asia to obtain spices. Herbs are the

Bay leaves come not from annual or perennial plants, as most herbs do, but from the bay tree. Bay leaves have woven themselves into food history since Apollo, the Greek god of prophecy, healing, and poetry, pursued the nymph Daphne. When Daphne turned herself into a bay tree to avoid him and his advances, Apollo declared the bay tree sacred and wore a crown of bay leaves on his head in memory of his lost love. The temple at Delphi, which is dedicated to Apollo, had a roof thatched with branches of bay leaves, and the priestesses there ate whole bay leaves before delivering prophecies.

leafy parts of plants or trees, and all are grown in temperate zones of the world. In contrast, spices, the dried roots, berries, seeds, or bark of tropical plants, are mostly grown in the Far East. Use herbs and spices to enhance the flavor of food, never to camouflage it.

For the best aroma and taste, fresh herbs stand out. To use fresh herbs, strip the little leaves from the tough stems by hand or with scissors. Chopping the herbs finely will best release the flavor. Sprinkle herbs on hot foods at the last minute so that they keep their color and texture. Chopped herbs can be added to cold dishes several hours before.

Herbs also come in dried form, and here is where you want to fill your pantry with wonderful flavors. It is best to buy dried herbs in small quantities if possible; their shelf life is usually no more than two years. Try to buy the more fragile dried herbs such as thyme and tarragon as leaves because they will last longer. They can be crushed easily if necessary.

Fresh and dried herbs can be used interchangeably, but remember this rule of thumb when cooking: *1 tablespoon of fresh herbs equals 1 teaspoon of crushed dried herbs.*

Use your creativity and imagination when cooking with herbs and spices. You may even want to conduct family taste tests to find everyone's favorites. The charts on the following pages give some guidelines to help spice up your family meals.

Bringing Herbs and Spices Home: Quick Hints for the Kitchen

- Store fresh herbs in the refrigerator wrapped in a wet paper towel, or place the stem ends of herbs in a glass jar filled 1/3 with water.

- Before using fresh herbs, always give them a quick cleaning. Just rinse in cool water to remove dirt, then shake a few times to remove excess water. Pat dry with a paper towel.

- Store dried herbs and spices in a cool, dry pantry or drawer in nontransparent containers. Check for freshness and bright color after six months, and replace frequently.

- When using dried herbs in recipes, soak them in

A GUIDE TO HERBS AND SPICES

Herb or Spice	Options	Favorite Uses	Grow at Home
Allspice Small, dried spiceberries. Clove- and nutmeg-flavored spice.	Whole dried berries, and ground	Great added to spice cakes, cookies, and fruit pies.	No
Anise Licorice-flavored spice	Whole, dried seeds, and ground	Adds flavor to cakes, cookies, and breads. Good in beef stews.	No
Basil Herb with a sweet, pungent flavor. Also try purple (opal) basil and curly leaf basil	Fresh leaves and dried or crushed	Marvelous in Mediterranean-style dishes such as tomato and pesto sauces, in soups and salads, or with chicken or fish.	Yes
Bay Leaf (Laurel) Herb with long green leaves and a woodsy, pungent flavor.	Whole dried leaves	Superb in beef stews, spaghetti sauces, and other long-cooking stocks and sauces. Always remove the leaves before serving; they are not edible.	Yes

A Guide to Herbs and Spices Continued

Herb or Spice	Options	Favorite Uses	Grow at Home
Caraway Aromatic seed with licorice flavor.	Whole dried seeds	Tasty in rye bread, eggs, and cheese spreads; great with cooked winter vegetables.	No
Cardamom Spice that is native to India. Aromatic, with a cinnamon-like flavor.	Whole dried seeds and ground	Adds flavor to baked goods. A key flavor in curries and Indian dishes. Perks up sweet potatoes and winter squash.	No
Cayenne The plump red fruit of the tropical capsicum plant. Sweet, pungent flavor.	Ground into powder	Adds heat to Mexican and Indian dishes. Good with eggs and sauces. Go gently.	No
Celery Seed Light brown, dried seed originally from India, with a strong celery-like flavor	Whole dried seeds	A great touch in potato salads, soups, and cabbage dishes. Use sparingly.	No

A Guide to Herbs and Spices Continued

Herb or Spice	Options	Favorite Uses	Grow at Home
Chervil Herb with feathery green leaves. Tastes slightly like licorice.	Fresh leaves and ground	Sprinkle in green salads or vegetable dishes, or with fish, shellfish, and chicken. Makes a great garnish.	Yes
Chili Powder Mix of ground chili peppers with other spices such as cumin and oregano	Ground	Awakens bean dishes, meat stews, and soups. Energizes egg and cheese dishes.	No
Chives Long, slender, green herb with mild onion taste	Fresh leaves and dried or frozen minced leaves	Delightful in soups and sauces, in fish and egg dishes, and on baked potatoes. Use as a garnish.	Yes
Cilantro Leafy, short-stemmed herb with very pungent flavor and refreshing taste	Fresh leaves	A popular addition to Mexican, South American, and Asian dishes. Great with ground meat, rice, and beans. Add fresh leaves at the last minute to fish, salads, salsas, and vegetables.	Yes

A Guide to Herbs and Spices Continued

Herb or Spice	Options	Favorite Uses	Grow at Home
Cinnamon Spice from the bark of a tropical tree. Sweet, mildly hot taste.	Quill-like sticks and ground	Delicious in French toast, spice cakes, and cookies. Great with sweet potatoes, carrots, and winter squash.	No
Clove Spice from a tropical evergreen tree. Strong, sweet, pungent taste.	Whole dried buds and ground	A versatile spice in baked goods and sauces. Good with pork, ham, and stews.	No
Coriander Spice with a mild fragrance and a flavor like blended lemon and carraway	Whole dried seeds and ground.	Ground seeds are nice in cakes, cookies, and buns. Whole seeds are tasty in pickling spice blends.	Yes
Cumin Hot, nutty-flavored spice	Whole dried seeds and ground	A basic spice in curry and chili powder mixtures. Great for vegetable soups, sausages, and lamb.	No

A GuiDe to HeRbS aNd SPicES CoNtiNueD

Herb or Spice	Options	Favorite Uses	Grow at Home
Dill Herb with feathery leaves and delicate, tangy taste or small pungent tan seeds	Fresh and dried leaves and seeds	Versatile herb with soups, green beans, cucumbers, tomatoes, potatoes, and fish. The seeds are good in pickling.	Yes
Fennel Herb with a slight licorice flavor	Fresh stalks and whole dried seeds	A unique addition to chicken, fish, lamb, and sausage dishes. Great in salads and breads, too.	Yes
Fines Herbes A French mixture of herbs including parsley, chives, chervil, and tarragon	Crumbled dry leaves	Sprinkle on fish, poultry, eggs, and cheese for a special taste	Yes
Ginger Sweet, peppery spice	Fresh; whole dried or ground; crystallized	Versatile; especially good in Asian and Indian dishes. The ground dried powder is good in baking, rice dishes, and marinades. Use crystallized ginger in baking; fresh ginger in marinades or with fish, meat, and vegetable dishes.	No

A GuiDe tO HeRbS aNd SPicES CoNtiNueD

Herb or Spice	Options	Favorite Uses	Grow at Home
Lemongrass A long, yellowish herb with a sour lemon taste and fragrance	Fresh and dried stalks. Not widely available.	An important herb in Thai and Indonesian cooking. Lovely with seafood or in soups and vinaigrettes.	No
Mace An orange-colored spice that tastes and smells like mild nutmeg	Dried and ground	A nice addition to spice cakes and cookies, custards, fruit desserts, and vegetable dishes	No
Marjoram Herb with mild oregano-like taste	Fresh leaves; whole dried leaves; and crumbled dried leaves	A versatile herb used in fish, meat, and poultry dishes	Yes
Mint Herb with spicy-sweet leaves. Thirty varieties, with peppermint and spearmint the most popular.	Fresh and crumbled dried leaves	Delicious added to desserts, fruit salads, and lamb and vegetable dishes. A Middle Eastern favorite. Great in iced tea and jellies.	Yes

A Guide to Herbs and Spices Continued

Herb or Spice	Options	Favorite Uses	Grow at Home
Nutmeg The spice seed from a tropical evergreen. It has a delicately warm, spicy, sweet taste and aroma.	Whole and ground seeds. For freshest flavor, buy whole nutmeg and grate what you need.	Terrific in cream sauces and soups, with different vegetables, and in all kinds of desserts; and don't forget eggnog.	No
Oregano Herb with a sweeter, stronger, more pungent taste than marjoram	Fresh and crumbled dried leaves	A basic herb in Italian, Greek, and Mexican cooking. Marvelous in tomato sauces and meat, poultry, and seafood dishes.	Yes
Paprika Spice made by grinding sweet red pepper pods. The pungent flavor can be mild or hot.	Sweet or hot; ground	A lively touch to potato and egg salads, fish, shellfish, and poultry. A basic spice in Hungarian goulash and paprikash.	No
Parsley Herb with a fresh, slightly peppery flavor. Two common varieties are Italian flat leaf and curly leaf.	Fresh and dried leaves	Good in salads, dressings, and soups, and with poultry, meats, fish, and seafood. Terrific in vegetable dishes. Great garnish.	Yes

A GuiDe to HeRbS aNd SPicES CoNtiNUeD

Herb or Spice	Options	Favorite Uses	Grow at Home
Poppy Seeds Small, blackish seeds of the poppy flower	Whole seeds and ground paste	Nice in baked goods. Also good with noodles and fresh fruit.	No
Rosemary Herb with needle-like leaves and piney, lemony flavor and aroma	Fresh and whole dried leaves	Delicious with lamb, pork, veal, and beef. Also good with roasted potatoes and mushrooms.	Yes
Saffron An expensive spice that comes from the dried stigma of a small crocus. Tiny, bright red or yellow threads.	Whole dried saffron threads that have a deep orange color are best. Also available ground or as dried whole stigmas.	Adds rich flavor to risotto, paella, and seafood dishes. A French and Spanish favorite. A little goes a long way.	No
Sage Herb with a musty-mint flavor and aroma. Pretty silver-green leaves make a great garnish.	Fresh leaves; whole dried and crumbled leaves; ground	Wonderful used with pork and in poultry stuffing, sausages, and dried bean soups and stews	Yes

A GUIDE TO HERBS AND SPICES:

Herb or Spice	Options	Favorite Uses	Grow at Home
Savory Herb with both summer and winter varieties	Fresh and crumbled dried leaves	A special touch in bean dishes. Good with most meats, in stuffing, or in tomato and onion dishes.	Yes
Tarragon Herb with a licorice-like flavor and long, thin leaves.	Fresh whole leaves and dried whole and crumbled leaves	A perky addition to salads, vinaigrettes, chicken, fish, shellfish, veal, and egg dishes. Gives energy to vegetables.	Yes
Thyme Herb with tiny, light green leaves and a minty, lemony aroma and flavor. Varieties: lemon, English, and French.	Fresh whole leaves and dried whole and crumbled leaves	Wonderful in sausage and stuffing, and in poultry, fish, and vegetable dishes. A basic herb in bouquet garni.	Yes
Turmeric A bright yellow spice with a bitter, pungent flavor	Ground dried	Vital to mustard and curry powder. Gives color to foods.	No

MINTED CuCUMBER DIP

This dip is refreshingly delicious and simple to prepare.

Makes about 1 1/2 cups

Preparation time: 5 minutes

1 **medium cucumber, peeled and seeded**

1 **cup yogurt**

1 **tablespoon finely chopped fresh mint**

1: Briefly puree the cucumber in a blender. Stir in the yogurt and mint.

2: Serve with raw vegetables, pita bread, or spicy foods.

PER SERVING: ABOUT 5 CALORIES, 0 CALORIES FROM FAT, 0 GRAMS PROTEIN, 1 GRAM CARBOHYDRATES, 0 GRAMS TOTAL FAT, 0 GRAMS FIBER, 3 MILLIGRAMS SODIUM

FOR SAFEKEEPING
Spicewise

Adding spices to food while cooking also gives protection against harmful bacteria, especially in hot climates. Recent research at Cornell University reported that widely used spices such as onions and garlic inhibited the growth of 30 microorganisms, and so did hot peppers, ginger, and other hot spices. In fact, the researchers believe that in hot climates like those of Mexico, India, South America, and Africa, spices play an important role in suppressing bacterial growth in food. Enjoy the flavor and get the benefit of food safety!

Growing Herbs

Amateur gardeners find that growing herbs is easy and rewarding. For me, a city girl, there is no simpler pleasure than bringing in homegrown herbs moments before cooking. The word "fresh" takes on a whole new meaning. Vast acres of land and a tractor are not necessary; in fact, if you are short on space, grow your herbs close to your kitchen in a windowbox or a few pots.

Children of all ages love taking care of the plants. Herbs do well in almost every region of the country, and there is an herb that is just right for every spot in the garden or sunny window. Get to know the endless variety of herbs and choose the ones that fit your site and your cooking needs.

- Basil, oregano, thyme, and parsley are easy-to-grow summer favorites. For Mexican and Chinese dishes, try cilantro.
- Herbs thrive in light, sandy soil, and grow especially well near the sea. Water at least once a week, and more frequently during hot, dry months. Give them plant food, too.
- Harvest herbs frequently for best results. Just snip the outside leaves with a small scissors and watch the new leaves spring from the center.

oil, lemon juice, or stock to get the most flavor and color.
- Use herbs as a garnish on plates or decorate with them by placing in a vase.

A Field of Flavor Favorites

Delicious-tasting meals are fun to prepare when you explore the fantastic array of flavors found in today's market. Discover the broad spectrum of ways to enhance taste while promoting everyone's health. The field of choices seems to be forever expanding. These ingredients can add those special touches to family meals.

Peppercorns: Probably the most valuable flavor player in the kitchen, fresh, ground pepper is a must-have for modern cooking. Preground pepper just does not compare. Green, black, and white peppercorns all come from the same plant. Green peppercorns are really unripened black peppercorns and taste milder than black or white peppercorns. They are not widely available. Black peppercorns have the strongest flavor; their complex taste is sweet, fruity, and warm. White peppercorns are fully ripened, and the skin is

> Growing herbs is the first step in getting close to food.
>
> —ANNIE SOMMERVILLE, CHEF, GREENS RESTAURANT, SAN FRANCISCO, CALIFORNIA

removed; they have a milder taste and less fragrance.

Chili Peppers: Though not a true herb or spice, chili peppers (capsicum) have become a popular flavor booster and are a great source of beta-carotene. Chilies come sweet, mild, hot, hotter, and hottest. Available in the market fresh, frozen, dried, flaked, and powdered, all chilies give a warm, tingling feeling on your tongue. The cuisines of Thailand, Mexico, the Caribbean, China, Vietnam, and many other countries depend heavily on the chili pepper.

There are over one hundred varieties of chilies. These favorites are most readily available:

Ground Red Chile: New Mexican dried ground chili pods.

Chipotle: A smoked jalapeño chili that comes dried, ground, or packed in adobo sauce. Very hot and terrific for sauces, soups, and salsas.

Serrano: Even hotter than the chipotle, and more flavorful. Good in salsas, pickled, or roasted.

Jalapeño: A small green pepper that is more peppery than hot. Milder than the serrano chili.

Red Pepper Flakes: Crushed, dried red chilies with seeds that add spark to dishes.

Small Dried Red Peppers: Many different kinds,

TIPS AND TRIVIA
Hot Tips for Cool Chilies

Some like it hot, but some are sensitive, too. Here is how to treat the chili peppers for best results:

* If your skin is sensitive or you are not used to handling chili peppers, wear rubber gloves. Avoid touching your eyes, nose, and mouth when your hands have chili oils on them.

* The hottest parts of chili peppers are the veins and seeds. For a milder taste, shake out the seeds and slice off the veins.

* To keep the potency of the chili pepper, whether it is ground or whole, buy a small amount at a time. Chilies have a short shelf life.

* When using whole chilies, remember to remove them before the dish is served.

NUTRITION POWER POINTS
The Generous Bulb

The garlic bulb doesn't just give us wonderful aroma and taste; it also gives us help against disease. Garlic plays a part in stimulating the immune functions. This means that it works against bacteria and viruses and assists in fighting cancer. So enjoy the flavor and the health benefits.

FIESTA SALSA

Lively and vibrant, hot or hotter, this is an all-purpose small dish you should not be without.

Makes about 1 cup

Preparation time: 15 minutes

2 Roma tomatoes, diced

1/4 cup diced red onion

1 teaspoon seeded and finely chopped jalapeño pepper

1/4 cup diced red or green pepper

1 tablespoon chopped cilantro

1 tablespoon fresh lime juice (about 1 lime)

Salt to taste

Freshly ground black pepper to taste

Hot sauce (optional)

1. Place the tomatoes, onion, jalapeño, pepper, cilantro, and lime juice in a bowl. Season to taste with salt, pepper, and hot sauce.
2. Serve with tortilla chips or pita bread.

PER SERVING (2 TABLESPOONS): ABOUT 7 CALORIES, 0 CALORIES FROM FAT, 0 GRAMS PROTEIN, 2 GRAMS CARBOHYDRATES, 0 GRAMS FAT, 0 GRAMS FIBER, 64 MILLIGRAMS SODIUM

including bird peppers, chili pequin, and others. All are hot, but the small ones are even hotter.

Onions and other members of the Allium family: These are probably the most widely used seasonings. Although technically the plant is closely related to herbs, it is considered by most people to be a vegetable (see page 41). Onions can be used to flavor almost anything and can be eaten raw, roasted, pickled, sautéed, or as a vegetable.

Chives: Grows well in the garden. Use as a garnish.

Garlic: A cook's best friend—both a vegetable and a pungent seasoning. Buy heads that are hard and tight.

Pearl Onions: Little, versatile onions with white and yellow skins.

Shallots: Small bulbs that grow in clusters and can be separated into two bulbs after being peeled. Its taste is something like a mix of onion, garlic, and leeks. It is often used raw in salads.

Scallions (Spring Onions): The shoots of young onions before they take mature shape. A delicious addition to salads.

Citrus: With acidic properties and aromatic peels, citrus fruits add interest and fragrance to cooking. They add taste to low-salt dishes while bringing out the natural flavors of the ingredients. A little squeeze of lemon, lime, or orange juice can bring out extra flavor from fruit. Lemon juice also prevents fruit such as apples and pears from discoloring.

Salt: The most universally used seasoning in the kitchen, salt gives flavor to foods and brings out the flavor of foods at the same time. It also draws out the moisture and bitter juices from vegetables and is often used as a preservative. For some people who are at risk for high blood pressure, medical experts recommend less consumption of salt or sodium.

When salt comes straight from sea water, it is a complex substance filled with trace minerals. After it has gone through processing and refinement, it has lost some of these minerals and some of its flavor. Here are the different forms of salt available:

- **Table:** The most finely grained variety. Additives are used to keep it free-flowing.

- **Iodized:** Because iodine is removed during processing, it is added back for nutritional reasons.
- **Sea:** Complex and saltier tasting; available as coarse or fine-grained. New coarse varieties, like Celtic sea salt, can be run through a pepper grinder.
- **Kosher:** Has a rough texture and is less salty than sea salt. It is a favorite of chefs because they can easily pick it up with their fingers. I keep a little bowl of kosher salt next to my stove for easy use.

Mustard: Every culture has its own distinct version of mustard, a favorite flavor enhancer. The cuisines of India, the Mediterranean, the Caribbean, northern Europe, Africa, and the United States all make wide use of mustard. There are more than three hundred varieties manufactured today.

The Romans first produced mustard thousands of years ago when they took fermented grape juice (must) and what we now call mustard seeds and turned it into paste. The word mustard comes from the French and means "burning" must. Mustard's acidic, pungent taste was always found on medieval tables and was a welcome relief from the sometimes bad-tasting meats.

Mustard is a "must" for kitchen pantries because it is so versatile. With many flavor dimensions, from subtle and discreet to assertive and bold, it is a welcome addition to many foods. A low-fat, low-calorie condiment, mustard is a great substitute for mayonnaise. These are some favorites:

- **Dijon:** With a secret recipe and French law protecting its name, Dijon mustard is the most famous of all. It is versatile in dressings and marinades and on sandwiches.

NUTRITION POWER POINTS
Salt: How Much Is Too Much?

Sodium and salt go together. Table salt is about half sodium, a mineral needed throughout your body to pump body fluids and nutrients where they need to go. You get plenty of sodium from foods without using the salt shaker. For blood pressure health, the American Heart Association suggests limiting sodium to about 3 grams per day, the amount found in a rounded teaspoon of salt. Sodium and salt are found primarily in processed foods, so it makes good sense to check the food label to learn the sodium content.

- **Coleman:** Regarded as an English treasure since the nineteenth century, this mustard has a vivid yellow color and hot flavor.
- **Dusseldorf:** A German variety with a bold taste that is good with dark rye breads and corned beef.
- **Prepared:** American-made mustard that is great on ham and cheese sandwiches and as a ballpark favorite.

Vanilla: Indispensable for baking and desserts, vanilla is available as an extract—pure or artificial—and as a bean. The pure extract has an excellent taste. Although it is a bit more expensive, a smaller quantity can be used. For the most intense taste use the vanilla bean. Here's how: Cut the beans in half lengthwise and scrape out the seeds. Add them to milk, heat, and allow to steep like tea. Use the milk in ice creams, custards, and puddings.

The Dynamic Duo: Vinegar and Oil

Vinegar: An all-purpose kitchen staple, vinegar is used as a condiment, as a food preservative, in canning and pickling, as a salad dressing, and as a flavor accent for just about any food. The wide variety of vinegar available today offers a chance to be creative and flexible. The word "vinegar" comes from the French, and it means sour wine. Vinegar was not even sold separately until the seventeenth century. Since then it has become a staple in kitchens everywhere. Here are some top choices for stocking up your pantry:

- **Balsamic:** Made from the unfermented juice of white grapes and aged for around twelve years; occasionally it has been aged for as long as one hundred years. Dark-colored and smooth, it has an intense sweet-tart taste. Makes a marvelous vinaigrette. Use in rice dishes or spoon over fresh fruit.
- **Cider:** Made from tart apples, it has a caramel color. Use in salad dressings, for smoked fish or meat, in curries, and in sautéed fruit dishes.
- **Malt:** Made from ale and used often in England. Serve with English fish and chips; use in salad dressings.
- **Rice:** An Asian white vinegar made from fermented rice wine. Good when used with Asian sesame oil in salads.
- **Wine:** Made from fermented red or white wine, sherry, or champagne. An all-purpose mild-tasting vinegar for salad dressings, marinades, and sauces.

FOR SAFEKEEPING
Storing Oils

Oils stay freshest when kept capped in a cool, dark place. After opening, most oils keep longer if stored in the refrigerator. Olive and sesame oils are quite stable, so they keep well in a cool, dark pantry. For quick everyday use, keep a small amount of olive oil handy in a jar or little pitcher on the kitchen counter. You can tell that an oil is rancid by its stale, fishy, soapy odor. Toss it; do not use it!

About Oil

Oils are widely used in many kinds of foods. Oils contain a mix of polyunsaturated, monounsaturated, and some saturated fatty acids, but no cholesterol. The fatty acids found in oils aid in forming cell walls throughout the body and help vitamins do their work. The chart below shows the differences among oils. Each oil contains 14 grams of total fat and 126 calories per tablespoon.

Percent of Total Fat

Oil	Polyunsaturated Fatty Acid	Monounsaturated Fatty Acid	Saturated Fatty Acid
Canola	31	62	7
Corn	62	25	13
Olive	9	77	14
Peanut	34	48	18
Soybean	61	24	15
Walnut	67	24	9

Infusing Vinegar and Oil

Infusing vinegar and oil with herbs and other spices offers a new taste experience and is simple to do. They are available in supermarkets and at farmer's markets, but the real pleasure is found in doing it in your kitchen. It is a fun activity for children, too. They can help gather the herbs or pluck off the leaves before they are added to the vinegar and oil.

Vinegar can be infused with herbs and fruits. If you start with red or white wine vinegar or rice wine vinegar, add herbs such as tarragon, thyme, or basil, or try a combination of herbs. Fruit vinegar goes well with any kind of berries or with stone fruit such as peaches or plums.

Oil can be infused with herbs, garlic, or spices. Neutral oils such as canola, olive, and salad oil blend best with the added flavors.

To make a basic herb-infused vinegar or oil, choose a fresh herb such as basil, dill, parsley, thyme, or others. Wash the herbs and dry them well.

Place them along with 2 cups vinegar or oil in a blender. Blend on high speed to combine.

Refrigerate in a container. The vinegar becomes clear in several hours. The added ingredients will settle at the bottom.

To make a fruit vinegar, wash 1 cup berries and dry them well. Place the berries and 2 cups vinegar in a blender. Blend on high speed to combine.

Refrigerate in a closed container. The vinegar becomes clear in several hours. Leave the fruit in the bottom; it looks pretty.

To make garlic oil, blanch 5 garlic cloves in salted, boiling water for 2 minutes, then plunge them into ice water. Dry well. Place the cloves and 2 cups oil in a blender and blend on high speed to combine. Refrigerate in a closed container.

To make a spicy oil, heat 1 tablespoon oil with 1 teaspoon chili powder in a frying pan over medium heat until warm to release the flavorful oils from the spice. Add the chili oil to the remaining oil. Refrigerate in a closed container.

Oil: The two basic categories of oil are salad oils, which are used primarily to flavor salad dressings, sauces, and marinades, and cooking oils, which are used for sautéing and frying. The smoking point of oils is another separating factor. Different oils have different temperatures at which they smoke and break down chemically. If they are heated past this point, they will have a bad flavor. For example, salad oils have lower smoking points and therefore are not well suited to high-heat cooking.

The aroma of an oil should be sweet and should reflect where the oil comes from. Here are several kinds of oils:

- **Canola:** A golden, thick, flavorless oil. A healthy

choice because it is low in saturated fat and a unique source of omega-3 fatty acids, which medical studies have found helpful in preventing heart attacks and strokes. Good for basic cooking.

- **Corn.** Light-flavored with a hint of corn aroma, especially the unrefined versions. Best used in cooking. Can be mixed with olive oil in salad dressings and mayonnaise.
- **Olive:** With its Mediterranean roots, delicious taste, and health benefits, olive oil has become a favorite. Look for a rich green or golden color and fruity aroma. Extra-virgin is the highest quality, most expensive and has the lowest acidity. It is best used in salad dressing, on pasta, and for drizzling over vegetables. Lower-quality olive oils such as pure or virgin are more acidic and are good for cooking.
- **Peanut:** The refined version has a somewhat neutral flavor and a high smoking point, or temperature at which the oil begins to smoke. The roasted peanut oil has a more powerful flavor. Good for sautéing, frying, and stir-frying.
- **Safflower:** A neutral-flavored oil that is good for cooking.
- **Sesame:** Light color and light, nutty flavor. Really good for cooking; sometimes used in salad dressing.
- **Soybean:** Bland flavor and pale color. A major component of most "vegetable" oils. Use in cooking.
- **Walnut, hazelnut, and other nuts:** Strong-flavored, with rich aromas. Can be mixed with more neutral oils such as corn or peanut. Adds a nice touch to salads and can be drizzled over compatible hot foods.

World-Class Tastes

Modern American cooking, like our country itself, is a melting pot. The diversity of our rich cultural heritage translates into a fusion of different flavors. Today the flavor dynamics of Asian, Mexican, and Indian cooking are capturing tremendous interest, along with the flavors of the Mediterranean and the Middle East. These strong, bold tastes are a great complement to low-fat diets rich in grains, vegetables, and fruits.

This short guide to three worldly flavors highlights distinctive ingredients from near and far.

Asian: The cuisines of China, Japan, Korea, Vietnam, and Thailand are noted for their light cooking and emphasis on vegetables and grains. The healthy diets of Asia have resulted in a lower incidence of cancer, heart disease, and other chronic diseases common in the West. Although each country has its own unique flavors, there are common threads that run throughout. Try these Asian seasonings and discover how they can boost the flavors in your kitchen.

- **Chinese five-spice powder:** Adds zest to Chinese meat dishes.
- **Coriander (cilantro):** The distinctive, pungent taste is welcome in poultry and seafood dishes. Looks a lot like flat-leaf Italian parsley.
- **Fish sauce:** The Thai equivalent of soy sauce. Goes well with lemongrass and ginger.
- **Fresh gingerroot:** A lively, hot addition to stir-fries. A little goes a long way. Available in most produce sections.
- **Lemongrass:** Lemony-flavored stalks popular in Thai and Indonesian cooking. Good in stir-fries.

- **Miso:** A Japanese paste made from fermented soybeans and grains. Makes a delicious soup when combined with water, vegetables, soy sauce, and honey (see recipe on page 172).
- **Rice vinegar:** Mild, sweet-tasting vinegar. Good in salad dressings and seafood dishes.
- **Rice wine:** Very tasty in Japanese marinades for chicken, beef, and seafood.
- **Soy sauce:** Made from water, soybeans, wheat, and salt. Available in light and low-sodium. Used widely in Chinese and Japanese cooking.
- **Tamarind:** A tart, sweet pod fruit with dark, tasty juice. Available ground and as a canned paste. Perks up appetizers, soups, and barbecues. Also used in Indian and Mexican cooking.
- **Thai sweet chili sauce:** A condiment for simply prepared grilled and broiled meats.

Indian: Many different tastes, textures, and colors weave through the fabric of Indian cooking. Indian meals focus on grains, vegetables, and fruits; meat is used little if at all. This high-fiber diet has resulted in a lower incidence of many cancers and heart disease in India. The defining features of Indian cooking are the exotic spices and wonderful aromas. Take an Indian adventure and try these exciting ingredients:

- **Basmati rice:** Long-grain white rice with a nutlike fragrance. Use as the base for curry dishes.
- **Cardamom:** A spice with a wonderful aroma; available ground and in the pod. Use sparingly in rice and puddings.
- **Chutney:** A condiment that can be tangy or sweet and hot. Usually made from a mixture of fruit,

spices, vinegar, lemon, and sugar. Widely available in jars or make your own. Use to top baked or grilled chicken, or serve as a side dish.
- **Coriander (cilantro):** Use as a seasoning and garnish in a variety of dishes. See page 104.
- **Cumin:** A star spice of India, essential to curry dishes. Available ground and whole, it has a nutty smell and flavor. Use in salads, and in curry and rice dishes.

TIPS AND TRIVIA

Curry's Curious Origins

While the mention of curry might conjure up a vibrant Indian market, curry powder itself began as a Western adaptation. European traders who wandered through the streets and cities of India needed a way to describe the mixture of spices in the delicious meals they tasted there. Curry can refer to the blend of seasonings or to the whole dish itself; a curry is determined by its contents and can contain anywhere from five to more than fifty spices. Curry blends often feature fifteen to twenty spices, usually including tumeric, ginger, cumin, mustard seed, red and black peppers, and occasionally cinnamon and cloves. Whatever the blend, use it sparingly because it is a strong seasoning.

- **Garam masala:** A blend of ground-roasted spices from northern India that includes cardamom, cumin, cloves, black pepper, nutmeg, and cinnamon. Use in dishes that combine rice and vegetables or beans.
- **Tamarind:** Use in chutneys and vegetable bean dishes. See page 119.

Mexican: Simple and bold flavors give the cooking of Mexico and Latin America its unique spirit. Increasingly popular in modern American kitchens, Mexican dishes have their roots in market foods that provide a healthy balance of grains and vegetables to meat. Mexican cuisine also makes happy party food. It is inexpensive and can be heaped on platters for the whole family to enjoy. Here are some ingredients frequently used in Mexican dishes:

- **Achiote paste:** Bright orange-colored seasoning paste that tastes like a mixture of oregano, cinnamon, and peppers. Great for a marinade or sauce if thinned with vinegar or citrus juices.
- **Chili peppers:** See page 112 for the wide variety of choices. Taste the different kinds and discover which you like.
- **Cilantro (coriander):** A key herb in the Mexican kitchen, as it is in Asian and Indian cooking. See page 104.
- **Epazote:** A wild herb that grows easily in the garden and has a pungent aroma. A favorite in bean dishes and quesadillas.
- **Limes:** Popular in Mexican dishes because of

their bold acidity and taste.

- **Oregano:** Considered the most common and versatile cooking herb in Mexico. If using the dried herb, toast it first in a dry skillet. See page 107.
- **Tamarind:** See page 119. Use the pulp to make a really fruity sweet and sour juice that is great with spicy food.
- **Tomatillo:** A small, round, green fruit with a husk and a more acidic taste than tomatoes. Use raw and in all kinds of cooked dishes.

Thyme Tales

Thyme's pungent scent has been remarked upon for ages, and this spice has been believed to have a much stronger effect than mere taste. Egyptians used this herb to embalm their dead; the Romans used it as the most dependable cure for melancholy; and people in the Middle Ages believed that it gave people courage. An old tradition tells that a young girl who wears a sprig of thyme in a small bouquet with mint and lavender will surely lure her intended sweetheart.

YoUr ChEcKLISt oF PaNtRY PriOrItIeS

Before you continue the adventure of modern cooking, take a few minutes to stop and look around your kitchen. If you have a choice of ingredients on hand, it is easier to be spontaneous and creative. Although it might seem like a big deal to do a personal check-off and then shop and stock up, it really is more efficient in the long run. With a well-stocked and flavor-full pantry, you will be ready to enjoy cooking with a minimum of last-minute scrambling.

The priority list on the following two pages was prepared in consultation with lots of chefs and friends. Check off what you have in your pantry today and what you need for tomorrow. But remember, this is only meant to be a guide; your family should make its own priorities. ■

ESSENTIAL HERBS AND SPICES

BASIL, FRESH OR DRIED

BAY LEAVES

CAJUN SEASONING

CHILI POWDER

CINNAMON, GROUND AND STICKS

CLOVES, GROUND AND WHOLE

CORIANDER (CILANTRO), FRESH OR GROUND

CUMIN, GROUND

CURRY POWDER

DILL, FRESH OR DRIED

FENNEL SEEDS

FIVE-SPICE POWDER

GINGER, FRESH OR GROUND

MARJORAM, DRIED

MINT, FRESH OR DRIED

MUSTARD, DRY

NUTMEG, GROUND OR WHOLE

OREGANO, FRESH OR DRIED

PAPRIKA, HUNGARIAN SWEET

PEPPER, CAYENNE, DRIED RED FLAKES

PEPPERCORNS, DRIED BLACK

POPPY SEEDS

ROSEMARY, FRESH OR DRIED

SAGE, FRESH OR DRIED

SALT, TABLE AND KOSHER

SESAME SEEDS

TARRAGON, FRESH OR DRIED

THYME, FRESH OR DRIED

TURMERIC

CONDIMENTS

BARBECUE SAUCE

CAPERS

CHILI PASTE AND SAUCE

CHUTNEY

HOISIN SAUCE

HONEY

HORSERADISH

HOT PEPPER SAUCE

KETCHUP

MAPLE SYRUP

MOLASSES, DARK

MUSHROOMS, DRIED WILD, SUCH AS

    SHIITAKE AND PORCINI

MUSTARDS: DIJON, GRAINY, HONEY, DRIED

OILS: OLIVE, CANOLA, SESAME, PEANUT

OLIVES: BLACK, CALAMATA, GREEN

PICKLES

RAISINS

SHALLOTS

SOY SAUCE (REDUCED SODIUM)

TERIYAKI SAUCE

TOMATOES, SUN-DRIED

VINEGARS: BALSAMIC, CIDER, RED WINE,

    WHITE WINE, RICE

WORCESTERSHIRE SAUCE

STAPLES

BAKING POWDER

BAKING SODA

BEANS, CANNED: BLACK, RED KIDNEY, WHITE

    (NO SALT ADDED)

BEANS, DRIED: RED KIDNEY, GREAT NORTHERN,

    LIMA, LENTILS, SPLIT PEAS, BLACK, PINTO

BREAD CRUMBS, UNSEASONED

BULGUR, FINE GROUND

BROTHS: CHICKEN, BEEF, VEGETABLE (NO SALT ADDED;

    AVAILABLE PACKAGED AND CANNED)

CEREAL

CHOCOLATE: UNSWEETENED SQUARES,

    SEMISWEET MORSELS

CORNMEAL, GROUND (POLENTA)

CORNSTARCH

COUSCOUS, WHOLE WHEAT

CRACKERS AND BISCUITS

DRIED FRUITS: RAISINS, CURRANTS, APRICOTS

EXTRACTS: VANILLA, ALMOND, LEMON, ORANGE

FLOUR: UNBLEACHED, ALL PURPOSE, WHOLE WHEAT, CAKE

FRUIT PRESERVES, JAMS, JELLIES

GARLIC, FRESH AND MINCED IN OIL

GELATIN, POWDERED AND UNFLAVORED

LEMONS

LIMES

NUTS: ALMONDS (SLIVERED), PEANUTS (UNSALTED,

    ROASTED), WALNUTS, PECANS, PINE

ONIONS: RED, YELLOW

PASTA, DRIED: SPAGHETTI, LINGUINI, ANGEL HAIR,

    FETTUCCINE, PENNE, ETC.

PASTA SAUCE

PEANUT BUTTER

POTATOES

RICE: LONG-GRAIN CONVERTED, WILD,

    BASMATI, ARBORIO

SHALLOTS

SOUP: CANNED, PACKAGED

SUGAR: GRANULATED, SUPERFINE, CONFECTIONERS',

    LIGHT BROWN, DARK BROWN

TOMATOES: CANNED OR PACKAGED WHOLE, CRUSHED,

    CHOPPED, PUREE, SAUCE

TUNA, CANNED

WATER CHESTNUTS

YEAST, ACTIVE DRY

ESSENTIAL REFRIGERATOR AND FREEZER FOODS

BUTTER, UNSALTED

CHEESE: PARMIGIANO-REGGIANO, CHEDDAR, GOAT

EGGS

FRUITS AND VEGETABLES

MAYONNAISE, LOW-FAT

MILK, SKIM

ORANGE JUICE, FRESH OR FROZEN CONCENTRATE

YOGURT, NONFAT PLAIN

Quick Chicks: Mix and Match

For busy nights with a hungry family, here is a fast fun menu of ideas. Use four chicken breasts without skin; they are easy to prepare, quick-cooking, and delicious. Just reach into the pantry for these quick solutions.

1. Choose your side dishes.
2. Marinate the chicken for 15 minutes or season it.
3. Grill or broil the chicken for 6–8 minutes on each side.
4. Add sauce or glaze. Heat on the grill or in the broiler if using barbecue sauce, honey mustard, or tomato sauce.

Marinade or Seasoning	Sauce or Glaze	Side Dishes
Choose 1	Choose 1	Choose 2
1 teaspoon Cajun seasoning	3/4 cup barbecue sauce	Corn on the cob
1/2 cup Basic Vinaigrette (page 175)	1/2 cup honey mustard	Pasta (hot)
1 teaspoon Old Bay (or seafood seasoning)	3 cups tomato sauce	Low-fat baked beans
1 teaspoon chili powder	1 1/2 cups Fiesta Salsa (page 113)	Roasted Parslied New Potatoes (page 205)
1/2 cup low-fat Italian dressing	1 cup chutney	Cole slaw
		Green salad
		Goat Hill Farm Tomatoes Salad with Double Basil Vinaigrette (page 179)
		Steamed broccoli
		Rice Pilaf (page 81)

PART 2

COOKING ADVENTURES AT HOME

SIMPLE SECRETS TO COOKING WITH EASE

Use recipes as a guide, not a rigid formula, except when baking.

Start by reading through the recipe first and identifying the ingredients you need. Lay out everything before starting to cook. Then you won't have to stop and search for them while you are in the middle of cooking. As you grow more comfortable with how things work together, begin to let go of the recipe, using your own personal touch. But baking is more like chemistry, and following the recipe is the key to its success.

Use fresh, seasonal ingredients for easy cooking.

When the food is picked or harvested at the peak of the season, it just doesn't get any better. It also is the easiest way to cook because the flavors are so alive. Nature provides the great taste, and the cook needs to do very little.

Every time you cook, learn something new about how the flavors, colors, and textures work together.

Bring the different components of the dish together to form a delicious whole with a central place for grains, vegetables, and fruits.

Taste the food frequently as you cook.

Learn to trust your instincts by tasting as you go along. Cooking is a personal experience, not an exact science. Season well with salt and pepper to bring out the wonderful flavors. Taste often before you complete the dish.

Build your confidence by learning basic techniques and then making your own twists.

Learning to cook a few things well and then moving beyond these dishes is such a positive experience. As you reach out from these basic techniques, the door opens easily to adventuresome cooking. Except when baking, be flexible with ingredients and experiment with substitutions. Be brave and realize that disasters do happen—just ask my family. We all learn from them.

Turn up the flavors as you reduce the fat in cooking.

When you lower the fat in recipes, you'll want to intensify the flavors. Increasing the amounts of herbs and spices and adding salsas and sauces will add zip and vitality to family meals. Your choice of herbs and spices personalizes your recipe.

Be ready for last-minute meals by making wise use of leftover and prepared foods.

Cut preparation time by keeping convenience items in your pantry or refrigerator. Cut-up veggies and other salad bar foods or good canned organic tomatoes can be instant additions. Plan ahead so that you can use leftovers. I love seeing how many different dishes I can create with a roasted chicken or a spaghetti sauce.

Let your love and caring shine through.

Don't forget that cooking is very much about nurturing and taking care of those you love. Consider family favorites when planning, and encourage everyone to be a part of the process. Love and caring are the best ingredients.

> You need to cook by using your senses—every one of them. Touch, taste, see, feel, listen to it cook, smell. Use all of them in order to cook well.
>
> —BOB KINKEAD, CHEF AND OWNER, KINKEAD'S, WASHINGTON, D.C.

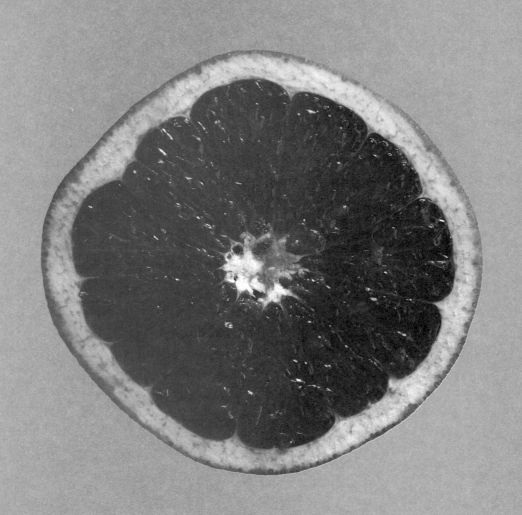

CHAPTER 5

BRIGHT AWAKENINGS: BeST BREAKFaSTS

Awake to a new day with energy, vigor, and the warmth of family gathered around the table. When we eat in the morning, we are breaking the fast after a night's sleep. Our bodies are on empty and need the energy, protein, vitamins, and minerals found at breakfast in order to get going. This first meal of the day is vital to our health and how well we do during the day.

Even though breakfast takes less time to prepare and eat than any other meal, many people skip breakfast, protesting that they do not have enough time. In fact, a 1994 survey found that 74 percent of Americans skip breakfast at least once a week. The biggest decline in breakfast eating has been among adolescents and young adults.

Beginning the day with breakfast brings benefits beyond health. In the rush of daily life, it is a time for parents and children to talk to each other and get ready for the day. And children are starting a pattern that they will carry throughout their life.

For Rick and Deann Bayless of Chicago's Frontera Grill, the most important meal of the day is breakfast with their daughter, Lanie. Rick calls it "a moment of calm before everyone leaves for the day" and says that for his family, weekend breakfasts are a highlight. That is when seven-year-old Lanie helps in the kitchen, and mom and dad eat breakfast in bed.

It is well documented that children who eat breakfast do better in school than children who don't. The knowledge that hungry children could not learn led to the creation of the School Breakfast Program in 1989. It has been growing fast, and in 1996 there were 6.6 million children participating. When I was responsible for the country's school meals programs, I shared breakfast with children all across the country. Teachers and principals told me that children often lined up as early as 6:30 A.M., often in the dark, to come into the cafeteria. Breakfast made a big difference in their school performance.

This chapter includes recipes, hints, and help to make everyday breakfasts special and birthday breakfasts memorable. Breakfast gets a fresh start with Fruit First. This section includes recipes to sweeten the morning and deliver energy at the same time. Get up and go with Rising Grains and find new healthy ways to begin the day in a flash. Good Egg Mornings includes creative ideas for celebrating breakfast. Finally, there is a word or two about Anytime Breakfasts and those "no rules" mornings.

Five Good Reasons to Do Breakfast

1. Breakfast gives you energy to think better, learn better, and do better. An increased metabolism improves all-around performance.

2. Breakfast makes it easier to reach the Food Guide Pyramid's goals for eating healthy foods, especially fruits, grains, and dairy products.

3. Breakfast gives you approximately one-quarter of the day's calories and nutrients, and helps moderate your appetite all day long, protecting against unhealthy snacking and overeating.

4. Breakfast is a time to share the comfort of food and family, to talk about the day ahead.

5. Breakfast need take only fifteen minutes from start to finish, and it builds healthy eating patterns for children.

" The honest simplicity of breakfast is so captivating. "

—MARION CUNNINGHAM, *THE BREAKFAST BOOK*

TIPS AND TRIVIA
Raising Math and Reading Scores

Students who eat breakfast before starting school have higher math and reading scores, according to a 1997 State of Minnesota study. When children got a jump-start on the day by eating breakfast, they also showed increased attention spans, reduced visits to the nurse, and improved behavior. Quite a good report card!

FRUIT FIRST

Any way you cut it, fruit is a refreshing way to begin the day. Fruits and fruit juices package essential vitamins, minerals, and fiber. Fruits also offer fructose, a fast-absorbing form of sugar that provides a burst of morning energy.

HARVEST APPLES

A family-friendly way to serve apples at breakfast or any time of day. Makes a welcoming after-school treat or autumn dessert.

Serves: 4

Preparation Time: 15 minutes

Cooking time: 30 to 40 minutes

1/4 cup raisins

1/4 cup coarsely chopped walnuts

1/4 cup brown sugar

1/4 teaspoon ground cinnamon (optional)

Dash of nutmeg (optional)

4 firm, tart apples such as Granny Smith

---

1. Preheat the oven to 350° F.

2. In a small bowl, mix the raisins, walnuts, brown sugar, cinnamon, and nutmeg together.

3. Wash and core the apples using an apple corer or a small knife.

4. In a baking dish, arrange the apples with the tops up. Fill each apple with one-fourth of the raisin mixture.

5. Pour water into the baking dish to the depth of 1/2 inch.

6. Bake for 30 to 40 minutes. Baste the apples once or twice with the cooking liquid. The apples are done when they still hold their shape and yield to a knife when pierced. Serve the apples when they are cooled slightly.

　　To warm in the microwave: Place the apple in a microwave-safe dish and microwave on low for 1-minute blasts until warm.

Twist: Substitute dried apricots and pecans for the raisins and walnuts.

Per Serving: About 251 calories, 45 calories from fat, 3 grams of protein, 54 grams carbohydrates, 5 grams total fat, 7 grams fiber, 8 milligrams sodium

CARAMELIZED GRAPEFRUIT

A warm way to capture the fruit's sweetness, along with a lot of vitamin C and fiber. Within minutes, everyday breakfasts come alive.

1 grapefruit makes 2 servings

Preparation time: 5 minutes

Cooking time: 5 minutes

1 grapefruit, cut in half

About 2 tablespoons brown sugar

---

1. Preheat the broiler.

2. Place the grapefruit halves in a baking dish and sprinkle with brown sugar.

3. Broil about 5 inches away from the heat source, until the sugar is caramelized and its color deepens, about 5 minutes.

4. Transfer to individual dishes and serve.

PER SERVING: ABOUT 91 CALORIES, 0 CALORIES FROM FAT, 1 GRAM PROTEIN, 23 GRAMS CARBOHYDRATES, 0 GRAMS TOTAL FAT, 1 GRAM FIBER, 5 MILLIGRAMS SODIUM

TIPS AND TRIVIA
Easy Peels

Here is the best way to peel and section citrus fruit to remove all the bitter white pith and still keep the beautiful shape of the fruit:

1. With a serrated knife, cut the top and bottom off to expose the flesh of the fruit at both ends.

2. Stand the fruit up on one of the cut ends. Cut the peel off in thin strips that extend from the top of the fruit to the bottom. Continue around the fruit until all of the peel is removed.

3. Remove the sections by cutting on each side of the membranes that separate them.

The World of Sun-Drenched Citrus

Many different varieties of zesty oranges, grapefruits, and other citrus fruits have traveled to our shores from all over the world. Citrus fruits were probably first cultivated more than four thousand years ago in southern China. They did not arrive in the Americas until Columbus's second voyage in 1493.

Today, citrus fruits are grown in more than one hundred countries with sunny climates, and they are probably the world's most commonly propagated fruit. In the United States, the biggest citrus-growing states are Florida, California, Arizona, and Texas. The worldwide popularity of citrus fruits is well deserved because of their sweet taste and the many health benefits they provide. They are an excellent source of vitamin C, which helps prevent colds and makes it harder for the body to become infected. Whole fruits provide fiber along with B vitamins. Try these tasty varieties and start the day off healthy and happy:

Sweet Orange. The most popular citrus fruit, its flesh contains a blend of sugar and acid.

- **Navel:** Known for its easy peeling and separation. A great table fruit.
- **Jaffa:** Originally from Israel. Good for juice and cooking.
- **Blood orange (Moro):** Has a sweet flavor and an exotic red color.
- **Valencia:** Mostly used for processing into juice. Represents 50 percent of the Florida crop.

Mandarin. A hardy citrus variety that includes tangerines and is known for its thin, loose peels.

- **Clementine:** A deep orange fruit with the flavor of apricot nectar. It separates easily.
- **Dancy tangerine:** A Christmastime favorite with a very sweet taste.
- **Honey mandarin:** A bright orange, easily separated fruit that is very juicy and contains many seeds.
- **Tangelo:** A cross between a mandarin orange and a grapefruit. Rich and tangy.
- **Temple orange:** A cross between a mandarin orange and a navel orange. Spicy flavor and easy to peel.
- **Ugli:** Not so pretty but very juicy, sweet, and easy to peel.

Grapefruit. A natural cross between a sweet orange and a pomelo. Available with or without seeds.

- **Burgundy:** Has sweet, juicy flesh and a deep red color.
- **Ruby Red:** A popular, red-pigmented grapefruit with few seeds.
- **Triumph:** Has whitish yellow, seedy flesh. Sweet, not bitter.

Here are five easy ways to add citrus fruits to your breakfast lineup:

1. Mix together orange and grapefruit pieces with sliced bananas and a touch of orange juice.
2. Sprinkle raspberries over orange sections. Top with a squirt of lime juice.
3. Create your own mixed citrus juice using grapefruits and different kinds of oranges.
4. Serve tangerine sections topped with granola for crunch.
5. Sprinkle berries on half a grapefruit.

MiXED-uP fRUIt COMPoTE

Enjoy a mellow morning with this comforting mixture of luscious, sweet fruits. Use it to top breakfast pancakes or serve it with yogurt and a sprinkling of granola. Heat it for a delicious dessert topping.
Make a double batch and use it all week.

Serves: 4-6

Preparation time: 10 minutes

Cooking time: 40 minutes

1 cup sugar (more or less, depending on taste)

1/2 cup water

One 1/2-inch slice lemon zest (yellow part only)

4 cups pitted plums or peaches, or a combination

1. Bring the sugar, water, and lemon zest to a boil over high heat. Simmer for 5 minutes. This will extract flavor from the peel, dissolve the sugar, and make a syrup.

2. Add the fruit and continue to cook for about 5 minutes, until just tender.

3. Remove the fruit from the juice and set aside. Discard the lemon zest. Reduce the juice over medium-high heat until it becomes syrupy, about 5 minutes. Pour the reduced syrup over the cooked fruit. Serve warm.

For Safekeeping: Cool the compote. Refrigerate up to 5 days.

Twists: Substitute for the plums and/or peaches:

   4 cups pitted cherries, peeled or sliced rhubarb, or a combination

   4 cups mixed seasonal berries

   3 cups apples, pears, or a combination, and 1 cup chopped walnuts.

   Substitute orange zest for lemon zest.

PER SERVING: ABOUT 192 CALORIES, 0 CALORIES FROM FAT, 1 GRAM PROTEIN, 49 GRAMS CARBOHYDRATES, 0 GRAMS TOTAL FAT, 2 GRAMS FIBER, 1 MILLIGRAM SODIUM

Yes to Yogurt

In a hurry but want a healthy start? Just do it with yogurt. An 8-ounce container of plain nonfat yogurt gives protein, potassium, and vitamin B12 as well as small amounts of other nutrients. What is more, it can contain as much as 400 milligrams of bone-building calcium—more than a glass of 1 percent or fat-free milk. Here are a few ways to add power to plain nonfat yogurt:

- Top it with cut-up bananas, peaches, or apples, then sprinkle on some wheat germ or granola.
- Top with Mixed-up Fruit Compote (see page 136).
- Berries and yogurt are a dream team. Mix in strawberries, raspberries, blueberries, and/or blackberries to your family's delight.
- Swirl in defrosted concentrated fruit juice for a delicious difference. Top with honey and raisins.

BANANA FRUIT SMOOTHIE

Get moving with this quick, healthy breakfast drink. Check out the seasonal twists. Brimming with vitamin C, it's also a great after-school refresher.

Serves: 1

Preparation time: 5 minutes

1/4 cup orange juice

1/2 cup plain low-fat yogurt

1 small banana, peeled and cut into pieces

Honey to taste (optional)

Place all the ingredients in a blender. Blend on high speed until smooth.

Twists: Very Berry: substitute 1/2 cup seasonal berries (blueberries, strawberries, or raspberries) for the banana
Peaches 'n' Cream: Substitute 1/2 cup peeled, pitted peaches for the banana.

PER SERVING: ABOUT 198 CALORIES, 27 CALORIES FROM FAT, 8 GRAMS PROTEIN, 39 GRAMS CARBOHYDRATES, 3 GRAMS TOTAL FAT, 3 GRAMS FIBER, 88 MILLIGRAMS SODIUM

LIGHT CANTALOUPE SMOOTHIE

Experience the passion of the tropics with this deliciously low-cal smoothie. In less than five minutes the pleasure begins. Be creative and mix up your family favorite.

Serves: 1

Preparation time: 5 minutes

1/2 cup orange juice

1/2 cup peeled, seeded, and cubed cantaloupe

Honey to taste (optional)

1/2 cup ice

Place the juice, fruit, and honey in a blender. Blend on high speed for 30 seconds. Add ice and blend until smooth.

Twists: Mango Madness: Substitute 1/2 cup peeled and pitted mango for the cantaloupe.

Pineapple Passion: Substitute 1/2 cup fresh or canned pineapple for the cantaloupe.

PER SERVING: 105 CALORIES, 0 CALORIES FROM FAT, 2 GRAMS PROTEIN, 25 GRAMS CARBOHYDRATES, 0 GRAMS TOTAL FAT, 1 GRAM FIBER, 9 MILLIGRAMS SODIUM

NUTRITION POWER POINTS
Cantaloupe's Sweet Prize

Not only is cantaloupe a lusciously sweet fruit, but it really is a nutrition prizewinner. Cantaloupe contains fiber, many vitamins, including beta-carotene and folic acid, and all minerals, including potassium and calcium.

BROILED TOMATOES

An old English breakfast tradition, broiled tomatoes are delicious any time of day. They're a wonderful complement to eggs.

Serves: 4

Preparation time: 5 minutes

Cooking time: 5 minutes

4 plum tomatoes

Drizzle of olive oil

Salt to taste

Freshly ground black pepper to taste

1 tablespoon chopped fresh herbs (optional)

1. Preheat the broiler.

2. Slice the tomatoes in half lengthwise and place them, skin side down, on a cookie sheet. Drizzle each half with olive oil and season liberally with salt and pepper.

3. Place the cookie sheet in the oven on a rack that is about 4 inches away from the heating element. Broil until the tomatoes brown slightly, about 2 to 4 minutes.

4. Remove the tomatoes from the oven and sprinkle with fresh herbs if desired.

PER SERVING: ABOUT 44 CALORIES, 36 CALORIES FROM FAT, 1 GRAM PROTEIN, 3 GRAMS CARBOHYDRATES, 4 GRAMS TOTAL FAT, 1 GRAM FIBER, 151 MILLIGRAMS SODIUM

NUTRITION POWER POINT
Milky Ways

All types of milk contain all the major nutrients except vitamin C and fiber. The valuable nutrients milk contains give great energy, build better bones, and contribute to good health.

For fat and calories, though, there is a real difference in what you drink. Here is how they compare for calories from fat per 8-ounce glass: .

Milk	Whole	2%	1%	Skim
Fat Calories	68	39	22	4

The Food Guide Pyramid recommends two to three servings of milk and milk products a day, yet many Americans do not reach that goal. So enjoy milk as a part of your family's diet. It's especially important to the growth and development of children's bodies. But remember to check how much fat is in the mix.

SUMMER FRUIT SIZZLE

The vibrant colors of berries and peaches at their summer peak easily transform pancakes and waffles into something special. These fruits are also great on nonfat yogurt or sorbet.

Serves: 4

Preparation time: 5 minutes

Cooking time: 5 minutes

1 teaspoon butter

1 cup blueberries

1/2 cup maple syrup

Dash of nutmeg

1. In a small skillet, melt the butter over medium heat. Add the fruit and cook until it begins to soften slightly, about 2 to 3 minutes.

2. Add the maple syrup and nutmeg. Bring to a boil, then pour over pancakes.

Twists: Substitute the following for the blueberries:

Spring: 3/4 cup cherries and 1/4 cup sliced almonds

Fall: 3/4 cup apples or pears and 1/4 cup walnuts

Winter: 3/4 dried apricots and 1/4 cup dried cranberries

PER SERVING: ABOUT 138 CALORIES, 9 CALORIES FROM FAT, 0 GRAMS PROTEIN, 23 GRAMS CARBOHYDRATES, 1 GRAM TOTAL FAT, 1 GRAM FIBER, 16 MILLIGRAMS SODIUM

FAMILY JAMMIN'

Making jam is as easy as can be, and it's tremendous fun for the kids to help. The taste gets even better when the whole family picks the berries. This simple method does not require special jars or other equipment.

Makes 2 pints

Preparation time: 5 minutes

Cooking time: 15 minutes

4 cups mixed berries

2 tablespoons lemon juice

1 package powdered fruit pectin

1 1/2 cups honey

1. Mix the berries, lemon juice, and pectin in a heavy-bottomed, stainless-steel pot.

2. Stir over high heat and bring to a boil. The berries begin to render liquid quickly, which prevents the mixture from burning. Stir in the honey.

3. Return to a boil and stir slowly for 10 to 12 minutes. The mixture will resemble a thick syrup when done. Let cool, then pour into a storage container, cover, and refrigerate.

Twist: Substitute 5 cups peeled, pitted, and chopped peaches, plums, or nectarines for the mixed berries. Boil only 4 to 6 minutes after the addition of the honey.

For Safekeeping: Keeps in the refrigerator up to 2 weeks.

PER SERVING: 1 TABLESPOON IS ABOUT 30 CALORIES, 0 CALORIES FROM FAT, 0 GRAMS PROTEIN, 8 GRAMS CARBOHYDRATES, 0 GRAMS TOTAL FAT,

0 GRAMS FIBER, 1 MILLIGRAM SODIUM

HEALTHY TIMESAVERS
Grab and Go

Faced with absolutely no time to fix breakfast? Just grab these healthy choices and go straight out the door:

- a banana, orange, or any fruit
- nonfat yogurt with or without fruit
- a muffin and a container of juice
- a bagel topped with jelly or peanut butter
- dried cereal, granola, or dried fruit in a plastic bag

GROOvY APPlESAUCE

An all-time family favorite that packs good nutrition with fantastic flavor. Make a batch and enjoy it from morning until night. Gather apples at an orchard for a fresh taste and fun times.

Makes 5 cups

Preparation time: 10 minutes

Cooking time: 25 minutes

5 cups peeled and cored apples, cut into chunks

3/4 cup water

2 tablespoons lemon juice

1/2 cup honey

Cinnamon to taste (optional)

Nutmeg to taste (optional)

1. Place the apple chunks in a large, heavy-bottomed, stainless-steel pot. Add the rest of the ingredients.

2. Bring to a boil over medium-high heat, stirring occasionally. Cook until the fruit becomes tender, about 20 minutes.

3. Drain the apples in a colander. Puree in a food mill or blender.

4. Cool and refrigerate.

For Safekeeping: Keeps in the refrigerator up to 2 weeks.

Twist: Substitute pears for the apples to make pear sauce. Add 10 twists of freshly ground black pepper to the pears for a surprising complement.

PER SERVING: ABOUT 84 CALORIES, 0 CALORIES FROM FAT, 0 GRAMS PROTEIN, 22 GRAMS CARBOHYDRATES, 0 GRAMS TOTAL FAT, 1 GRAM FIBER, 1 MILLIGRAM SODIUM

RISING GRAINS

Eat whole grains for the get-up-and-go feeling you need to do your best throughout the day. They get high marks because they provide complex carbohydrates, a slower-burning form of energy that helps prevent midmorning sluggishness. To top it off, whole grains contain fiber, which promotes intestinal health. Read on for easy recipes that make everyone rise and shine!

MUESLI WITH RED AND GREEN GRAPES

A soothing way to start a fast-paced, event-filled day. The bright color of the grapes contrasts with the light tones of the oats. Make ahead and wake to a delight.

Makes about 5 cups

Preparation time: 5 minutes

2 cups rolled oats

Ground cinnamon to taste

1/2 cup raisins

1 cup skim milk

1/2 cup chopped walnuts

1 cup seedless red grapes

1 cup seedless green grapes

1. Place the oats, cinnamon, and raisins in a bowl. Add the milk. Cover and refrigerate overnight.

2. Stir in the nuts and grapes when ready to serve.

For Safekeeping: Keeps up to 3 days in the refrigerator.

PER SERVING: 1/2 CUP IS ABOUT 160 CALORIES, 45 CALORIES FROM FAT, 5 GRAMS PROTEIN, 26 GRAMS CARBOHYDRATES, 5 GRAMS TOTAL FAT, 3 GRAMS FIBER, 16 MILLIGRAMS SODIUM

GOLDEN GRAIN GRIDDLE CAKES

When our family has something to celebrate, we start the day with these griddle cakes. The whole-grain buckwheat flour gives an extra health boost. Have fun tossing in sweet summer berries, chopped nuts, or a topping of fruits. Makes a great supper, too.

Makes 5 servings of 3 cakes each

Preparation time: 10 minutes

Cooking time: 15 minutes

1/2 cup buckwheat flour

1/2 cup all-purpose flour

2 teaspoons baking powder

1/2 teaspoon salt

2/3 cup milk

1 large egg

2 tablespoons melted butter

2 tablespoons honey

1. Mix the flours, baking powder, and salt in a bowl. (This can be done the night before and kept covered on the counter.)

2. Lightly beat the milk, egg, butter, and honey together.

3. Add the liquid ingredients all at once to the flour mixture. Stir with a wooden spoon until just moistened. Do not overmix; a few lumps are fine.

4. Warm a lightly greased griddle pan over medium heat. The pan is ready when a few drops of water sprinkled on the griddle form fast-moving bubbles.

5. Pour batter onto the griddle: 1/8 cup for small or 1/4 cup for large pancakes. When the tops of the pancakes are covered with holes and the bottoms are golden brown, flip over. Keep warm in the oven.

Twists: *Buttermilk*: Substitute 1/2 cup all-purpose flour for the buckwheat flour, 2/3 cup buttermilk for the milk, and 1/2 teaspoon baking soda for the baking powder.

Whole Wheat: Substitute 1/2 cup whole wheat flour for the buckwheat flour.

PER SERVING: ABOUT 188 CALORIES, 63 CALORIES FROM FAT, 5 GRAMS PROTEIN, 27 GRAMS CARBOHYDRATES, 7 GRAMS TOTAL FAT, 2 GRAMS FIBER, 459 MILLIGRAMS SODIUM

HEALTHY TIMESAVERS
'Twas the Night Before Breakfast

Enlist the whole family's help to get a head start on breakfast, then enjoy it together as the sun comes up.

- Set the table with placemats, napkins, silverware, dishes, and nonperishable foods. I also love to add a few flowers to the table.
- Get out the equipment you will use, such as a frying pan and mixing bowls.
- Try making cooked cereals and refrigerating them overnight. The next morning, zap them for a minute in the microwave.
- Make muffins ahead of time and freeze or refrigerate them. Reheat in the oven for a few minutes.
- Be creative: Mix together a variety of whole-grain cereals, place the mixture in a bowl on the table, and cover with plastic wrap.

FAMILY FUN
Getting Into the Act

Weekend breakfasts are a great time for children to learn to cook and become a part of the total food experience. Here are some jobs they can have to make those pancakes or eggs taste even better. Just pull up a chair for them to stand on, if needed, roll up your sleeves, and see the smiles when you show them how. In no time they will be making breakfast.

- Breaking an egg into the bowl with no shells takes a little practice, but it's great fun for kids.
- Measuring the flour for the pancakes or waffles teaches both cooking and math skills.
- Mixing the pancake or French toast batter is a favorite job.
- Adding berries to batter or cut-up herbs to eggs allows kids to provide the finishing touch.

TIPS AND TRIVIA
Light and Lively Pancakes and Waffles

The amount of milk used in the batter helps to determine how light the pancakes or waffles will be. More milk makes them thinner and lighter.

To make light, delicate pancakes and waffles, separate the eggs. Beat the egg yolks until they are pale yellow and thick. Gently stir in the other liquid ingredients. Stir this mixture into the dry ingredients. In a separate bowl, whip the egg whites until they are stiff but not dry. Fold the egg whites into the batter and follow the cooking instructions.

JASON'S FAVORITE FRENCH TOAST

Morning French toast, soft and sweet, always makes my son Jason feel ready for anything. This recipe is easy to make and is best when made with day-old bread. I have yet to meet anyone who did not love it.

Serves: 4

Preparation time: 5 minutes

Cooking time: 10 minutes

2 large eggs

1 1/2 cups skim milk

1/4 cup sugar

1/2 teaspoon ground cinnamon

1/4 teaspoon nutmeg

1/2 tablespoon vanilla extract

Peanut oil as needed

8 slices slightly stale bread

1. Whisk together the eggs, milk, sugar, cinnamon, nutmeg, and vanilla until thoroughly mixed. (This can be done ahead and refrigerated overnight.)

2. Heat a well-greased griddle or large frying pan with peanut oil until hot but not smoking.

3. Soak the bread slices in the egg mixture until moistened. Place the soaked slices on the griddle. Discard any leftover mixture.

4. When the bottoms are golden brown, flip with a spatula and brown the other side. Keep them in a warm oven until ready to serve.

PER SERVING: ABOUT 344 CALORIES, 117 CALORIES FROM FAT, 12 GRAMS PROTEIN, 50 GRAMS CARBOHYDRATES, 13 GRAMS TOTAL FAT, 0 GRAMS FIBER, 479 MILLIGRAMS SODIUM

FAMILY FUN
Birthday Breakfasts

We have a family tradition of celebrating birthdays first at breakfast. The table is set the night before with presents and cards for the birthday person. Everyone gathers together to share in the excitement and warmth and enjoy a favorite morning meal. My son Jason always wanted French toast, and Lisa always loved lots and lots of strawberries and cereal. Light a candle set in a muffin and have everyone sing "Happy Birthday." What a way to start a special day!

SeASoNAL MuFFiNS

A simple, basic way to fix marvelous muffins. Add different fruits, nuts, or bran for a seasonal twist. Great to make ahead, then warm in the oven or pop in the microwave for a minute. Watch them disappear!

Makes about 36 mini-muffins

Preparation time: 15 minutes

Baking time: 12 to 15 minutes

2 cups flour

1 cup sugar

2 teaspoons baking powder

1/4 teaspoon salt

1 large egg at room temperature

1 cup milk at room temperature

4 tablespoons melted butter

---

1. Preheat the oven to 400° F. Coat a muffin pan with nonstick spray.

2. Sift the flour, sugar, baking powder, and salt together. (This can be done the night before and kept covered on the counter.)

3. Whisk together the egg, milk, and melted butter. If the egg and milk are cold, the butter may solidify.

4. Make a well in the center of the dry ingredients and add the liquid all at once. Stir with a wooden spoon until the dry ingredients are just moistened. The batter will be a little lumpy; do not overmix.

5. Fill the tins two-thirds full, being careful not to drip batter on the edge of the tins where it will burn and cause sticking.

6. Bake until golden brown and set in the center, approximately 12 to 15 minutes. The muffins are done when a knife inserted in the center of a muffin comes out dry. Cool for 5 minutes before removing.

Twists: *Spring Muffins*: Fold the finely chopped zest of 2 lemons and 1/4 cup poppy seeds into the batter at the end of Step 4.

Summer Muffins: Fold 1 cup lightly floured fresh berries into the batter at the end of Step 4.

Fall Muffins: Fold 1/2 cup lightly floured dried fruit and 1/2 cup nuts into the batter at the end of Step 4.

Winter Muffins: Substitute 1 cup bran for 1 cup flour. Add the bran to the egg mixture and let sit for 10 minutes before stirring into the dry ingredients in Step 4.

PER SERVING: 1 MUFFIN IS ABOUT 64 CALORIES, 18 CALORIES FROM FAT, 1 GRAM PROTEIN, 11 GRAMS CARBOHYDRATES, 2 GRAMS TOTAL FAT, 0 GRAMS FIBER, 62 MILLIGRAMS SODIUM

DOWN-HOME CORN BREAD

Freshly baked, piping-hot corn bread is a breakfast-time treat, especially when drizzled with honey. It also is a terrific partner for stews, chilies, vegetable soups, and all kinds of Mexican and Cajun cooking.

Serves: 12

Preparation time: 10 minutes

Cooking time: 15 minutes

1/2 cup flour

1 1/2 cups cornmeal

1 teaspoon salt

1 teaspoon sugar

1 tablespoon baking powder

3 large eggs at room temperature

1 1/4 cups low-fat milk at room temperature

8 tablespoons (1 stick) butter, melted

1. Preheat the oven to 400° F. Coat a 9 x 9-inch pan with nonstick spray.

2. Sift the flour, cornmeal, salt, sugar, and baking powder together in a mixing bowl. (This can be done the night before and kept covered on the counter.)

3. Stir in the eggs, milk, and butter with a wooden spoon until the dry ingredients are just moistened. Do not overmix.

4. Pour into the pan and bake until golden brown around the edges, about 15 minutes. The cornbread is done when a small knife inserted in the center comes out dry. Best when served warm from the oven.

PER SERVING: 178 CALORIES, 81 CALORIES FROM FAT, 4 GRAMS PROTEIN, 18 GRAMS CARBOHYDRATES, 9 GRAMS FAT, 1 GRAM FIBER, 405 MILLIGRAMS SODIUM

HEALTHY TIMESAVERS

Cereal Toppers

Cold cereal tops the list as a popular, healthy timesaver—especially if it is made from whole grains.

Mix up several cereals to enjoy the varied tastes and textures, then add these terrific toppers:

- sliced banana, strawberries, or other berries
- a summer mixture of peaches, berries, and nectarines
- raisins and slivered almonds
- dried fruit such as apricots, dates, or prunes

Good Egg Mornings

When breakfast includes eggs, you get a nutrition bonus because eggs are such a good source of vitamins, minerals, and high-quality proteins. The egg white contains ten different proteins and lots of vitamins, while the egg yolk has every vitamin but C and such minerals as iron and zinc. Yes, egg yolks also contain 200 milligrams of cholesterol, which can raise the level of cholesterol in the blood. For that reason, moderation is the key. The American Heart Association recommends eating no more than four eggs per week.

"An egg is always an adventure," Oscar Wilde once said. Discover new ways to prepare them and spark everyone's energy and enjoyment.

FOR SAFEKEEPING
Egg-Wise Tips

Keep the health benefits of eggs and prevent salmonella contamination by following these tips:

- Buy the best possible grade (AA Fresh Fancy) that has been boxed the most recently. Look closely for hairline cracks on the eggshells. *Never use cracked eggs.*
- Always store eggs in the refrigerator in cartons in which they were sold to keep them from absorbing odors. Use uncooked eggs within three to five weeks.
- To avoid eating eggs from a sick hen, break each egg individually into a small cup before using. Discard any eggs with a large splash of bright red blood.
- Cook eggs to at least 140° F. or when no longer runny to prevent risks from bacteria.

EGGS SCRAMBLED WITH TOMATOES AND HERBS

This late-summer favorite looks as good as it tastes with vivid red tomatoes that contrast with the bright green of the herbs. The kids will love to help mix the eggs, gather the herbs from the garden, or just enjoy the wonderful flavors.

Serves: 4

Preparation time: 5 minutes

Cooking time: 5 minutes

1 teaspoon olive oil

1/2 cup diced tomatoes

8 large eggs

Salt to taste

Freshly ground black pepper to taste

2 tablespoons chopped dill

---

1. Heat the oil in a 10-inch nonstick frying pan over medium-high heat.

2. Add the tomatoes and cook for about 2 minutes. Drain the tomatoes. Wipe the pan clean so that it can be reused for the eggs.

3. Whisk the eggs with the salt and pepper until well blended.

4. Pour the eggs and tomatoes into the frying pan and stir constantly over low heat with a rubber spatula. When the eggs begin to set, add the dill and continue stirring.

5. When the eggs have reached the desired degree of consistency, put them on warm plates and serve immediately.

Twists: Experiment with different herbs and vegetables. Try fresh basil, dill, oregano, or scallions. Add cooked green or red peppers.

PER SERVING: ABOUT 166 CALORIES, 108 CALORIES FROM FAT, 12 GRAMS PROTEIN, 50 GRAMS CARBOHYDRATES, 12 GRAMS TOTAL FAT, 0 GRAMS FIBER, 479 MILLIGRAMS SODIUM

Memorable Morning Walks

Early morning is a great time to get energized for the day by taking an exhilarating walk. Parents

and children can spend time together and talk about the busy day ahead. It's a favorite way for nutritionist Patty

Morris and her daughter Stephanie to begin the day. Get going and start feeling great.

- Find a comfortable stride and swing your arms naturally.

- Keep your head up and your eyes forward.

- Try to avoid arching your back.

- Work up a sweat and exhale through your mouth for the best results.

ANNE ROSENZWEIG's BREAKFAST BURRITOS

Bringing food to the table is great fun for Anne Rosenzweig, the chef and owner of the Lobster Club restaurant in New York City. She loves to share the experience with her daughter, Lilly, and they give a cooking class together. "When children cook, they have a greater investment," she says. Sometimes Anne and Lilly go to the squash patch in the country and pick vegetables for an afternoon of soup-making.

This child-friendly breakfast burrito has its origins south of the border. The burrito is filled with lots of energy, flavor, and freshness. It certainly can make an everyday morning into something special.

Serves: 4

Preparation time: 15 minutes

Cooking time: 10 minutes

For the relish:

1 tomato, finely diced

1/2 small red onion, minced

1 small hot fresh chili, seeds removed and minced

1/2 cup chopped fresh parsley

1/2 cup chopped fresh cilantro

1 tablespoon fresh lime or lemon juice

Salt to taste

Mix all the ingredients together and chill. (This can be made ahead and refrigerated overnight.)

For the burritos:

8 small fresh corn tortillas

3/4 cup cooked red or black beans, or refried beans

4 large eggs

4 large egg whites

Salt to taste

Freshly ground pepper to taste

1 tablespoon canola oil

1. Preheat the oven to 350° F. Wrap the tortillas in aluminum foil and warm in the oven.

2. Heat the beans in a small pan or in the microwave until hot.

3. Break the eggs into a bowl. Add the egg whites, salt, and pepper, and mix well with a fork.

4. Heat the oil in a large skillet over medium-high heat. Pour the eggs into the pan and scramble until the eggs are just cooked, about 1 1/2 to 2 minutes.

5. To put it together: Place a spoonful of beans in the center of each tortilla. Divide the scrambled eggs among the tortillas, spooning them over the beans. Spoon a teaspoon of relish on top of the eggs. Roll up the tortillas and place 2 burritos, seam side down, on each plate. Top with more relish and serve immediately.

PER SERVING: ABOUT 274 CALORIES, 81 CALORIES FROM FAT, 15 GRAMS PROTEIN, 33 GRAMS CARBOHYDRATES, 9 GRAMS FAT, 4 GRAMS FIBER, 416 MILLIGRAMS SODIUM

EASY HERB OMELET

Omelets taste wonderful, but I've always been intimidated at the thought of flipping them. Not anymore. This easy method gets omelets right every time. The secret to success is speed, high heat, and using the right size nonstick omelet pan. The best omelets are made one at a time.

Serves: 1

Preparation time: 5 minutes

Cooking time: 1 minute

2 large eggs

Salt to taste

Freshly ground black pepper to taste

1 teaspoon peanut oil

1 tablespoon chopped chives, parsley, or dill

---

1. Crack the eggs into a bowl. Season with salt and pepper. Whisk to combine completely.

2. Heat the peanut oil over medium-high heat in a 6- or 8-inch nonstick omelet pan until almost smoking.

3. Pour in the egg mixture and immediately stir with a spatula. While stirring, quickly shake the skillet in a back-and-forth motion directly on the heat surface. (Do not lift the pan off the heat because this will cool the pan.) This step should not take more than 15 seconds.

4. When the eggs are almost set, remove the pan from the heat and add the desired filling across the center of the omelet.

5. Fold the omelet in half and turn it out onto a warm plate.

Twists: *Vegetable*: Add 1/4 cup cooked mushrooms, spinach, onions, or peppers.

South of the Border: Add shredded Monterey jack cheese (this should be added before other fillings so it has an extra moment to melt) and Fiesta Salsa (see page 113).

Scandinavian: Add 1/4 cup smoked salmon and chopped dill and top with low-fat sour cream.

PER SERVING: ABOUT 190 CALORIES, 135 CALORIES FROM FAT, 13 GRAMS PROTEIN, 2 GRAMS CARBOHYDRATES, 15 GRAMS TOTAL FAT, 0 GRAMS FIBER, 400 MILLIGRAMS SODIUM

The Spreads Spreadsheet

Before you spread your morning toast, here are a few points to consider: Butter tastes great but is high in fat and cholesterol. It is minimally processed, and its balance of omega-3 and omega-6 fatty acids is beneficial. If you use margarine, remember that the softer it is, the healthier it is likely to be. Also, canola and soybean oils add a healthy balance to the fatty acids found in margarine.

The main thing is portion control, says Dr. George Blackburn of Harvard Medical Center. Whatever way you go in the morning, think of how you will balance the rest of the day. A little goes a long way.

Here is a chart, using USDA data, that compares the fat and cholesterol in these spreads. For more information on the different fats, see page 8.

Spread	Fat Grams	Saturated Fats (g)	Monounsaturated Fats (g)	Polyunsaturated Fats (g)	Cholesterol (mg)
Butter	12	7	3	0	31
Margarine (stick)	11	2	5	4	0
Margarine (tub)	11	1	3	6	0
Imitation Margarine	6	1	2	2	0

ITALIAN FRITATTA WITH POTATOES, ONIONS, AND HERBS

Satisfaction is guaranteed with this cozy Italian version of an open-faced omelet. Explore different twists from the Mediterranean and Greek kitchen, or add leftover veggies like chopped broccoli or spinach. Serve it warm, hot, or cold, and make it ahead if you like. Any way is delicious.

Serves: 6

Preparation time: 15 minutes

Cooking time: 25 minutes

8 large eggs

1 cup freshly grated Parmesan cheese

1 tablespoon chopped parsley

Salt to taste

Freshly ground black pepper to taste

1 tablespoon olive oil

1/2 cup chopped onion

1 cup cooked and peeled potatoes, cut into 1/2-inch cubes

---

1. Whisk the eggs, cheese, parsley, salt, and pepper together until thoroughly combined.

2. In an 8- or 10-inch ovenproof skillet, heat the oil over medium heat.

3. Add the onion and cook until soft and translucent, about 5 minutes.

4. Add the potatoes and turn the heat to low.

5. Add the egg mixture (do not stir) and cook over low heat until the eggs are set, about 15 to 20 minutes. Meanwhile preheat the broiler.

6. Place under the broiler for 30 to 45 seconds to finish cooking the top.

Twists: *Mediterranean*: Add 1/2 cup chopped cooked tomatoes with the potatoes and use basil for the herb of choice. During this time, preheat the broiler.

Greek: Add 1/2 cup cooked, well-drained, and chopped spinach with the potatoes. Use oregano and feta cheese.

Ham: Add 1 cup chopped cooked ham with the potatoes. Use chives and Swiss cheese.

PER SERVING: ABOUT 215 CALORIES, 126 CALORIES FROM FAT, 16 GRAMS PROTEIN, 6 GRAMS CARBOHYDRATES, 14 GRAMS TOTAL FAT, 0 GRAMS FIBER, 493 MILLIGRAMS SODIUM

Anytime Breakfasts

There are times in every family when you are faced with the morning challenge of getting everyone to eat his or her breakfast and get going on time. Breakfast need not be rigid; sometimes it can even look like lunch or dinner.

For the times when you need to call on your imagination to answer the morning challenge, here are a few unconventional ideas for doing breakfast. Offer glasses of juice and milk along with:

A PEANUT BUTTER AND BANANA SANDWICH

A PITA POCKET WITH COTTAGE CHEESE AND SLICED OR CHOPPED APPLES

A SLICE OF PIZZA OR A TACO

TORTILLA ROLL-UP SANDWICHES WITH LIGHT CREAM CHEESE AND CHOPPED VEGETABLES

STRING CHEESE AND ORANGE SLICES

CHAPTER 6

VERSATILE FAVORITES: SOUPS, SALADS, AND SMALL DISHES

Menu planning in today's fast-paced, demanding world is made much easier when you discover the wonderful versatility of soups, salads, and small dishes. These healthy dishes are not meant to be pigeonholed into only one type of meal. Instead, the recipes found on the following pages can be enjoyed in many different and exciting ways. The soups are marvelous when served at lunch, dinner, or in between; the salads are a great accompaniment to the meal or can be served as the main attraction; and the small dishes are terrific as late-afternoon snacks or as part of a dinner of several components.

Use these dishes to capture the seasons in fun and creative ways. With each new season there is a wide variety of ingredients in the market to choose for these recipes (see the guides beginning on page 35). Try the many possibilities for making delicious meals happen with ease.

THE SOOTHING COMFORT OF SOUP

Humble of origin, soup is the supreme food to nurture those you love. I have fond memories of my mother making chicken soup every Friday night when I was growing up. She passed that recipe on to me more than thirty years ago, and it has become a family favorite.

Making soup is a chance to use your creativity and respond to what looks good in the market. Most often, vegetables used in soup are easily interchangeable.

"The key to good soup," says chef Bob Kinkead of Kinkead's in Washington, D.C., "is starting with very clear, good stock and then building from there." Stock is best when made at home. The recipes that follow use Basic Chicken Stock (see page 158), but when you do not have the time and have none in the freezer, canned broth works well. Buy low-sodium broth; you can always add salt as you go along.

Making vegetable soup can be a fun family activity for a weekend afternoon. Get everyone into the act.

Here is an easy, basic soup framework:

- Begin with a soup base that uses a combination of vegetables cooked over low heat to get rich layers of flavor. Onions, shallots, celery, leeks, garlic, and carrots all work well to highlight the predominant flavor of the soup.

- Add dried herbs and spices at the start of cooking so that they have plenty of time to release their flavor.

- Add stock and simmer to get the flavor from the base, then add the main vegetables and simmer until tender. There should be enough stock to cover the vegetables in the pot.

- Puree if you wish. The consistency of the soup can vary depending on personal tastes. Enjoy the vegetables swimming in broth or puree part or all of the soup.

- Add fresh herbs at the end for the best smell and taste. As a last step, taste the soup and finish it by adjusting the salt and pepper.

On the pages that follow are basic techniques and wonderful recipes to warm the hearts and stomachs of your family.

Taking Stock

With stock on hand, good taste always follows. Making your own stock is easy and satisfying; best of all, it needs no extra attention once the pot starts simmering.

Here is a key to the different terms:

Stock: A liquid made by simmering bones and vegetables, extracting proteins that give flavor and body.

Broth: A thinner liquid than stock made by simmering meat and/or vegetables.

Bouillon: The French word for broth.

Consommé: A very clear, flavorful stock that has been reduced.

Stock is valuable and versatile because it adds flavor and nutrition without fat. Here are some favorite uses:

- It can replace water when cooking rice or dried beans or when poaching fish, shellfish, chicken, and vegetables.
- It can replace some of the oil in vinaigrettes.
- It makes a delicious sauce when added to a hot pan to release the roasted little bits that are left after roasting or sautéing.
- It makes a great low-fat sauce when reduced slowly or pureed with vegetables or fresh herbs.
- It replaces water as a base for bean and vegetable soups and stews.
- It makes a wonderful pasta sauce when reduced and mixed with cooked vegetables, salt, pepper, and fresh herbs.

BASIC CHICKEN STOCK

Using homemade chicken stock will make a tremendous difference in your soups and other dishes. Make a big batch and freeze what you don't use immediately. It is easy and fun to make stock on Sunday afternoon or immediately after dinner. The stockpot requires little attention from you while it is simmering.

Makes about 2 quarts

Preparation time: 10 minutes

Cooking time: 2 hours, 10 minutes

2 pounds raw chicken bones, excess skin and fat removed (see Note)

4 carrots, roughly chopped into 1-inch pieces

4 medium onions, roughly chopped into 1-inch pieces

4 stalks celery, roughly chopped into 1-inch pieces

3 cloves garlic, peeled

10 peppercorns

1 bay leaf

1/2 cup parsley, stems included

---

1. Place all the ingredients in a stockpot large enough to hold everything easily. Cover with cold water.

2. Bring to a boil quickly over high heat.

3. Lower the heat and skim off any foam or fat that rises to the surface. Simmer for at least 2 hours, uncovered.

4. Strain and cool quickly. Refrigerate.

5. When the stock is thoroughly chilled, fat will rise to the top and solidify. Remove the fat and discard it.

Note: If you are using previously cooked bones, return the stock to the stove after straining in Step 4 and simmer until it has good flavor.

For Safekeeping: Refrigerate up to 3 days or freeze for longer storage.

Per Serving: 1 cup is about 34 calories, 18 calories from fat, 3 grams protein, 0 grams carbohydrates, 2 grams total fat, 0 grams fiber, 85 milligrams sodium

MY MOTHER'S CHICKEN SOUP

Making chicken soup is a ritual in our family that has been passed down for generations. Every time I take out the big soup pot and begin, I think of all the love that my mother and grandmother brought to the kitchen. The secret, my mother says, is to cook the chicken until it falls off the bone and to make sure that you use lots of celery leaves to give it a fresh taste. For the best flavor don't forget the dill and parsley at the end.

Makes about 2 quarts

Preparation time: 10 minutes

Cooking time: 2 1/2 hours

1 raw chicken, 3 to 4 pounds

2 carrots, chopped into 1/2-inch pieces

2 onions, chopped into 1/2-inch pieces

3 stalks celery with leaves, chopped
into 1/2-inch pieces

2 parsnips, chopped into 1/2-inch pieces

Freshly ground black pepper to taste

Salt to taste

1/2 cup chopped fresh dill

1/2 cup chopped fresh parsley

---

1. Place the chicken, carrots, onions, celery, parsnips, and pepper in a stockpot large enough to hold everything easily. Season lightly with salt. Cover with cold water.

2. Bring to a boil quickly over high heat.

3. Lower the heat and skim off any foam or fat that rises to the surface. Simmer, uncovered, until the chicken is thoroughly cooked and tender, at least 2 hours.

4. Remove the chicken from the pot and let it cool for a few minutes. Remove the meat from the bones, cut the meat into bite-size pieces, and return to the pot. Discard the bones.

5. Add the dill and parsley, and simmer 30 minutes more.

6. Adjust the salt and pepper to taste.

For Safekeeping: Cool the soup. Refrigerate up to 3 days or freeze for longer storage.

Per Serving: About 191 calories, 27 calories from fat, 26 grams protein, 14 grams carbohydrates, 3 grams total fat, 3 grams fiber, 181 milligrams sodium

SOUPS FOR ALL SEASONS

Create spectacular soups all year long by using the best the market has to offer. These four recipes use the same basic ingredients and technique, with a special twist for each season.

SPRING ASPARAGUS SOUP

The arrival of spring is captured in this delicate, smooth soup. The sweet flavor of woodsy green asparagus makes a fantastic beginning to any meal.

Serves: 6

Preparation time: 10 minutes

Cooking time: 40 minutes

About 1 tablespoon peanut oil

1/3 cup finely chopped carrot

1/3 cup finely chopped celery

1/3 cup finely chopped onion

Salt to taste

Freshly ground black pepper to taste

About 1 quart Basic Chicken Stock (see page 162) or vegetable stock

5 cups asparagus stalks, cut into 1-inch pieces

Fresh or dried chopped dill to taste (optional)

1. Heat the peanut oil in a saucepan over low heat. Add the carrots, celery, and onion, season lightly with salt and pepper, and cook for 10 minutes.

2. Add the stock and bring to a boil quickly over high heat.

3. Lower the heat and simmer until the vegetables are completely tender, about 15 minutes.

4. Add the asparagus and simmer until just tender, about 5 to 7 minutes.

5. Puree in a blender and strain.

6. Add the chopped dill if desired.

7. Adjust the salt and pepper to taste.

For Safekeeping: Cool the soup. Refrigerate up to 3 days or freeze for longer storage.

PER SERVING: 59 CALORIES, 19 CALORIES FROM FAT, 5 GRAMS PROTEIN, 7 GRAMS CARBOHYDRATES, 2 GRAMS TOTAL FAT, 3 GRAMS FIBER, 454 MILLIGRAMS SODIUM

SUMMER ROASTED RED PEPPER SOUP

Vibrant red peppers fresh from the farmer's market add an exciting spark to summer meals. Roasting the peppers is easily done and delivers extra flavor. Great served hot or cold.

Serves: 6

Preparation time: 10 minutes

Cooking time: 40 minutes

About 1 tablespoon peanut oil

1/3 cup finely chopped carrot

1/3 cup finely chopped celery

1/3 cup finely chopped onion

Salt to taste

Freshly ground black pepper to taste

About 1 quart Basic Chicken Stock (see page 162) or vegetable stock

5 cups roasted red peppers (see page 185)

Chopped fresh basil to taste (optional)

1. Heat the peanut oil in a saucepan over low heat. Add the carrot, celery, and onion, season lightly with salt and pepper, and cook for 10 minutes.

2. Add the stock and bring to a boil quickly over high heat.

3. Lower the heat and simmer until the vegetables are completely tender, about 15 minutes.

4. Add the roasted red peppers and simmer 15 minutes more.

5. Puree in a blender.

6. If adding, chop the basil at the last minute so that it does not discolor. Add it to the soup.

7. Adjust the salt and pepper to taste

For Safekeeping: Cool the soup. Refrigerate up to 3 days or freeze for longer storage.

PER SERVING: ABOUT 65 CALORIES, 18 CALORIES FROM FAT, 3 GRAMS PROTEIN, 9 GRAMS CARBOHYDRATES, 2 GRAMS TOTAL FAT, 2 GRAMS FIBER, 455 MILLIGRAMS SODIUM

FALL LENTIL SOUP

The rich flavor and texture of lentils are a family-friendly start to any autumn meal. Served with crusty bread and a salad, this soup makes a wonderful lunch with virtually no fat and lots of fiber and nutrients.

Serves: 6

Preparation time: 10 minutes

Cooking time: 1 hour

About 1 tablespoon peanut oil

1/3 cup finely chopped carrot

1/3 cup finely chopped celery

1/3 cup finely chopped onion

1 sprig fresh or 1/4 teaspoon dried thyme

Freshly ground black pepper to taste

About 1 1/2 quarts Basic Chicken Stock (see page 162) or vegetable stock

2 cups dried lentils

Salt to taste

1. Heat the peanut oil in a saucepan over low heat. Add the carrot, celery, onion, and thyme, season lightly with pepper, and cook for 10 minutes. (Do not add salt until the lentils are fully cooked.)

2. Add the stock and lentils, and bring to a boil quickly over high heat.

3. Lower the heat and simmer until the lentils are tender, about 1 hour.

4. Puree 2/3 of the soup in a blender and stir it into the remaining 1/3.

5. If the soup is too thick, thin it by adding a little more stock. Raise the heat and bring the soup to a boil for 15 seconds.

6. Add salt and more pepper to taste.

For Safekeeping: Cool the soup. Refrigerate up to 3 days or freeze for longer storage.

PER SERVING: 238 CALORIES, 18 CALORIES FROM FAT, 17 GRAMS PROTEIN, 38 GRAMS CARBOHYDRATES, 2 GRAMS TOTAL FAT, 10 GRAMS FIBER, 473 MILLIGRAMS SODIUM

WINTER POTATO AND LEEK SOUP

Winter white and cozy as can be, this soup is the ultimate comfort food. When temperatures rise, try it chilled.

Serves: 6

Preparation time: 10 minutes

Cooking time: 40 minutes

About 1 tablespoon peanut oil

1/2 cup finely chopped onion

2 cups chopped and well rinsed leeks (white part only)

1 sprig fresh or 1/4 teaspoon dried thyme

Salt to taste

White pepper to taste

About 1 1/2 quarts Basic Chicken Stock (see page 162) or vegetable stock

2 cups peeled potatoes cut into 1/2-inch cubes (keep in a bowl of water so they do not discolor)

1 tablespoon chopped fresh chives

1. Heat the peanut oil in a saucepan over low heat. Add the onion, leek, and thyme, season lightly with salt and pepper, and cook for 15 minutes.

2. Add the stock and bring to a boil quickly over high heat.

3. Lower the heat and simmer for 15 minutes, or until the leeks are completely tender.

4. Add the potatoes and simmer about 10 minutes more, or until the potatoes are tender.

5. Puree in a blender.

6. Adjust the salt and pepper to taste.

7. Serve garnished with chives.

For Safekeeping: Cool the soup, then refrigerate up to 3 days or freeze for longer storage.

PER SERVING: ABOUT 122 CALORIES, 36 CALORIES FROM FAT, 4 GRAMS PROTEIN, 18 GRAMS CARBOHYDRATES, 4 GRAMS TOTAL FAT, 2 GRAMS FIBER, 456 MILLIGRAMS SODIUM

TIPS AND TRIVIA
Souping It Up

Add these imaginative toppings to your favorite soups:

- toasted pumpkin seeds
- croutons
- fresh chopped herbs, especially parsley
- chopped blanched vegetables
- toasted nuts
- nonfat yogurt or low-fat sour cream
- diced ham or poultry

Bob Kinkead's Summer "Salad" Soup

With family roots in New England, Bob Kinkead, chef and owner of Kinkead's in Washington, D.C., first became a master at cooking seafood and soups. But it is when he talks about vegetables that he really gets going. "Vegetables are an integral part of a meal," he says, and he plans meals by thinking about "the wraparound of the dish—the vegetables." He suggests checking out what looks best in the market.

Filled with Italian flavor, this chilled soup is a sensational way to enjoy the pleasures of summer-ripe, fresh vegetables. It's easy to make, and as Bob says, "It doesn't get any healthier"—low in calories and fat but filled with vitamins. Best of all, it soars with good taste.

Serves: 8

Preparation time: 45 minutes

Cooking time: 10 minutes

12 cups Basic Chicken Stock (see page 162)

2 cups broccoli florets

1 cup cauliflower florets

1 tablespoon extra-virgin olive oil

2 cloves garlic, minced

1 small zucchini, cut into 1/2-inch cubes

Juice of 1 lemon

1/2 cup red wine vinegar

Salt to taste

Freshly ground black pepper to taste

4 small radishes, finely sliced

2 tomatoes, peeled, seeded, and diced

1 small red onion, sliced

3 scallions, chopped

1 large cucumber, diced

1 medium carrot, peeled and finely sliced

2 celery stalks, finely sliced on the diagonal

1 red pepper, diced

1 small fennel bulb, finely sliced

20 fresh basil leaves, shredded

1/2 cup coarsely chopped parsley

1/4 cup chervil leaves (optional)

Garnish:

1 cup shredded radicchio

1 cup shredded arugula

Continued >

1. Bring the stock to a boil and simmer until it has reduced by half. Refrigerate until well chilled.

2. Blanch the broccoli and cauliflower florets in boiling salted water until slightly cooked but still crunchy, about 1 minute. Plunge the florets into ice water, strain, and refrigerate.

3. Heat the olive oil in a skillet over medium heat. Add the garlic and cook until transparent, not brown, about 1 minute.

4. Add the zucchini and cook until the skin turns bright green but is still firm, about 3 minutes. Remove from the heat and chill.

(Steps 1 through 4 can be done ahead and the ingredients kept separately in the refrigerator up to 2 days.)

5. Add the lemon juice, vinegar, salt, and pepper to the cold stock. Add all the vegetables and herbs and let stand for 5 to 10 minutes.

6. Adjust the salt and pepper to taste.

7. Divide the soup among 8 bowls. Top with the radicchio and arugula, and serve

PER SERVING: ABOUT 128 CALORIES, 45 CALORIES FROM FAT, 8 GRAMS PROTEIN, 14 GRAMS CARBOHYDRATES, 5 GRAMS TOTAL FAT, 5 GRAMS FIBER, 250 MILLIGRAMS SODIUM

FOR SAFEKEEPING
Cautious Cut-ups

Cutting-board safety reduces the likelihood of bacterial contamination and food-borne illness. While both wood and plastic cutting boards are available, the USDA Meat and Poultry Hotline recommends using only plastic boards for cutting raw meat, poultry, and seafood. If you have wooden boards, use a separate one for cutting each of these items.

It is essential to wash the cutting boards thoroughly in hot, soapy water after each use. Then rinse them well and pat dry with fresh paper towels. Every so often, sanitize the boards with a solution of 2 teaspoons bleach per quart of water. Rinse thoroughly and let stand a few minutes; rinse again and pat dry with a paper towel.

Finally, cutting boards should be replaced when they show signs of wear.

NORA POUILLON'S ROASTED BUTTERNUT SQUASH SOUP WITH TOASTED SEEDS

My good friend Nora Pouillon has a passion for fresh, organically grown ingredients. With a strong commitment to good health, she cooks exceptional dishes at Restaurant Nora and Asia Nora in Washington, D.C.

Eating seasonally is a joy, Nora says, because "you get in touch with what is going on around you, the nutritional value is high, and you are also keeping local farmers in business." This simple, smooth soup is a luscious way to enjoy the farmer's autumn harvest. Children love toasting the squash seeds and sprinkling them on top of the soup.

Serves: 6

Preparation time: 15 minutes

Cooking time: 1 hour

1 butternut squash, 2 to 2 1/2 pounds

2 teaspoons canola oil

1 onion, chopped

1 stalk celery, chopped

4 cups low-fat milk or stock

2 tablespoons fresh lemon juice

1/4 teaspoon cumin

1 pinch allspice

2 tablespoons dry sherry or marsala

Sea salt to taste

Freshly ground black pepper to taste

2 tablespoons pumpkin seeds or reserved butternut squash seeds

1. Preheat the oven to 350° F.

2. Cut the butternut squash in half, scrape out the seeds, and set them aside. Place the squash, cut sides down, on a baking sheet and bake until tender and easily pierced with a fork, about 40 minutes. Let cool about 10 minutes.

3. While the squash is baking, heat the oil in a small skillet over medium heat. Add the onion and celery, and cook until soft and translucent, about 3 minutes.

4. Scoop the squash pulp out of the skin with a spoon and put it into a large bowl. Add the onion, celery, and milk or stock. Stir to combine.

(Steps 2 through 4 can be done ahead and refrigerated up to 3 days or frozen for longer storage.)

5. Puree this mixture in a blender in batches, being careful not to overfill the blender. Strain the blended mixture through a colander to remove any remaining fiber or seeds.

6. Add the lemon juice, cumin, allspice, and sherry or marsala. Season with salt and pepper to taste.

7. Spread the cleaned, reserved seeds on a baking sheet and toast in the oven until lightly browned, about 10 minutes.

8. Reheat the soup, adding milk or stock if it is too thick. Divide it among 6 warmed soup bowls and sprinkle with the toasted seeds.

PER SERVING: ABOUT 133 CALORIES, 36 CALORIES FROM FAT, 5 GRAMS PROTEIN, 21 GRAMS CARBOHYDRATES, 4 GRAMS TOTAL FAT, 6 GRAMS FIBER, 166 MILLIGRAMS SODIUM

MiCHAEL FOLEY's CREAMY CREAMLESS MISO SOUP WITH POTATOES

Appreciating food for its cultural value as well as its taste is important to Michael Foley's broad vision. Printers Row, the restaurant in Chicago where he has been owner and chef for many years, began as part of his dream of urban renewal. He helped to transform the rundown neighborhood of Printers Row while he created a focal point for midwestern cooking. For years he owned a 475-acre sustainable farm that also produced the food for the restaurant.

Michael also seriously studies nutrition and is concerned about "how food is a link to health and how it works in the body." He enjoys using ingredients that have health benefits, such as miso. This Asian-inspired miso soup has a silky smooth texture and the surprise tangy taste of lemongrass.

Serves: 6

Preparation time: 15 minutes

Cooking time: 20 minutes

2 tablespoons butter or canola oil

5 to 6 leeks, white part only, diced and rinsed well

1 tablespoon finely chopped lemongrass

1 tablespoon finely chopped ginger

Salt to taste

White pepper to taste

4 cups vegetable or chicken stock

1 medium potato, peeled and cut into 1/2-inch cubes

1 medium sweet potato, peeled and cut into 1/2-inch cubes

4 teaspoons miso of your choice

Juice of 1 lemon

1 teaspoon chopped chives or scallions

---

1. Melt the butter in a 2-quart saucepan over medium heat. Add the leeks and stir to coat with the butter. Add the lemongrass and ginger. Season with salt and pepper. Cook until the leeks are tender and translucent.

2. Add the stock and potatoes, and simmer until the potatoes are cooked through. Puree in a blender.

3. Add the miso. Blend to combine.

4. Add the lemon juice and adjust the salt and pepper to taste.

5. Serve hot in simple, small cups. Garnish with the chives or scallions.

PER SERVING: ABOUT 161 CALORIES, 45 CALORIES FROM FAT, 3 GRAMS PROTEIN, 28 GRAMS CARBOHYDRATES, 5 GRAMS TOTAL FAT, 3 GRAMS FIBER, 308 MILLIGRAMS SODIUM

About Miso

Miso is made from soybeans, such grains as rice and barley, plus salt, water, and an active culture. It is becoming increasingly available in the refrigerated cases of the supermarket. To get the high-protein benefits of miso, don't overcook it; add it just before serving. The nutrition is in the enzyme, and cooking it only slightly keeps it alive. Try the many kinds of miso available such as red, brown, and white. Chef Michael Foley recommends the light misos for use with vegetables and fish and the darker misos for use with meat.

THE SPARKLE oF SaLaD

The vivid colors and diversity in textures and taste are living testament to the wide appeal of salads. Enjoy them before the meal, after the meal, or as the meal. Salads offer a chance to be creative and add variety to everyone's diet.

There seems to be no limit to the kinds of greens available in the market. All are low in fat but rich in valuable nutrients, especially the deep green and leafy vegetables, which have plenty of health-promoting carotenoids and vitamin C. The Greens Salad Bar below will help you introduce a kaleidoscope of new greens to your next salad.

The Greens Salad Bar

Arugula. Smooth, dark green leaves with a strong peppery taste. Mixes well with a vinaigrette of milder lettuces such as Bibb.

Belgian Endive. Pale leaves edged in yellow; crunchy and a bit bitter tasting. Use in tossed salads with other mild greens and a creamy dressing. Braise it as a side dish.

Bibb/Boston. Small, tender head of light green leaves with a sweet flavor. Mixes well with other greens and vinaigrette or a light creamy dressing.

**Chicory/Frisee.** Curly green leaves that taste best when young. Frisee is the sweetest member of the chicory family. Mixes well with other greens and vinaigrettes.

Escarole. Crisp, light green leaves and a pale yellowish heart. Slightly bitter flavor. Serve alone as a salad with red wine vinaigrette or just lemon juice.

Iceberg. Crisp, light green leaves with a mild taste. Best mixed with other lettuces and a light, creamy salad dressing.

**Loose-leaf Lettuce.** Fluffy, soft red or green leaves with a sweet flavor. Mixes well with hardy watercress, arugula, or radicchio and vinaigrette.

**Mâche.** Small, round, deep green leaves with a delicate, nutty flavor. Best in salad by itself or mixed with Belgian endive and vinaigrette.

**Mesclun.** A mix of tiny, young greens that may include arugula, chervil, dandelion, and oak leaf lettuce. Toss with herbs and a light vinaigrette.

**Radicchio.** A small, tight head of vibrant, deep red–colored leaves with a tangy flavor. Toss in a salad with lighter lettuces and a hardy dressing such as walnut vinaigrette.

Romaine. A large head of green or red leaves that has a sweet flavor. Toss with other greens in Italian-type salads such as Caesar.

Watercress. Small, round, dark green leaves with a spicy flavor. Toss with milder greens or by itself with a vinaigrette.

TIPS AND TRIVIA
Lettuce Lineage

Honored, revered, and always enjoyed, lettuce can be traced back to the Roman Empire. Caesar Augustus so worshipped lettuce as a cure-all that he erected a statue in its honor. The Romans introduced it to England, where it quickly became popular. Early American settlers brought many different varieties with them, but by the 1950s supermarket shelves were dominated by iceberg lettuce, which became popular as a response to the growth of cities and the need to ship produce long distances. The pendulum started to swing again in the 1980s with the growth in popularity of tasty lettuces such as Mesclun.

Simple Salad Solutions

There are endless ways to prepare salads. Greens mix well with all kinds of vegetables, grains, and protein-rich ingredients such as beans, chicken, beef, or seafood. To enhance the flavor of salads try adding chopped shallots, citrus fruits, and chopped chili peppers. For simple, sensational salads:

- Start with ingredients that are in season, look fresh, and are appealing to the eye.
- Pluck the leaves apart by hand, never with a knife, being careful to handle the lettuce gently to avoid bruising.
- Wash the leaves carefully in a large bowl of cold water and swish them with your hand. If they are very dirty, let them soak for a few minutes. Lift the leaves out and dry them in a salad spinner or pat them gently with a towel.
- Balance tastes and textures such as bold with mild, and soft with crisp.

- Place the leaves and salad dressing in a bowl with lots of room. With washed hands or salad forks, toss the leaves until the dressing covers them.
- Always dress salads lightly at the last minute to avoid a soggy texture.

About Vinaigrette

Basic vinaigrette is one part vinegar to three parts olive oil. Change the taste by adding more or less vinegar.

Red wine vinegar is probably the best all-around vinegar to use; balsamic is a close second; and white wine, sherry, and flavored vinegars are also good.

Olive oil should be high quality and extra-virgin. You can really taste the difference. Walnut oil and other flavored oils are also good.

Minced shallots, salt, and pepper are standard ingredients; they complement any vinaigrette. Chopped fresh herbs can be added as desired.

BASIC VINAIGRETTE

Makes about 1 cup

Preparation time: 5 minutes

1/4 cup red wine vinegar

3/4 cup olive oil

1 tablespoon finely chopped shallots

Salt to taste

Freshly ground black pepper to taste

Place all the ingredients in a jar with a tight-fitting lid. Shake well.

For Safekeeping: This can be made ahead and refrigerated up to 1 week. Shake well before using.

Twist: For Basic Mustard Vinaigrette, add 1/4 cup

Dijon mustard to the other ingredients. It will be thicker than Basic Vinaigrette.

PER SERVING: 2 TABLESPOONS IS ABOUT 174 CALORIES, 174 CALORIES FROM FAT, 0 GRAMS PROTEIN, 0 GRAMS CARBOHYDRATES, 20 GRAMS FAT, 0 GRAMS FIBER, 141 MILLIGRAMS SODIUM

SpINacH, OrANGE, AND ALMOND sALAD WiTH SoY-LiME vINAIGREtTE

The light, fresh taste of this original salad sings with Asian influences. It is simple to put together, pleasantly sweet to enjoy, and loaded with plenty of good nutrients and vitamins.

Serves: 6

Preparation time: 15 minutes

For the vinaigrette:

1 tablespoon soy sauce

2 tablespoons fresh lime juice

1 tablespoon finely chopped shallots

1/3 cup olive oil

Salt to taste

Freshly ground black pepper to taste

1. Place all the ingredients in a container with a tight-fitting lid. Shake well.

2. Add the salt and pepper to taste

For the salad:

1/2 cup slivered almonds

4 cups spinach, cleaned and torn into bite-size pieces

1 orange, peeled and sectioned (see page 134)

1. Preheat the oven to 350° F.

2. Spread the almonds on a baking sheet and toast in the oven until lightly browned, about 5 minutes.

3. Place the spinach in a bowl and toss with the vinaigrette.

4. Transfer the dressed spinach leaves to a serving plate. Arrange the orange sections on top and sprinkle with the almonds.

Twist: Grapefruit sections are a delicious alternative to oranges.

PER SERVING: ABOUT 199 CALORIES, 162 CALORIES FROM FAT, 3 GRAMS PROTEIN, 8 GRAMS CARBOHYDRATES, 18 GRAMS TOTAL FAT, 2 GRAMS FIBER, 286 MILLIGRAMS SODIUM

ANNIE SOMERVILLE'S SUMMER BEANS WITH CHERRY TOMATOES AND TARRAGON

"Down-to-earth and inviting" describes both Annie Somerville and the marvelous food she cooks at Greens, a sunny vegetarian restaurant overlooking the bay in San Francisco. Annie's love of food came from her years growing up in the Midwest and watching her mother and grandmother cook. Annie gives cooking classes in San Francisco that focus on tasting everything and becoming familiar with how ingredients work together.

This salad is great for a picnic in late summer when fresh beans are plentiful. Try using three or four varieties, such as green and yellow Romano beans, Blue Lake green beans, and yellow wax beans. The dish is wonderfully colorful and delicious.

Serves: 6

Preparation time: 10 minutes

Cooking time: 1–6 minutes

2 shallots, thinly sliced

2 tablespoons champagne vinegar or white wine vinegar

Salt

1 pound fresh beans, any kind or a combination of green and yellow wax-type

3 tablespoons extra-virgin olive oil

1 tablespoon coarsely chopped fresh tarragon

Freshly ground black pepper to taste

2 tablespoons sherry vinegar or red wine vinegar

1 cup cherry tomatoes, cut in half if large

1. In a medium-size bowl, toss the shallots with the champagne or white wine vinegar to draw out their pink color.

2. Bring a medium-size pot of water to a boil and add 1/2 teaspoon salt. Drop in the beans and cook until just tender, 1 to 2 minutes for small young beans and up to 6 minutes for larger beans. Drain.

3. Immediately toss the hot beans with the olive oil, shallots, tarragon, 1/2 teaspoon salt, and pepper. The beans will soak up the flavors as they cool to room temperature.

(Steps 1 through 3 can be done ahead and kept in the refrigerator for 1 day.)

4. Just before serving, add the sherry or red wine vinegar and toss in the cherry tomatoes.

5. Adjust the salt and pepper to taste.

PER SERVING: 97 CALORIES, 63 CALORIES FROM FAT, 2 GRAMS PROTEIN, 9 GRAMS CARBOHYDRATES, 7 GRAMS TOTAL FAT, 3 GRAMS FIBER, 395 MILLIGRAMS SODIUM

FOR SAFEKEEPING
On the Road

Family picnics and long car rides mean packing food for the ride. Food-to-go can be both a money- and time-saver. Keep everyone happy by filling plastic bags with handy snacks such as carrots, broccoli florets, and sliced apples or other fruit. To enjoy the trip from start to finish, follow these food safety tips:

- Keep perishable food such as meat, poultry, eggs, fish, and mayonnaise in a cooler.
- To pack the cooler safely, take the food directly from the refrigerator or freezer. Full coolers stay cold longer, so pack any remaining space with ice, fruit, and nonperishable foods. Add more ice as soon as it starts melting. Keep the cooler in the passenger section rather than a hot trunk.
- Toss out any foods that feel above refrigerator temperatures (40° F.). Bacteria that can cause foodborne illness grow rapidly at warm temperatures.

Always make sure hands and utensils are clean before eating. Moist towelettes are a handy way to keep clean.

HEALTHY TIMESAVERS
Isabella's Favorite Food

Isabella is not yet a teenager, but she loves hanging out in the kitchen, says her father, chef Todd English of Olives restaurant in Charlestown, Massachusetts. Isabella's favorite dish is a quick and easy combination of potatoes and applesauce. All you need to do is boil a few potatoes, rice them or mash them, and then add a little applesauce to taste (see page 142 for the Groovy Applesauce recipe). It is a surprising yet deliciously healthy combination that children like.

> **Tomatoes, when they are ripe, stop the conversation at the table.**
> —GORDON SINCLAIR, CHEF AND OWNER, GORDON'S, CHICAGO, ILLINOIS

GOAT HILL FARM TOMATOES WITH DOUBLE BASIL VINAIGRETTE

I will never forget the crisp autumn day in the rolling hills of Rappahannock County, Virginia, when I visited Terri Lehman and John Burns at their rustic farmhouse. At Goat Hill Farm they grow more than twenty-nine varieties of tomatoes, a wide variety of lettuces and berries, and many other wonderful things that they sell at local farmer's markets.

Terri's fantastic rainbow tomato salad is a feast for the eyes as well as the tastebuds. On that day we relished raw heirloom tomatoes such as Persimmons, Green Zebras, Purple Cherokees, and Arkansas Travelers. With no cooking and no pots to clean, this salad is the ultimate easy, delicious recipe.

Serves: 4

Preparation time: 10 minutes

For the vinaigrette:

2 tablespoons Basil-Infused Red Wine Vinegar (see page 117)

⅓ cup Basil Oil (see page 117)

Salt to taste

Freshly ground black pepper to taste

1. Place all the ingredients in a container with a tight-fitting lid. Shake well.

2. Adjust the salt and pepper to taste.

For the salad:

4 large ripe tomatoes, assorted varieties and colors, sliced

4 slices red onion

Basil leaves for garnish

Freshly ground black pepper to taste

Arrange the tomato and onion slices on 4 serving plates. Sprinkle generously with the vinaigrette. Garnish with basil leaves and a few twists of pepper.

PER SERVING: ABOUT 205 CALORIES, 171 CALORIES FROM FAT, 2 GRAMS PROTEIN, 10 GRAMS CARBOHYDRATES, 19 GRAMS FAT, 3 GRAMS FIBER, 160 MILLIGRAMS SODIUM

ROASTED BEETS, GREENS, AND GOAT CHEESE WITH PINE NUT VINAIGRETTE

Contrasting colors, tastes, and textures give this showpiece salad major appeal. The ruby-red beets glisten against the green-and-white backdrop. Perfect for a festive dinner.

Serves: 4

Preparation time: 15 minutes

Cooking time: 1 hour

For the vinaigrette:

1 tablespoon finely chopped shallots

2 tablespoons red wine vinegar

1/3 cup olive oil

1/4 cup pine nuts

Salt to taste

Freshly ground black pepper to taste

1. Place all the ingredients in a blender. Blend on high speed to combine.

2. Adjust the salt and pepper to taste.

For the salad:

2 medium beets, unpeeled

2 cups red- or green-leaf lettuce, washed and torn into bite-size pieces

1/2 cup goat cheese

1. Preheat the oven to 350° F.

2. Wrap the beets in aluminum foil. Roast in the oven until tender, about 1 hour.

3. Peel the beets when they are cool enough to handle but are still warm. Cut into wedges.

4. Toss the beets with half of the vinaigrette.

5. In another bowl, toss the greens with the remaining vinaigrette.

6. Arrange the greens on a serving plate. Place the beets on top of the greens. (Rinse your hands well to remove the red beet juice.)

7. Crumble the goat cheese and sprinkle over the top of the salad.

PER SERVING: (INCLUDES 2 TABLESPOONS VINAIGRETTE): ABOUT 270 CALORIES, 216 CALORIES FROM FAT, 9 GRAMS PROTEIN, 8 GRAMS CARBOHYDRATES, 24 GRAMS TOTAL FAT, 2 GRAMS FIBER, 267 MILLIGRAMS SODIUM

Head Starts

Get a head start on your next meal. When you are chopping herbs, garlic, shallots, or onions for any reason, chop some extra for future use. They last in the refrigerator for a day or two, but keep them well sealed in plastic wrap so that their odors do not affect other food.

GREENS WITH APPLES, WALNUTS, BLUE CHEESE, AND BALSAMIC VINAIGRETTE

This hearty salad recalls the crispness of fall and winter. The crunch of the apples and walnuts is a great contrast to the smooth texture of the blue cheese and the balsamic vinaigrette. Take the family to pick apples and have the kids help to toss them with the salad.

Serves: 6

Preparation time: 15 minutes

For the vinaigrette:

1 tablespoon finely chopped shallots

2 tablespoons balsamic vinegar

1/3 cup olive oil

Salt to taste

Freshly ground black pepper to taste

1. Place all the ingredients in a container with a tight-fitting lid. Shake well.

2. Adjust the salt and pepper to taste.

For the salad:

4 cups red- or green-leaf lettuce, washed and torn into bite-size pieces

1 apple, cored and sliced (peeling is optional)

1/2 cup chopped walnuts

1/2 cup crumbled blue cheese

1. Toss the lettuce and apple with the vinaigrette in a bowl.

2. Transfer to a serving plate and sprinkle with the walnuts and blue cheese.

Twists: Experiment with different combinations of fruits, nuts, and cheeses. For example, try pears, pecans, and goat cheese.

PER SERVING: ABOUT 242 CALORIES, 198 CALORIES FROM FAT, 4 GRAMS PROTEIN, 10 GRAMS CARBOHYDRATES, 22 GRAMS TOTAL FAT, 2 GRAMS FIBER, 260 MILLIGRAMS SODIUM

SMALL DISHES WITH BIG BENEFITS

Preparing small dishes is a wonderful way to break away from routine cooking and add zip to family meals. Small dishes are a delicious way to add new vegetables, fruits, and grains to the day's menu and get great health benefits. Make a terrific meal with several small components that complement each other, or serve small dishes with simply prepared main dishes. Try serving a small dish to start off dinner, as an easy lunch, or as a snack for when everyone comes into the kitchen asking, "What is there to eat?"

ZUCCHINI AND TOMATO TART

The vibrant contrasting colors of zucchini and tomato make this small dish a visual delight. It is a sunny summer favorite because it tastes so good. Use prepared piecrust to save time; whole wheat piecrusts add extra nutrition. Superb!

Serves: 6

Preparation time: 15 minutes

Cooking time: 10 minutes

One 8- or 9-inch piecrust (store-bought is fine)

1/4 cup grated Gruyère cheese

20 fresh basil leaves

2 tablespoons olive oil

1 clove garlic, finely chopped

Salt to taste

Freshly ground black pepper to taste

1 medium zucchini, sliced 1/8-inch thick

3 small plum tomatoes, sliced 1/8-inch thick

1. Preheat the oven to 350° F. Prick the piecrust with a fork several times and bake until golden brown, according to the directions on the package.

2. Chop 10 of the basil leaves. Mix together with the oil, garlic, salt, and pepper. Reserve.

3. Sprinkle the cheese on the bottom of the pie shell. Arrange the remaining whole basil leaves on top of the cheese.

4. Brush each slice of zucchini and tomato with the basil-garlic oil. Arrange the zucchini and tomato slices alternately, overlapping by half, in a single layer in the pie shell. Brush the entire layer again with the basil-garlic oil.

5. Bake until the vegetables are warmed, about 8 to 10 minutes. Serve warm.

PER SERVING: 204 CALORIES, 126 CALORIES FROM FAT, 4 GRAMS PROTEIN, 16 GRAMS CARBOHYDRATES, 14 GRAMS TOTAL FAT, 1 GRAM FIBER, 310 MILLIGRAMS SODIUM

GRILLED EGGPLANT ROLL-UPS STUFFED WITH GOAT CHEESE

Inspired by the tastes of the Mediterranean, this dish is a modern celebration of the garden's best vegetables. These easy roll-ups cause a sensation at the table.

Serves: 4

Preparation time: 20 minutes

Cooking time: 20 minutes

For the roll-ups:

About 3 tablespoons olive oil

2 cups spinach leaves, washed

Salt to taste

Freshly ground black pepper to taste

8 slices eggplant, sliced lengthwise about 1/4-inch thick

1/2 cup goat cheese

1 tablespoon chopped parsley

8 strips roasted red pepper (see page 185), cut 1 inch wide

1. Preheat the grill to medium and the oven to 350° F.

2. Heat 1 teaspoon of the olive oil in a skillet. Add the spinach and a pinch each of salt and pepper and toss in the pan for about 1 minute. Remove from the pan and let cool.

3. Brush the eggplant slices with olive oil and season with salt and pepper. Grill for 1 to 2 minutes on each side, taking care not to overcook.

4. Mix the goat cheese and parsley together. Season with salt and pepper. Shape the cheese into 8 cork-size pieces.

5. To assemble: On the top of each slice of eggplant, place a strip of pepper, a few leaves of spinach, and a "cork" of cheese. Begin with the wide end of the eggplant and roll toward the narrow end. Place on a lightly oiled cookie sheet, seam side down.

(Steps 2 through 5 can be done ahead and kept in the refrigerator up to 2 days.)

6. Warm the roll-ups in the oven until thoroughly heated, about 8 to 10 minutes, longer if they have been refrigerated. While the roll-ups are warming, make the sauce.

For the sauce:

1 tablespoon olive oil

1 tablespoon chopped shallots

1/4 cup fresh tomatoes, seeded and chopped

1/4 cup balsamic vinegar

1. Heat 1 teaspoon olive oil in a small skillet over low heat. Add the shallots and cook until soft and translucent, about 2 minutes. Add the tomatoes and sauté for 1 minute. Add the balsamic vinegar and quickly bring to a boil. Remove from the heat.

2. Place 2 roll-ups on each plate. Spoon sauce over the top and serve.

PER SERVING: 251 CALORIES, 180 CALORIES FROM FAT, 7 GRAMS PROTEIN, 13 GRAMS CARBOHYDRATES, 20 GRAMS TOTAL FAT, 4 GRAMS FIBER, 271 MILLIGRAMS SODIUM

ALICE WATERS'S RAINBOW TOMATO PIZZA

Alice Waters, the chef and owner of the restaurant Chez Panisse in Berkeley, California, lives to share her joy for irresistible food. Alice has made a tremendous difference to those who have tasted the food at her restaurant: the children at the King Middle School of Berkeley, California; the former San Francisco prison inmates who grow organic vegetables as part of the Garden Project, and thousands of others.

With Alice's leadership, the community of the King Middle School transformed a neglected open field behind the school into an amazing garden. When I last visited this edible landscape, the variety of vegetables grown was amazing, and children gathered around the pizza oven to make their own pizzas. Here is a simple recipe for a spectacular pizza, inspired by this school garden and the student growers.

Makes one 14-inch pizza or 2 smaller pizzas

Preparation time: 15 minutes (plus rising times)

Cooking time: 15 minutes

For the pizza dough:

3/4 cup warm water

1 tablespoon milk

2 teaspoons active dry yeast

2 cups all-purpose flour, plus extra

1 teaspoon salt

1/2 teaspoon olive oil, plus extra

For the Rainbow Tomato Topping:

2 to 4 tomatoes of various varieties and colors

2 cloves garlic, chopped

About 1/8 cup olive oil

4 ounces mozzarella cheese, grated

1 teaspoon chopped parsley

Salt to taste

Freshly ground black pepper to taste

To make the dough:

1. Mix the water, milk, and yeast together in a large bowl and stir with a wooden spoon.

2. Add the flour, salt, and olive oil. Mix together with the wooden spoon until the dough is too thick and sticky to stir.

3. Spread a little flour on a work surface and place the dough on top of the flour. Knead the dough by pulling the dough from the sides and folding it into the middle. Keep kneading until the dough becomes a

continued ›

mooth ball. If it sticks to the table or to your hands, add a little more flour.

4. Rub a clean bowl with olive oil and put the dough in it. Cover the bowl with a towel and put it in a warm place. Let the dough rise for about 1½ hours, or until doubled in volume.

5. Punch the raised dough down with your fist. Turn the dough over, form it into a ball again, cover, and let rise for another hour.

6. Heat the oven to 450° F. Roll out the dough with a rolling pin or use your hands to pat the dough into a circle about 12 to 14 inches across and 1/4 inch thick. Place the dough on an oiled baking sheet.

To make the pizza:

1. Cut the tomatoes into very thin rounds.

2. Sprinkle the garlic and spread the olive oil over the rolled dough. Sprinkle with the mozzarella cheese, leaving the edge of the pizza free. Put the tomato slices on top of the cheese.

3. Bake until nicely browned and crispy, about 15 minutes. Remove from the oven, drizzle a little olive oil over the edge, and sprinkle with chopped parsley. Season with salt and pepper.

PER SERVING: ABOUT 446 CALORIES, 135 CALORIES FROM FAT, 18 GRAMS PROTEIN, 60 GRAMS CARBOHYDRATES, 15 GRAMS TOTAL FAT, 4 GRAMS FIBER, 337 MILLIGRAMS SODIUM

TIPS AND TRIVIA
Roasted Garlic

Slice off the top of a bulb of garlic in order to barely expose the garlic inside each clove. Place the bulb in an ovenproof dish and drizzle with olive oil. Place the dish, uncovered, in a 350° F. oven for 15 to 20 minutes, until the garlic is golden brown and soft. Let cool. It is delicious in mashed potatoes, spread on bruschetta, and in vinaigrettes.

TIPS AND TRIVIA
Roasted Peppers

Slice the pepper in half lengthwise and remove the ribs and seeds. Place the 2 halves on a cookie sheet and press down so they lie flat with the skin side up. Place the peppers under a hot broiler until the skin is evenly blistered, about 5 to 8 minutes. Carefully remove the peppers from the cookie sheet and place in a bowl. Cover tightly with plastic wrap and let sit for 5 minutes. Uncover and peel off the skin.

SEASONAL BRUSCHETTA

Bruschetta is toasted slices of rustic bread rubbed with garlic, drizzled with extra-virgin olive oil, and topped in ways to fit the season. This simple, down-to-earth dish can be a hearty snack if the bread is thickly sliced or an appetizer if it's thinly sliced. Whatever the season, it is sure to be a crowd pleaser. But remember: It's the good extra-virgin olive oil that makes the difference.

Serves: 4

Preparation time: 10 minutes

Cooking time: 5 minutes

BASIC BRUSCHETTA

12 slices French bread, about 1/4-inch thick for an appetizer or 1/2-inch thick for a hearty snack

1 tablespoon extra-virgin olive oil

2 to 3 cloves garlic

1. Toast the bread on both sides in a toaster oven, under the broiler, or on the grill.

2. While the toasted slices are still warm, rub them with garlic and drizzle them with olive oil on one side.

3. Top with a seasonal variation (see below).

PER SERVING: ABOUT 80 CALORIES, 18 CALORIES FROM FAT, 2 GRAMS PROTEIN, 13 GRAMS CARBOHYDRATES, 2 GRAMS FAT, 1 GRAM FIBER, 152 MILLIGRAMS SODIUM

SPRING: CARAMELIZED ONION BRUSCHETTA

1 tablespoon olive oil

1 large onion, sliced

1 sprig fresh thyme or 1/4 teaspoon dried

Salt to taste

Freshly ground black pepper to taste

6 olives, pitted and halved

1. Heat the olive oil in a skillet over medium heat. Add the onion, thyme, and a little salt and pepper.

Cook until the onions begin to get soft. Turn the heat up a little and cook until the onions turn golden brown. Adjust the salt and pepper to taste.

2. Place a dollop of caramelized onions on each slice of bruschetta and top with half an olive.

PER SERVING: ABOUT 97 CALORIES, 27 CALORIES FROM FAT, 2 GRAMS PROTEIN, 13 GRAMS CARBOHYDRATES, 3 GRAMS FAT, 3 GRAM FIBER, 172 MILLIGRAMS SODIUM

Summer: Tomato Bruschetta

2 tablespoons seeded and diced fresh tomatoes

1 teaspoon chopped fresh basil

Salt to taste

Freshly ground black pepper to taste

1 tablespoon extra-virgin olive oil

1. In a mixing bowl, combine the tomatoes, basil, salt, pepper, and olive oil.

2. Put a dab of the tomato mixture on each slice of bruschetta and serve.

Per Serving: About 91 calories, 27 calories from fat, 2 grams protein, 13 grams carbohydrates, 3 grams fat, 1 gram fiber, 152 milligrams sodium

---

Fall: Roasted Garlic and Red Pepper Bruschetta

3 or 4 cloves Roasted Garlic (see page 185)

1 teaspoon extra-virgin olive oil

Salt to taste

Freshly ground black pepper to taste

1 Roasted Red Pepper (see page 185), diced

1/2 teaspoon chopped parsley

1. Mash the roasted garlic with the olive oil and a generous amount of salt and pepper to make a paste.

2. Mix the roasted pepper and parsley together and season with salt and pepper.

3. Spread each slice of bruschetta with the garlic paste and top with a spoonful of the roasted pepper mixture.

Per Serving: 85 calories, 18 calories from fat, 2 grams protein, 14 grams carbohydrates, 2 grams fat, 1 gram fiber, 152 milligrams sodium

---

Winter: Olive Tapenade Bruschetta

2 tablespoons pitted and finely chopped black or green olives

1 teaspoon capers

1/2 teaspoon extra-virgin olive oil

Freshly ground black pepper to taste

1. Mash the olives, capers, olive oil, and pepper together.

2. Put a dab of the olive mixture on each slice of bruschetta.

Per Serving: About 83 calories, 18 calories from fat, 2 grams protein, 13 grams carbohydrates, 2 grams fat, 1 gram fiber, 173 milligrams sodium

GRILLED PORTOBELLO SANDWICH

A satisfying sandwich treat that is filled with lots of bold tastes and earthy pleasures.

Serves: 6

Preparation time: 10 minutes

Cooking time: 10 minutes

2 tablespoons olive oil

2 cloves garlic, finely chopped

2 teaspoons chopped fresh basil

Salt to taste

Freshly ground pepper to taste

3 to 4 Portobello mushrooms

4 tablespoons low-fat cream cheese or goat cheese

6 slices focaccia or other good-quality bread, split in half

1 cup washed and dried spinach or arugula leaves

6 slices tomato

---

1. Preheat the grill.

2. Mix the olive oil, garlic, 1 teaspoon of the basil, salt, and pepper together. Remove the stems from the mushrooms and brush both sides of the caps with the olive oil mixture. Set aside.

3. Mix the cheese, the remaining teaspoon of basil, salt, and pepper together. Set aside.

4. Grill the mushrooms until they are soft in the center, about 3 to 4 minutes on each side. Slice each cap on the diagonal into 1-inch strips.

(Steps 2 through 4 can be done ahead. The ingredients will keep in the refrigerator for up to 3 days.)

5. Spread 6 halves of bread with the cheese mixture, then top with the spinach or arugula, a slice of tomato, and the sliced Portobello. Place the other half of the bread on top.

PER SERVING: ABOUT 233 CALORIES, 72 CALORIES FROM FAT, 10 GRAMS PROTEIN, 34 GRAMS CARBOHYDRATES, 8 GRAMS FAT, 5 GRAMS FIBER, 389 MILLIGRAMS SODIUM

HEALTHY TIMESAVERS
Beyond Thanksgiving Sweet Potatoes

With their top nutrition profile, mellow flavor, and soothing texture, sweet potatoes are a super snack or side dish any time of the year. Sweet potatoes are a terrific source of beta-carotene, a valuable antioxidant compound, as well as potassium, fiber, and carbohydrates. Try microwaving them on high for 15 minutes (be sure to prick with a fork so they do not explode). Kids love them topped with applesauce for a wonderful lunch or afternoon snack.

RISOTTO WITH FRESH PEAS

You'll delight in this special Italian dish with its fusion of creamy rice and sweet fresh peas. It is best made with Italian Arborio rice, which has tender starch that dissolves as it cooks and clings to all the ingredients. The rice needs to absorb the chicken stock slowly, but when you are finished, the taste will be *magnifico!* Try seasonal twists on the basic recipe.

Serves: 6

Preparation time: 10 minutes

Cooking time: 40 minutes

About 4 cups Basic Chicken Stock (see page 162)

1 tablespoon olive oil

1/2 cup diced onion

1 1/2 cups Arborio rice

1/2 cup freshly grated Parmesan cheese

Salt to taste

Freshly ground black pepper to taste

1 cup freshly shelled peas

1. Heat the stock in a saucepan and keep hot over low heat.

2. Meanwhile, heat the olive oil over medium heat in a separate medium-size pot. Add the onion and cook for 2 to 3 minutes, until the onion turns translucent.

3. Add the rice to the onion mixture and stir.

4. Turn the heat to low, add about 1 cup of the hot stock to the rice mixture, and stir slowly until the stock is absorbed, about 6 minutes per cup.

5. Continue to add the stock 1 cup at a time, stirring slowly, letting the rice absorb the stock before adding more.

6. While the risotto is cooking, blanch the peas in boiling salted water for 30 seconds. Drain.

7. The risotto is cooked when it is creamy on the outside and *al dente* in the center. Stir in the Parmesan cheese and half of the peas. Season with salt and pepper to taste. If the risotto is too thick, add a little more stock until it becomes creamy.

8. Divide the risotto into serving dishes and sprinkle with the remaining peas.

Twists: Substitute for the peas:

> 1 cup sliced sautéed mushrooms
>
> 1 cup sautéed shrimp or scallops
>
> 1/2 cup thin strips cooked ham
>
> 1 cup blanched asparagus, cut in 2-inch pieces

PER SERVING: 272 CALORIES, 9 CALORIES FROM FAT, 10 GRAMS PROTEIN, 42 GRAMS CARBOHYDRATES, 1 GRAM TOTAL FAT, 1 GRAM FIBER, 299 MILLIGRAMS SODIUM

CHAPTER 7

MAIN ATTRACTIONS:
ALL-TIME GOOD DINNERS

The best dinnertime experience is sharing delicious food with those you care most about. Getting there may require a little planning but need not take hours and hours of complicated cooking. Discover the pleasure of putting together a wonderful meal of healthy components, diverse colors, varied textures, and fresh flavors.

Our time is precious, and it can be difficult to balance the needs of family, home, and work. But with whatever time you do have, you can create meals that everyone enjoys. Try one-dish meals or serve simply prepared chicken, meat, or fish alongside vegetables or grains. On these pages you will find ideas for everyday meals as well as recipes for dishes that take a bit longer to cook and are perfect for the weekend. Also included in this chapter are complete dinners with side dishes.

Now you can serve family dinners that are fast, seasonal, and delicious, and give everyone time to relax together after a long day.

Solving the Dinner Plate Puzzle

This chapter helps you figure out the puzzle of putting together a dinner plate that supports your priorities of time, taste, and good health. When my children were hungry and tired after a long day of school and sports, and I was exhausted from a grueling day at the office, it was always helpful to have an action plan for when I hit the kitchen. It is too hard to serve up a delicious dinner if you only start thinking about it at 6 P.M. Instead, begin tying your shopping and cooking together by following these strategies and techniques:

1. **Plan ahead.** Map out the next night's dinner the night before and check to see if you have everything you need.

2. **Visualize the plate.** Take a fresh look at the different components and give vegetables and grains a starring role. By contrasting color, texture, and taste, you will add nutrition and interest.

3. **Expand your menu ideas.** Move beyond the "same old thing" syndrome by adding a twist when you feel comfortable with the recipe.

4. **Let the season be your guide.** Use local seasonal produce to spark your creativity. The fresh, ripe flavors are sure to be a big hit.

5. **Take advantage of available resources.** A well-stocked pantry and refrigerator provide the ingredients you need for cooking great dinners. And when time gets extremely tight, make the most of convenience foods found in your local supermarket. On page 225 you will find all kinds of ideas for using what you have on hand.

RIGATONI WITH TURKEY, OLIVES, AND TOMATO SAUCE

The Mediterranean influence weaves through this deliciously simple dinner. The final step of short baking intensifies the wonderful flavor of the olives, tomatoes, and herbs. Make a double batch and freeze it for a future meal.

Serves: 6

Preparation time: 20 minutes

Cooking time: 30 minutes

12 ounces rigatoni

2 tablespoons olive oil

1/2 cup diced onion

2 cloves garlic, crushed

1 pound lean ground turkey or beef

Salt to taste

Freshly ground black pepper to taste

3 cups tomato sauce

1 cup halved and pitted black olives

1/2 cup chopped fresh basil

1 cup shredded low-fat mozzarella cheese

1/2 cup freshly grated Parmesan cheese

1. Preheat the oven to 350° F.

2. Bring 1 gallon of salted water to boil. Add the rigatoni and cook until *al dente,* about 8 to 10 minutes. Drain and rinse with cold water.

3. Meanwhile, heat the olive oil in a large skillet over medium heat. Add the onion and cook until soft and translucent, about 4 to 5 minutes. Add the garlic and cook 30 seconds more. Add the ground meat, season with salt and pepper, and brown. Drain off the excess fat.

4. Add the tomato sauce and olives, and simmer for 5 minutes. Adjust the seasoning.

5. In a casserole dish, toss the rigatoni, meat sauce, and basil together. Sprinkle with the cheeses. (This can be made ahead and stored unbaked in the refrigerator up to 2 days, or it can be frozen.)

6. Bake until the cheese is bubbly and brown and the dish is thoroughly heated, about 15 to 20 minutes; bake longer if the dish has been refrigerated.

PER SERVING: 411 CALORIES, 135 CALORIES FROM FAT, 25 GRAMS PROTEIN, 44 GRAMS CARBOHYDRATES, 15 GRAMS TOTAL FAT, 3 GRAMS FIBER, 1142 MILLIGRAMS SODIUM

TODD ENGLISH'S GRILLED CHICKEN MARINATED IN YOGURT AND HERBS WITH A TOMATO CHUTNEY

"The table is a place that is sacred," believes Todd English, owner and chef of Olives restaurant in Charlestown, Massachusetts. "It is a great place to gather." The dinnertime moments he shares with his three children and wife are precious to him. They have fun exploring different foods, especially vegetables. A leader in regional New England cooking, Todd values the close natural bond between farmers and chefs. When you support local farmers by buying their products, he says, "you can taste the difference."

In this exciting yet mellow dish, the low-fat yogurt tenderizes the chicken while adding calcium and vitamins, and the mint and curry give a tremendous flavor accent. Any leftover chutney can jazz up other simple grilled or roasted dishes.

Serves: 4

Preparation time: 20 minutes

Cooking time: 40 minutes

For the marinated chicken:

1 cup plain low-fat yogurt

Zest of 1 lemon

1 tablespoon curry powder

2 cloves garlic, minced

2 tablespoons honey

1/4 cup minced red onion

2 tablespoons chopped fresh mint

4 boneless, skinless chicken breasts

1. Mix all the ingredients except the chicken in a large bowl.

2. Add the chicken to the mixture and coat evenly.

3. Cover the bowl and refrigerate overnight.

For the chutney:

2 teaspoons olive oil

1 cup diced white onion

4 large tomatoes, diced

3/4 cup dried currants

1/4 cup cider vinegar

1 cup orange juice

1/2 cup tomato juice

1 jalapeño pepper, seeded and diced

1 teaspoon kosher salt

1. Heat the oil in a small saucepan over medium heat. Add the onions and tomatoes, and cook until soft, about 3 to 4 minutes.

2. Add the currants, vinegar, and juices, and cook until reduced by one-third, about 12 to 15 minutes.

3. Add the jalapeño and cook for 5 minutes.

4. Add the salt and set aside.

(The chutney can be made ahead and refrigerated for several days. Bring to room temperature before serving.)

To cook the chicken:

4 marinated chicken breasts

1 teaspoon kosher salt

1/2 teaspoon black pepper

2 tablespoons chopped fresh mint

2 tablespoons chopped fresh cilantro

2 tablespoons chopped scallions

1. Preheat the grill.

2. Remove the chicken from the marinade and discard the marinade. Sprinkle the chicken with the salt and pepper.

3. Place the chicken on the hot grill and cook until the juices run clear, 6 to 8 minutes per side.

4. Garnish the chicken with the mint, cilantro, and scallions. Serve with rice and the chutney on the side.

PER SERVING: ABOUT 720 CALORIES, 270 CALORIES FROM FAT, 59 GRAMS PROTEIN, 3 GRAMS CARBOHYDRATES, 30 GRAMS TOTAL FAT, 0 GRAMS FIBER, 1100 MILLIGRAMS SODIUM

Chicken Nuggets

Here's a chart to help you compare the nutrition in white and dark meat and skinless and skin-on pieces of chicken. For 3 ounces of roasted chicken:

	Calories	Calories from fat	Cholesterol (mg)
White meat, skinless	140	27	58
White meat, skin	167	63	72
Dark meat, skinless	178	81	80
Dark meat, skin	210	117	81

Marketwise Poultry Picks

The market for chicken overflows with health- and budget-conscious choices. This list will help you make the best poultry picks:

- Chicken and other poultry products are best when they have moist skin, a plump breast, and a fresh smell. The skin color varies from creamy white to golden yellow depending on the region and the bird's diet.

- The "sell by" date on the label helps ensure freshness. Check the label for the last day to purchase.

- Choose USDA Grade A for best flavor and tenderness. It is the most common grade.

- The package should contain little or no liquid. Too much liquid in the package means it has been frozen and then thawed, which means the poultry will be dry when cooked.

- Know your bird sizes:

    3 to 3 1/2-pound whole chicken = 4 servings

    3/4 to 1 pound bone-in chicken pieces = 1 serving

    1/2 breast or 2 drumsticks = 1 serving

- Free-range poultry are raised in an open, uncaged environment, while organic poultry is raised on chemical-free grain on land without pesticides. Free-range poultry is often more expensive but is considered more flavorful. Do your own taste test and choose your favorite.

WINTER CHICKEN STEW WITH MUSHROOMS AND PEARL ONIONS OVER SKINNY ROASTED MASHED POTATOES

For a dinner filled with cozy warmth, this chicken stew can't be beat. Cooking over a low, moist heat makes this a tender, tasty dish. Serve the chicken with mashed potatoes or over rice. It is easy to make more for a crowd.

Serves: 6

Preparation time: 30 minutes

Cooking time: 2 hours

3 pounds chicken thighs and/or legs

Salt to taste

Freshly ground black pepper to taste

About 4 tablespoons flour

2 tablespoons canola oil

1 carrot, coarsely chopped

1 onion, coarsely chopped

1 stalk celery, coarsely chopped

1 bay leaf

1 sprig fresh thyme or 1/4 teaspoon dried

1/4 cup red wine

2 quarts Basic Chicken Stock (see page 162)

1 cup quartered mushrooms, sautéed

1 cup pearl onions, peeled and blanched

1. Season the chicken with salt and pepper. Dust the chicken with flour.

2. Heat the oil in a wide, shallow pot over medium-high heat. Add the chicken and brown on all sides, about 2 minutes on each side. The oil should be hot enough to sear in the juices but not burn. Remove the chicken from the pan and drain off the excess fat.

3. Turn the heat down to medium and add the vegetables. Cook for 3 to 4 minutes, until they begin to soften. Turn up the heat and brown slightly.

4. Add the bay leaf, thyme, and red wine, and cook until the wine is almost completely evaporated.

5. Put the seared chicken back in the pot and cover with stock. Bring to a simmer and cook, uncovered, for 1 1/2 hours. Do not let it boil.

6. Strain the stew over a bowl and retain the chicken and liquid. Discard the vegetables. Return the liquid to the pot and simmer to reduce its volume by half.

7. Remove the skin from the chicken; discard the skin. Add the chicken (either on or off the bone), mushrooms, and onions to the reduced liquid.

8. Adjust the seasoning with a generous amount of salt and pepper.

(This can be made ahead and kept in the refrigerator up to 3 days or frozen.)

Per Serving: About 405 calories, 198 calories from fat, 35 grams protein, 14 grams carbohydrates, 22 grams total fat, 2 grams fiber, 382 milligrams sodium

sKINNY RoAsTED MASHED PoTATOES

The cartoon character Skinny Minnie never had it so good. Here is the ultimate comfort food with virtually no fat but the benefit of great taste. A hungry family will devour these potatoes in a flash.

Serves: 6

Preparation time: 10 minutes

Cooking time: 30 minutes

4 large potatoes, Idaho or russet

About 1 cup Basic Chicken Stock (see page 162)

1 bulb Roasted Garlic (see page 185)

Salt to taste

Freshly ground black pepper to taste

1. Peel the potatoes and cut them in half. Place them in a pot and cover with cold water. Bring to a boil over high heat and simmer until the potatoes are tender when pricked with a fork, about 30 minutes depending on the size of the potatoes. Drain.

2. Bring the stock to a boil.

3. Squeeze the roasted garlic bulb to release the garlic inside each clove. Mash the garlic with a fork and throw the skins away.

4. Mash the potatoes with a potato masher or fork, or use a food mill. Add the roasted garlic. Slowly add the stock until the desired consistency is reached.

5. Adjust the salt and pepper to taste.

Per Serving: About 105 calories, 18 calories from fat, 3 grams protein, 20 grams carbohydrates, 2 grams total fat, 2 grams fiber, 118 milligrams sodium

CHARLIE TROTTER'S SMOKED TURKEY AND MIDDLE EASTERN COUSCOUS SALAD WITH ARTICHOKES AND LEMON-CHIVE VINAIGRETTE

Charlie Trotter is both a sensualist and a pragmatist. Food, he says, "is the only sensual pleasure that we all enjoy every single day." But he believes as well in simplifying preparations to make daily cooking easier. Charlie also limits fat in the dishes he serves at his restaurant, Charlie Trotter's, in Chicago because he believes that too much fat blocks taste.

This refreshing salad combines varied textures, colors, and flavors with a lemon-chive vinaigrette to make a fantastic main or side dish. What a joy!

Serves: 6 to 8

Preparation time: 30 minutes

Cooking time: 20 minutes

For the vinaigrette:

1/4 cup lemon juice

5 tablespoons olive oil

Salt to taste

Freshly ground black pepper to taste

4 tablespoons chopped chives

1. In a mixing bowl, whisk the lemon juice and olive oil together. Season with salt and pepper. (This can be done ahead and kept in the refrigerator for 1 day.)

2. Add the chives.

For the salad:

1 1/2 cups raw Middle Eastern couscous, Israeli couscous

4 tablespoons olive oil

1 red onion, thinly sliced

1 tablespoon balsamic vinegar

Freshly ground black pepper to taste

1 red pepper, sliced in thin strips

1 cup cherry tomatoes, halved

1 cup canned artichokes, drained and cut into small wedges

1 cucumber, peeled and diced

1 cup chopped scallions

1 1/2 pounds smoked turkey, sliced in thin strips

Salt to taste

1. Preheat oven to 375° F.

2. Rinse the couscous in a sieve under cold water until the water runs clear. Add the couscous to 3 cups boiling salted water. Simmer over medium heat, stirring occasionally, until *al dente*, about 12 to 15 minutes. (Check the package directions for more exact

cooking times.) Cover, remove from the heat and let stand 10 minutes. All the liquid should now be absorbed. Return the couscous to the sieve and rinse under cold water for about 3 minutes, until cool. Drain and place in a large bowl.

3. Toss the couscous with 3 tablespoons olive oil.

4. Toss the onion with the remaining tablespoon olive oil and the balsamic vinegar and season heavily with pepper. Spread the onion slices evenly on a baking sheet and roast in the oven until caramelized, about 15 to 20 minutes.

5. Toss the couscous with the onion, red pepper, cherry tomatoes, artichokes, cucumber, scallions, turkey, and lemon-chive vinaigrette. Season with salt and pepper, and chill in the refrigerator until ready to serve. If the salad is too dry, spritz it with lemon juice and olive oil.

PER SERVING: ABOUT 482 CALORIES, 189 CALORIES FROM FAT, 26 GRAMS PROTEIN, 50 GRAMS CARBOHYDRATES, 21 GRAMS TOTAL FAT, 6 GRAMS FIBER, 1422 MILLIGRAMS SODIUM

Chicken Checks

Poultry packs great nutrition but can also contain bacteria that cause foodborne illness. Check out these guidelines for handling and storage to help prevent contamination:

- Keep raw poultry refrigerated at 40° F. or below and use within two days of buying. Cooked poultry can be kept in the refrigerator up to four days.
- Store raw poultry in clean containers that do not leak. Be careful not to allow raw poultry or its juices to touch any other food.
- Thaw frozen poultry slowly in the refrigerator, under cold running water in the sink, or in the microwave. Do not leave it sitting at room temperature.
- Wash all utensils and cutting boards with hot, soapy water after preparing poultry.
- Wash your hands thoroughly with hot, soapy water after working with raw poultry.

Is It Done Yet?

When cooking, it is critical to control temperature in order to inhibit bacterial growth. According to the USDA, using a meat thermometer is the safest and most reliable way to decide when the food is "done": cooked to an internal temperature high enough to kill any harmful bacteria that might have been in the food. Most pathogenic bacteria (those than can cause disease) are destroyed when the internal temperature of the meat reaches between 140° and 165° F. Visual indicators such as color are not adequate for determining safety, especially when cooking meat and poultry. To prevent undercooking, use a food thermometer to check the temperature. After using the food thermometer, remember to wash the probe with hot, soapy water.

JOYCE GOLDSTEIN'S ORECCHIETTE WITH BROCCOLI RABE

A mother, grandmother, cooking teacher, chef, restaurateur, and cookbook author, Joyce Goldstein understands a great deal about food. "Food is comfort. It is how we take care of the ones we love," she says. Her children and grandchildren have inherited her love of food. She now shares trips to the San Francisco farmer's market with her granddaughter, Elena. Together they taste almost everything. Elena especially loves to look at pictures of the farmers' goats while she eats goat cheese.

Joyce says she has never met a kid who did not like pasta, and this dish is one that everyone will love. Refreshingly easy to make, it comes alive with the bright green broccoli rabe. It also is an excellent source of vitamin C, folic acid, and iron. The cooked white beans or chickpeas add protein.

Serves: 6

Preparation time: 10 minutes

Cooking time: 20 minutes

1 1/2 pounds broccoli rabe (about 5 cups)

1 pound orecchiette

1/4 cup olive oil

1 tablespoon finely minced anchovy fillets, or to taste

3 cloves garlic, minced

Freshly ground black pepper to taste

1/2 cup Basic Chicken Stock (see page 162)

1 cup cooked white beans or chickpeas

1/2 cup grated Pecorino cheese

1. Bring 1 gallon salted water to a boil. Wash the broccoli rabe and trim away any tough stalks. Roughly chop the greens into 2-inch lengths. Cook in the boiling water until tender, about 3 to 4 minutes. Remove with a slotted spoon and save the water for the pasta. Drain the greens well and set aside.

2. Bring the water back to a boil and cook the orecchiette until *al dente,* about 8 minutes. Drain.

3. Meanwhile, heat the olive oil in a skillet over medium heat. Add the anchovies and garlic, and cook for 1 minute. Add the broccoli rabe, orecchiette, pepper, stock, and white beans or chickpeas, and toss until thoroughly heated. Transfer to a warm bowl, sprinkle with the cheese, and serve.

Twists: Substitute 5 cups broccoli or cauliflower florets for the broccoli rabe. You can also increase the heat by substituting hot red pepper flakes for the black pepper.

PER SERVING: ABOUT 506 CALORIES, 126 CALORIES FROM FAT, 21 GRAMS PROTEIN, 76 GRAMS CARBOHYDRATES, 14 GRAMS TOTAL FAT, 9 GRAMS FIBER, 197 MILLIGRAMS SODIUM

MICHAEL ROMANO'S PENNE WITH ASPARAGUS AND RED PEPPERS

Michael Romano grew up in a large family in New York City, and he says that "nothing in the family ever happened without food." Now the renowned chef and owner of the Union Square Café in New York City shows his love of food through his support of the community. The young children at Public School 2 on the Lower East Side of Manhattan will never forget the day he came to their school to cook lunch for USDA's Team Nutrition.

This springtime pasta dish sparkles with bright green asparagus and roasted red and yellow peppers. The tiny touch of butter in the stir-fry gives a warm, nutty flavor, and finishing the penne with chicken stock adds a wonderful depth.

Serves: 4

Preparation time: 20 minutes

Cooking time: 15 minutes

1 tablespoon kosher salt

12 ounces penne (ziti and rigatoni also work well)

4 tablespoons butter

1 pound asparagus, ends snapped off and stalks cut into 2-inch pieces

2 yellow bell peppers, roasted, peeled, and diced (see page 185)

2 red bell peppers, roasted, peeled, and diced (see page 185)

1 teaspoon minced garlic

1 1/2 cups Basic Chicken Stock (see page 162)

1 1/2 tablespoons minced fresh thyme

2/3 cup grated Parmigiano-Reggiano cheese

Freshly ground black pepper to taste

1. Bring 1 gallon water and 1 tablespoon kosher salt to a boil. Add the pasta and cook until just before it becomes *al dente.* Drain.

2. Meanwhile, melt 2 tablespoons butter in a 10-inch skillet over medium heat. Add the asparagus and cook, stirring occasionally, until tender and lightly browned, about 5 to 7 minutes. Add the peppers and garlic, and cook 1 minute more. Add the stock, bring to a boil, and lower the heat to medium.

3. Add the penne and thyme. Stir to combine the ingredients and simmer until the pasta is *al dente,* about 5 to 7 minutes. Stir in half of the cheese and the remaining 2 tablespoons butter. Adjust the salt and pepper to taste. Transfer to a warm bowl, sprinkle with the remaining cheese, and serve.

PER SERVING: ABOUT 548 CALORIES, 171 CALORIES FROM FAT, 22 GRAMS PROTEIN, 75 GRAMS CARBOHYDRATES, 19 GRAMS TOTAL FAT, 8 GRAMS FIBER, 1845 MILLIGRAMS SODIUM

Safe Ways with Meat

Follow these safety guidelines for meat to help prevent foodborne illnesses from salmonella, *E. coli,* and other bacteria:

- Select meat just before checking out of the supermarket and go directly home.

- If not using immediately, freeze the meat in its original wrapper for use within two weeks. For longer storage, use freezer paper or a plastic freezer bag. Ground beef will keep in the freezer for three or four months; other meats for six to twelve months.

- Refrigerate meat leftovers promptly after serving. Leftover cooked meat can be frozen for two or three months.

- The day before the meat is needed, defrost it on a tray in the refrigerator. Never defrost at room temperature.

- Keep raw meat and meat juices away from other foods during preparation.

GRILLED ROSEMARY FLANK STEAK WITH ROASTED PARSLIED NEW POTATOES

Simply delicious when grilled outdoors on a lovely summer evening, this lean beef cut has very little fat and is best when sliced thinly on the bias. The twist that substitutes soy sauce for balsamic vinegar is a favorite of my children. The touch of rosemary adds spark and goes well with the roasted parslied potatoes and Magical Greens (see page 50).

For the Flank Steak:

Serves: 6

Preparation time: 5 minutes

Marinating time: 1 hour or overnight

Cooking time: 10 minutes

1/4 cup olive oil

1 tablespoon balsamic vinegar

2 cloves garlic, crushed

1 sprig rosemary, chopped

Salt to taste

Freshly ground black pepper to taste

2 pounds flank steak

continued >

1. Mix the oil, vinegar, garlic, rosemary, salt, and pepper, and brush on the flank steak. Refrigerate for 1 hour or overnight.

2. Preheat the grill.

3. Grill the flank steak for 4 to 8 minutes on each side, depending on the desired doneness. Let the steak rest on a carving plate for 1 or 2 minutes.

4. Slice the steak on the bias.

Twist: *Asian*: Substitute 1 tablespoon soy sauce for the balsamic vinegar. Also add 1 teaspoon minced ginger and 1 teaspoon Dijon mustard to the marinade.

PER SERVING: 192 CALORIES, 99 CALORIES FROM FAT, 22 GRAMS PROTEIN, 0 GRAMS CARBOHYDRATES, 11 GRAMS TOTAL FAT, 0 GRAMS FIBER, 360 MILLIGRAMS SODIUM

For the Roasted Parslied New Potatoes:

Serves: 6

Preparation time: 5 minutes

Cooking time: 20 minutes

12 red bliss new potatoes

1 tablespoon olive oil

Salt to taste

Freshly ground black pepper to taste

2 tablespoons chopped parsley

1. Preheat the oven to 350° F.

2. Wash the potatoes and cut them in half. Toss with the olive oil and a generous amount of salt and pepper.

3. Roast in the oven until tender, about 20 minutes.

4. Sprinkle with parsley and serve.

PER SERVING: ABOUT 79 CALORIES, 18 CALORIES FROM FAT, 2 GRAMS PROTEIN, 14 GRAMS CARBOHYDRATES, 2 GRAMS TOTAL FAT, 1 GRAM FIBER, 102 MILLIGRAMS SODIUM

RICK BAYLESS'S TOMATO, RICE, AND BEEF CASSEROLE

When he visits classrooms and teaches children about food, Rick Bayless, the chef and owner of Chicago's Frontera Grill, inevitably talks about the cultural roots of a particular dish and fills the lesson with geography and history. Through these lessons, Rick says, "we are building a community around our foods."

Inspired by the regional cooking of Mexico, this casserole, with roasted poblano chilies and melted cheese, is filled with warmth and comfort. Rick says that "when caring and love are there, you can taste them." Rick uses the chilies for their remarkable flavor, not for spiciness.

continued >

Serves: 6

Preparation time: 20 minutes

Cooking time: 20 minutes

For the roasted poblano chilies and tomatoes:

6 poblano or Anaheim chilies

6 ripe Roma tomatoes

1 tablespoon olive oil

1 large white onion, sliced 1/4-inch thick

3 cloves garlic, finely chopped

1/2 teaspoon dried oregano

About 1 teaspoon salt

1. Preheat the broiler.

2. Roast the chilies and tomatoes under a very hot broiler until blackened on all sides, about 10 minutes for the chilies and 12 minutes for the tomatoes.

3. Cover the chilies with a clean kitchen towel and let stand for 5 minutes. Peel the chilies and remove the stems and seedpods. Rinse the chilies briefly to remove specks of skin and seeds. Slice the chilies into 1/4-inch strips.

4. Cool, peel, and roughly chop the tomatoes. Set aside the tomatoes and their juices.

5. Heat the oil in a medium-size skillet over medium heat. Add the onion and cook until golden brown, about 5 minutes. Add the garlic and oregano, and cook 1 minute longer. Add the chilies, tomatoes, and their juices. Stir until the juices have reduced, about 3 to 4 minutes. Season with salt. Remove from the heat and set aside.

(This can be made ahead and refrigerated up to 3 days.)

For the rice casserole:

1 teaspoon salt

1 cup medium or long-grain rice

1 cup grated Monterey jack or Mexican
   Chihuahua cheese

1 1/2 cups cooked and shredded boneless beef
   (grilled skirt or flank steak works well)

1. In a large pot, bring 3 quarts water and the salt to a boil. Add the rice and simmer, uncovered, for about 15 minutes, until all the grains are tender but not mushy or splayed. Strain the rice and spread on a tray to cool.

2. Preheat the oven to 350° F.

3. Spread half the rice over the bottom of a lightly greased 8 x 8-inch baking dish. Spoon on half the chili-tomato mixture and sprinkle with half the cheese. Spread all the beef over the cheese. Cover with the remaining rice, chili-tomato mixture, and cheese. (This can be assembled a day in advance and refrigerated.)

4. Bake until bubbly and brown, about 20 to 30 minutes, but longer if it was refrigerated. Let stand 10 minutes, then serve.

Twists: Substitute 1 1/2 cups cooked and shredded chicken or pork for the beef.

Per Serving: About 493 calories, 144 calories from fat, 47 grams protein, 40 grams carbohydrates, 16 grams total fat, 3 grams fiber, 977 milligrams sodium

Making the Grade

The quality grading system for beef, developed by the USDA, is the key indicator of the meat's tenderness, juiciness, and flavor. In the early 1980s, consumers were concerned that the grading system favored the fattier beef. The organization I headed then, Public Voice, petitioned the government to change the grades. The government responded and today there is a great deal more lean beef available in the marketplace; in fact, the beef you buy today is 27 percent leaner than that of twenty years ago.

The grading is performed by the USDA and is based on the amount of marbling (flecks of fat within the lean) and the age of the animal. After grading, the product is marked with a shield-shaped stamp bearing one of the following terms.

U.S. Select.   Has the least amount of marbling and the least amount of fat. Leaner beef, but not as juicy as other grades, so use a slow, moist cooking such as braising or stewing. It is the most economical in price.

U.S. Choice.   The most widely available grade. Use for everyday broiling, roasting, and other cooking methods. This grade has fat content and tenderness between that of Select and Prime. It is moderate in price.

U.S. Prime.   Contains the most marbling and the most fat. This grade is sold mostly to restaurants and specialty meat markets because of its tenderness. It is the most expensive in price.

Family Affair

Helping hands make preparing dinner more fun. Younger helpers can tear lettuce and scoop up ingredients to put in salad bowls or serving dishes; they can also help stir. Older family members can cut up the raw ingredients and handle the hot ones. Help in chopping is always welcome when stir-fries, salsas, and stews are on the menu, as long as parents keep a close and cautious eye on these activities.

When children participate in dinner preparation, they learn lessons they will carry with them for a lifetime. It may be messy and take longer when little hands help, but the strong sense of accomplishment and closeness that children feel makes it all worth it. To make things easier, read the recipe first and assemble the ingredients before you start cooking. When the whole family is involved, everyone's eating pleasure grows.

BARBECUED PORK CHOPS WITH PECANS, SWEET POTATO PUREE, AND SAUTÉED GREEN BEANS, ONIONS, AND MUSHROOMS

The lively taste of barbecued pork works great with the Cajun seasoning and lime juice that take the flavor of the sweet potatoes to a new level. The pecans add interesting texture, and the meal is made complete when accompanied with sautéed green beans, mushrooms, and onions—a quick-cooking, tricolored dish that is full of valuable nutrients and flavors.

For the Sweet Potato Puree:

Serves: 6

Preparation time: 10 minutes

Cooking time: 45 minutes

**2 pounds sweet potatoes, peeled and cut into
2-inch pieces**

Juice of 2 limes

1/2 cup milk

Cajun seasoning to taste

Salt to taste

1. Place the sweet potatoes in a pot and cover with cold water. Bring to a boil over high heat. Lower the heat and simmer about 20 to 30 minutes, until the potatoes are done. Check for doneness by piercing with a fork; there should be no resistance. Drain well.

2. Mash the sweet potatoes with a potato masher or fork, or use a food mill.

3. Add the lime juice and stir well. Add the milk and stir.

4. Season with Cajun seasoning and salt to taste. (This can be made ahead and refrigerated up to 3 days.)

PER SERVING: ABOUT 176 CALORIES, 9 CALORIES FROM FAT, 3 GRAMS PROTEIN, 39 GRAMS CARBOHYDRATES, 1 GRAM TOTAL FAT, 4 GRAMS FIBER, 147 MILLIGRAMS SODIUM

For the Sautéed Green Beans, Pearl Onions, and Mushrooms:

Serves: 6

Preparation time: 10 minutes

Cooking time: 5 minutes

2 cups green beans

1/2 cup pearl onions, peeled

Splash of peanut oil

continued >

Salt to taste

Freshly ground black pepper to taste

1 cup quartered mushrooms

1. Bring 1 gallon of salted water to a boil. Cook the green beans and pearl onions separately in the boiling water until just tender, about 4 minutes for the beans and 8 minutes for the onions.

2. Cut the onions in half.

(The green beans and pearl onions can be cooked ahead and kept in the refrigerator up to 1 day.)

3. Heat the oil over high heat. Add the onions, salt, and pepper, and cook for 1 minute. Add the mushrooms and cook for 2 more minutes. Add the green beans and cook for 2 more minutes.

4. Adjust the salt and pepper to taste. Serve immediately.

PER SERVING: ABOUT 48 CALORIES, 12 CALORIES FROM FAT, 2 GRAMS PROTEIN, 8 GRAMS CARBOHYDRATES, 1 GRAM TOTAL FAT, 3 GRAMS FIBER, 202 MILLIGRAMS SODIUM

For the pork chops:

Serves: 6

Preparation time: 10 minutes

Cooking time: about 15 minutes

6 1/2-inch-thick center-cut pork loin chops

1/2 teaspoon Cajun seasoning

About 1/2 cup barbecue sauce

1/2 cup finely chopped toasted pecans

1. Preheat the oven to 350° F.

2. Spread the pecans on a baking sheet and toast in the oven until lightly browned, about 5 minutes.

3. Preheat the grill or broiler.

3. Rub the pork chops with Cajun seasoning and brush with barbecue sauce.

4. Grill or broil for 5 to 8 minutes on each side, depending on thickness. Baste with extra barbecue sauce as needed.

PER SERVING: ABOUT 340 CALORIES, 180 CALORIES FROM FAT, 36 GRAMS PROTEIN, 4 GRAMS CARBOHYDRATES, 20 GRAMS TOTAL FAT, 1 GRAM FIBER, 280 MILLIGRAMS SODIUM

Putting It Together: Sprinkle each pork chop with pecans and serve with the sweet potato puree and sautéed green beans, mushrooms, and onions.

NUTRITION POWER POINTS
The Slim Story of Pork

Pork producers have worked modern magic in the last twenty years by making a leaner meat. In fact, pork today has 31 percent less fat and 14 percent fewer calories than it did in the 1970s. The leanest pork choice is the pork tenderloin. With only 4 grams of fat per serving, it is as lean as a skinless chicken breast. Pork is also a good source of iron, phosphorous, thiamin, riboflavin, and niacin. All this means that you get health benefits along with good taste.

MARY SUE MILLIKEN AND SUSAN FENIGER'S PORK CHILI VERDE WITH POSOLE AND RED RICE

Mary Sue Milliken and Susan Feniger make cooking an adventure at Santa Monica's Border Grill Ciudad Restaurant and on cable television where they are known as "The Too Hot Tamales." They buy organic vegetables because it makes them feel closer to the land and the taste is noticeably better, especially tomatoes. Mary Sue and Susan suggest looking for foods that are grown locally and building meals around them. They even brought their ideas to the Los Angeles school lunch program and helped change the menus to make them healthier.

Cooking soups and stews is a favorite weekend activity for both women. This stew, with its Mexican roots, is vibrant and bold. The rich, slow-cooked pork is a great counter to the tanginess of tomatillos and the heat of the chilies—all perfect for a family gathering or a potluck supper with friends.

For the Pork Chile Verde with Posole:

Serves: 8

Preparation time: 20 minutes

Cooking time: 1 1/2 hours

1 pound tomatillos, husked and washed,
    or green tomatoes

2 pounds pork stew meat, cut in 1 1/2–inch
    cubes (pork shoulder works well)

Salt to taste

Freshly ground black pepper to taste

Flour for dredging

2 tablespoons canola oil

1 yellow onion, chopped

2 Anaheim or poblano chilies, cut into 1-inch cubes

2 green peppers, cut into 1-inch cubes

2 to 3 jalapeño peppers, seeds removed and diced

3 cloves garlic, peeled and minced

1 1/2 cups canned hominy (posole), drained

1/2 cup chopped cilantro leaves

1 tablespoon dried oregano

2 teaspoons ground cumin

3 cups Basic Chicken Stock (see page 162) or water

1. Preheat the broiler.

2. Roast the tomatillos on a baking sheet about 4 inches away from the broiler until charred on all sides, about 5 to 8 minutes. Let cool. Chop roughly and reserve with all the juices.

continued ›

3. Season the pork with 1 teaspoon salt and 1/2 teaspoon pepper. Flour it lightly. Heat the oil in a skillet over medium-high heat. Add the pork and brown on all sides. Remove the pork from the skillet and place in a soup pot. Drain off the excess fat in the skillet.

4. Using the skillet, turn the heat to medium and add the onion. Cook until soft and translucent, about 5 minutes. Add the chilies, green peppers, and jalapeños, and cook 3 to 4 minutes more. Add the garlic and cook 1 minute more.

5. Add the vegetables to the soup pot along with the roasted tomatillos and their juices, hominy, cilantro, oregano, and cumin. Cover with the stock, bring to a boil, and lower to a simmer. Cook, loosely covered, until the pork is very tender, about 1 1/2 hours.

6. Adjust the seasoning with salt and pepper to taste.

PER SERVING: ABOUT 381 CALORIES, 153 CALORIES FROM FAT, 27 GRAMS PROTEIN, 29 GRAMS CARBOHYDRATES, 17 GRAMS TOTAL FAT, 6 GRAMS FIBER, 832 MILLIGRAMS SODIUM

For the Red Rice:

Serves: 8

Preparation time: 15 minutes

Cooking time: 30 to 40 minutes

1/3 cup canola oil

3 cups long-grain rice

1 medium onion, chopped

5 serrano chilies, steamed and seeded

2 cloves garlic, minced

3/4 cup Basic Chicken Stock (see page 162)

3 cups Fiesta Salsa (see page 113), pureed and strained

1. Preheat the oven to 350° F.

2. Heat the oil in a saucepan over medium-low heat. Add the rice and stir occasionally until golden and crackling, about 5 minutes.

3. Add the onion and chilies, and cook until the onion just softens. Add the garlic and cook 1 minute more. Add the stock and salsa, and mix well to combine.

4. Transfer to a 4-quart baking dish, cover with foil, and bake until the liquid is absorbed and the rice is tender, about 30 to 40 minutes.

5. Stir and serve hot.

PER SERVING: ABOUT 191 CALORIES, 90 CALORIES FROM FAT, 3 GRAMS PROTEIN, 24 GRAMS CARBOHYDRATES, 10 GRAMS TOTAL FAT, 1 GRAM FIBER, 206 MILLIGRAMS SODIUM

NUTRITION POWER POINTS
Lean on the Lean

Look for lean cuts of beef, pork, and lamb when you go to the market. Meat is a great source of protein, iron, and zinc, but there is a natural difference in the fat content of the different cuts. Look for the loin, tenderloin, round, and flank, which are leaner than the shoulder, rib, and sirloin. When buying ground beef, choose the leanest, usually labeled "extra lean." It is no more than 5 percent fat. If you serve small portions of meat with grains, vegetables, and legumes, you cut the fat even more.

MARK MILLER'S BRAISED LAMB WITH SCARLET RUNNER BEANS AND RICOTTA

Mark Miller, the owner and chef of numerous restaurants, including Coyote Café in Santa Fe, New Mexico, has explored the food traditions of many cultures. He gets excited when he talks about new flavors and always shares his enthusiasm. "Trust yourself and your tastes," he says. "There is pleasure in knowing for yourself that a certain taste is different."

In this dish the tomatoes, carrots, and mushrooms blend together with the lamb, creating a rich contrast to the ricotta cheese and herb mixture. The final touch of the scarlet runner beans adds a wonderful depth.

Serves: 4

Preparation time: 20 minutes

Cooking time: 1 hour 50 minutes

4 fresh lamb shanks, about 8 to

10 ounces each

Salt to taste

Freshly ground pepper to taste

3 tablespoons olive oil

20 baby carrots

1 1/2 onions, peeled and diced

12 whole shallots, peeled

1 ounce dried mushrooms, any variety

8 cloves garlic

1 1/2 cups red wine

1/2 cup tomato puree

8 cups chicken stock

2 bay leaves

2 sprigs fresh thyme

1 cup ricotta cheese

1/4 cup chopped fresh basil

1/8 cup chopped fresh mint

1 cup cooked scarlet runner beans or fava beans

---

1. Preheat the oven to 350° F.

2. Season the lamb shanks with 1/2 teaspoon salt and 1/2 teaspoon pepper. Heat the olive oil over medium heat in a braising pan or stew pot. Add the shanks and brown well on all sides.

3. Remove the shanks from the pan and sauté the carrots, onions, shallots, and mushrooms, stirring occasionally until lightly browned, about 6 to 8 minutes. Add the garlic and cook about 1 to 2 minutes more.

continued >

4. Add the red wine and tomato puree, and simmer until the volume has reduced by half, about 6 to 8 minutes.

5. Add the stock, browned shanks, bay leaves, and thyme, and bring to a simmer. Cover and cook in the oven until the meat is tender, about 1 1/2 hours.

6. Meanwhile, combine the ricotta cheese with the basil and mint. Set aside.

7. Strain and reserve the stock and keep the shanks warm on the side. Return the strained stock to the stove and simmer until the volume has reduced by half, about 15 minutes. Adjust the salt and pepper to suit your taste. (This can be done in advance and kept in the refrigerator up to 3 days.)

8. Heat the scarlet runner beans in the sauce.

9. Place 1 shank in the center of each of 4 large warm bowls. Pour the sauce and beans over and around the shanks. Spoon the ricotta mixture on top of the beans.

PER SERVING: ABOUT 443 CALORIES, 171 CALORIES FROM FAT, 36 GRAMS PROTEIN, 25 GRAMS CARBOHYDRATES, 19 GRAMS TOTAL FAT, 4 GRAMS FIBER, 388 MILLIGRAMS SODIUM

ToP TEN FaVORiTE FISH

There are more than twenty thousand species of fish swimming in waters around the world. It may seem as if there are that many in the supermarket because there is an ever-increasing selection available with a wide variety of flavors and textures. Read this chart to learn about the different varieties and easy substitutions you can make.

Fish is a lean protein and a great source of B vitamins, phosphorous, iron, and zinc. Research shows that the omega-3 fatty acids found in oily fish help to prevent heart attacks and strokes by reducing the tendency of blood to form clots. The fattier fish are the richest in omega-3 fatty acids. The amount of fat found in fish varies according to season, age, food supply, and the environment. The information on fat obtained from the USDA, presented below, is only a rough guide.

The total fat values are based on the following, as cited by the USDA:

LOW FAT = 1 TO 20 GRAMS PER SERVING

MODERATE FAT = 21 TO 36 GRAMS PER SERVING

HIGH FAT = OVER 38 GRAMS PER SERVING.

Fish	Description	Fat	Substitutions	Best Uses
Bass	Firm, flavorful flesh. Many species.	Medium	Grouper, snapper, ocean perch	Bake, grill, fry, and poach
Catfish (often farm-raised)	Firm flesh with a mild flavor	Medium	Trout	Bake, broil, grill, and poach. Frying is a favorite southern method.
Cod	A popular, mild-flavored fish with lean, firm, white meat	Low	Scrod, flounder, haddock	Broil, grill, poach, and pan fry
Flounder	Delicate mild-tasting flesh that flakes readily	Low	Other flatfish such as sole and turbot	Pan fry and broil

ToP TEN FaVORiTE FISH CoNTInUED

Fish	Description	Fat	Substitutions	Best Uses
Grouper	Firm flesh with a mild taste	Low	Red snapper, halibut, black sea bass	Grill, broil, bake, pan fry, and poach
Halibut	Firm texture with a mild flavor	Low	Grouper, cod, turbot, Chilean sea bass	Grill, broil, and poach
Red Snapper	Red-colored skin, firm texture, and mild taste	Low	Cod, grouper, halibut, other snapper, orange roughy	Broil, grill, and bake
Salmon	Light orange flesh and silver skin. Firm texture and distinctive flavor	High	Trout, whitefish, char	Grill, broil, bake, sauté, and poach.
Sole	A flatfish with a firm texture and mild flavor	Low	Flounders	Sauté, bake, and poach
Tuna	Firm flesh ranging from beige to dark red. Tasty.	Medium	Shark	Grill, broil, and poach

ALLEN SUSSER'S PAN-ROASTED RED SNAPPER WITH ORANGE AND MANGO SALSA

The connection between family and food is a very strong one for Allen Susser, chef and owner of Chef Allen's restaurant in Miami, Florida. He remembers from his childhood in Brooklyn, New York, that "food and love were always there." He continues this commitment to his family today: He tries to leave the restaurant every day at 4:30 to help his young daughter with her homework, then has dinner with his wife and two daughters before going back to the restaurant. Allen believes it is at the table that "we pass on the values that are most important."

Florida mangoes are ripe from June through August and add a marvelous color, texture, and flavor to fish dishes. In this dish the tropical warmth and lushness of mangoes and oranges complement the delicate flavor of the pan-roasted red snapper. Served with rice, this family-friendly meal is also big on nutrition.

Serves: 4

Preparation time: 15 minutes

Cooking time: 10 minutes

For the salsa:

2 large sweet oranges, peeled, segmented, and diced

1 large mango, peeled, pitted, and diced

1/2 cup diced red onion

1 jalapeño pepper, seeded and diced

2 tablespoons chopped fresh cilantro

1/2 tablespoon olive oil

1 tablespoon freshly squeezed lime juice

1 teaspoon kosher salt

1/4 teaspoon freshly ground black pepper

In a stainless-steel bowl, combine all the ingredients and mix well. Set aside.

For the fish:

Four 6-ounce red snapper fillets

1 teaspoon kosher salt

1/4 teaspoon freshly ground black pepper

1 1/2 tablespoons olive oil

1 clove garlic, minced

1 cup fresh orange juice

1 tablespoon chopped fresh cilantro

1. Season the snapper fillets with salt and pepper, then drizzle with olive oil.

2. Place a sauté pan large enough to accommodate all the fillets over medium-high heat. Add the snapper fillets

continued >

and lower the heat to medium. Cook until well browned on one side, about 3 minutes. Turn the fillets over and cook 1 more minute.

3. Add the garlic and orange juice to the pan. Bring to a low simmer, then remove the fish and place on a warm platter. Continue to simmer the juice for 3 to 4 minutes to reduce. Add the cilantro.

4. Place each fillet in the center of a warm plate. Pour the orange-flavored cooking juice over the fish and serve the salsa on the side.

PER SERVING: ABOUT 217 CALORIES, 72 CALORIES FROM FAT, 32 GRAMS PROTEIN, 4 GRAMS CARBOHYDRATES, 8 GRAMS TOTAL FAT, 1 GRAM FIBER, 810 MILLIGRAMS SODIUM

FOR SAFEKEEPING
Safe Sea Catches

Make the most of today's market of nutritious seafood choices by being alert to possible risks and shopping wisely for good fresh fish. Potential hazards from contaminated fish are serious because seafood can carry bacteria, viruses, toxins, and parasites that are harmful to human health. Careful shopping can make a big difference in the quality and safety of the fish you buy.

"Seafood's shelf life is like nothing else," says chef Allen Susser. "The most important thing is to know your purveyor—really get to know the person behind the counter. He knows where it starts."

For the best sea catches, follow these tips:

- Check out the store or counter: It should be bright and clean, and fish should be displayed on ice or stored in a refrigerated case.
- Check out the fish: It should have a fresh, clean smell, not a strong fishy smell. It should have slick skin, flexible fins, and reddish-colored gills with no brownish tones. The eyes should be very clear and bulging.
- Ask where the fish comes from and when it came into the store. Avoid fish that is more than three days old.
- Shellfish, such as lobster and crab, should have signs of movement when touched.

SAUTÉED SEA BASS WITH MUSHROOM RAGOUT

This dish is always a showstopper. Surprisingly easy to prepare, it features bold colors and a medley of tastes. Serve it with polenta for a wonderfully earthy flavor.

Serves: 4

Preparation time: 15 minutes

Cooking time: 15 to 20 minutes

For the Mushroom Ragout:

1 tablespoon olive oil

1 tablespoon chopped shallots

1 cup sliced mushrooms

4 plum tomatoes, quartered and skinned, or 1 cup
    canned whole tomatoes

1 sprig fresh tarragon or 1/4 teaspoon dried

Salt to taste

Freshly ground black pepper to taste

1. Heat the oil in a skillet over medium heat. Add the shallots and cook until they begin to soften, about 2 minutes.

2. Turn the heat to medium-high, add the mushrooms, and sauté 2 minutes more.

3. Add the tomatoes, tarragon, salt, and pepper. Heat thoroughly. If using canned tomatoes, simmer for 30 minutes to reduce the acidic taste.

4. Adjust the salt and pepper to taste.

(This can be made ahead and kept in the refrigerator for up to 2 days.)

For the Polenta: see page 75.

For the Sautéed Sea Bass:

4 sea bass fillets, 4 to 5 ounces each (black and
    striped bass work well)

Salt to taste

Freshly ground pepper to taste

1 tablespoon canola oil

1. Generously season the fillets with salt and pepper.

2. Heat the oil over medium-high heat in a pan large enough to accommodate all the fillets.

3. Sear the fillets for 3 to 4 minutes on each side, turning only once. (Thin fillets will take less time, and thicker fillets will take more.)

4. Place a spoonful of polenta (see page 75) in the center of 4 warm plates. Place the sea bass on top of the polenta and spoon the mushroom ragout over and around the fish.

PER SERVING: 190 CALORIES, 81 CALORIES FROM FAT, 22 GRAMS PROTEIN, 4 GRAMS CARBOHYDRATES, 9 GRAMS TOTAL FAT, 1 GRAM FIBER, 374 MILLIGRAMS SODIUM

Twists: Substitute Chilean sea bass, a thicker fish, for the sea bass and cook in a 350° F oven for 5 to 8 minutes after searing in step 3.

ERiC RiPeRT's PoAchEd HaLiBuT IN A WaRm HeRB vInaIgReTTe

The seafood dishes that Eric Ripert prepares at New York City's Le Bernardin are simply exquisite. Growing up in Andorra, on the border of France and Spain, he noticed how even everyday food was presented, and now his dishes look as spectacular as they taste. "Cooking does not have to be complicated," he says. "Just add parsley, herbs, and lemon to make dishes more appealing."

Eric has a genuine respect for where food comes from and suggests weekend family visits to the harbor so children can see the fishermen bringing in the catch. This poached halibut in warm herb vinaigrette is splendid when served with young, tender asparagus. Perfect for welcoming spring or celebrating a good friend's birthday, it is both easy to make and lovely to behold. It will taste even better if you harvest the herbs from your own garden.

Serves: 4

Preparation time: 10 minutes

Cooking time: 15 minutes

1 tablespoon Dijon mustard

1 cup Basic Vinaigrette (see page 175)

1 tablespoon finely diced shallots

3 cups prepared fish stock or water

1 tablespoon white wine vinegar

Sea salt to taste

4 halibut steaks, about 8 ounces each

Freshly ground white or black pepper to taste

1/2 teaspoon chopped fresh tarragon

1 1/2 teaspoons chopped fresh Italian parsley

2 tablespoons chopped fresh chives

2 tablespoons chopped fresh chervil (optional)

1. Place the mustard in a mixing bowl and whisk in the vinaigrette and shallots. Pour into a small saucepan and set aside.

2. Bring the stock, white wine vinegar, and 1 teaspoon sea salt to a boil in a 10-inch pot. Season the halibut with salt and pepper on both sides. Add the halibut to the pot and adjust the heat so the liquid just simmers.

3. Remove the steaks from the liquid when done (5 to 7 minutes for rare steaks, longer for medium). Discard the poaching liquid.

4. Add the herbs to the saucepan containing the vinaigrette and warm over low heat.

5. Pull the skin off the halibut and place each steak in the center of a plate. Spoon the vinaigrette over and around the fish.

6. Serve with steamed asparagus (see page 35).

PER SERVING: ABOUT 605 CALORIES, 405 CALORIES FROM FAT, 48 GRAMS PROTEIN, 2 GRAMS CARBOHYDRATES, 45 GRAMS TOTAL FAT, 0 GRAMS FIBER, 1081 MILLIGRAMS SODIUM

BROILED SALMON WITH SIZZLE OF CORN AND TOMATOES

Sizzling with the summer tastes of sweet corn and ripe tomatoes, this simple seafood dish is a real winner. The blend of balsamic vinegar and jalapeño pepper adds zing to this terrific dish.

Serves: 6

Preparation time: 15 minutes

Cooking time: 15 minutes

For the Sizzle of Corn and Tomatoes:

1 tablespoon olive oil

1 teaspoon finely chopped shallots

1/2 cup chopped fresh tomatoes, or canned, drained

1 1/2 cups fresh corn kernels removed from the cob

1 teaspoon jalapeño pepper, seeds removed and
   finely chopped

Pinch of cumin

1/2 teaspoon sugar

2 tablespoons balsamic vinegar

Salt to taste

Freshly ground black pepper to taste

1. Heat the oil in a skillet over medium heat. Cook the shallots for 2 to 3 minutes, until soft but not dark in color.

2. Add the tomatoes, corn, and jalapeño pepper, and cook for 1 minute. Add the cumin and sugar, and cook 1 more minute.

3. Add the vinegar and cook until the liquid reduces slightly.

4. Add salt and pepper to taste.

Twist: Substitute quartered mushrooms for the tomatoes. Omit the cumin, sugar, and vinegar, and season simply with salt and pepper. Cook the mushrooms, corn, and jalapeño pepper for 5 minutes.

For the Broiled Salmon:

6 salmon fillets, 4 to 5 ounces each

Salt to taste

Freshly ground black pepper to taste

1 tablespoon canola oil.

1. Preheat the broiler.

2. Season the fillets generously with salt and pepper.

3. Broil the fillets for 3 to 4 minutes on each side, turning only once. (Thin fillets take less time, thicker fillets take more.)

4. Divide the Sizzle of Corn and Tomatoes among 6 warm plates. Put the fillets on top.
Serve immediately.

PER SERVING: ABOUT 344 CALORIES, 147 CALORIES FROM FAT, 45 GRAMS PROTEIN, 9 GRAMS CARBOHYDRATES, 13 GRAMS TOTAL FAT, 1 GRAM FIBER, 459 MILLIGRAMS SODIUM

Twist: Substitute halibut or cod for the salmon.

SHRIMP STIR-FRY WITH CHINESE CABBAGE, CARROTS, AND BROCCOLI

In this dish, lively ginger and other Asian flavors mix with bright contrasting colors. Shrimp is an excellent protein-rich food that is very low in calories, though quite high in cholesterol. Together with the veggies, this dish gives top-rated nutrition. Cook quickly over high heat to keep the veggies crunchy and preserve their nutrients.

Serves: 4

Preparation time: 15 minutes

Cooking time: 10 minutes

1 teaspoon chopped garlic

1 tablespoon peanut oil

1 teaspoon chopped ginger

1 cup Chinese cabbage, sliced 1/2-inch wide

1 cup very thinly sliced carrots

1 cup broccoli florets, cut in small pieces

1 pound medium-size shrimp, peeled and deveined

Freshly ground black pepper to taste

1/2 cup soy sauce

2 cups cooked rice

1. Heat a skillet or wok large enough to accommodate all the ingredients over medium-high heat.

2. Add the garlic, peanut oil, and ginger, and stir quickly for 30 seconds.

3. Raise the heat to high. Add the cabbage, then the carrots, then the broccoli, then the shrimp, stirring quickly after each addition.

4. Season with pepper.

5. Add the soy sauce and cook until the shrimp are fully cooked and opaque, about 2 minutes.

6. Place 1/2 cup rice on each of 4 warm plates. Make a well in the center of the rice and push it out to form a ring. Spoon the stir-fry into the center of the well.

PER SERVING: ABOUT 351 CALORIES, 45 CALORIES FROM FAT, 30 GRAMS PROTEIN, 45 GRAMS CARBOHYDRATES, 5 GRAMS TOTAL FAT, 2 GRAMS FIBER, 800 MILLIGRAMS SODIUM

TIPS AND TRIVIA
Parsley Pleasures

Parsley brings a lovely fresh taste to dinnertime dishes. For best results, vigorously swish the parsley in a bowl of cold water to remove dirt and sand, then dry it in a salad spinner. Remove the large woody stems and chop the rest with a sharp knife. Cover the chopped parsley with a damp paper towel and refrigerate until needed.

SUSAN SPICER'S JAMBALAYA

Down in New Orleans, cooking gets hot and the flavors spark. Susan Spicer, the chef and owner of Bayona Restaurant, leads the way by creating memorable Cajun dishes that combine different colors, textures, and flavors. A passionate gardener, she grows all kinds of herbs in her garden and adds them to her dishes.

Susan also loves to do "pot cooking," as I do, in which everything is thrown into one big pot. Not only is this jambalaya an easy one-pot dish, but it is also great party food. Turn up the spice as high as you want. It's marvelous!

Serves: 4 to 6

Preparation time: 15 minutes

Cooking time: 40 minutes

8 ounces Andouille or smoked sausage, cut into
　1/2-inch pieces

2 teaspoons peanut oil

8 ounces boneless chicken breast or thigh, cut
　into 1/2-inch strips

1 white onion, chopped

2 stalks celery, chopped

1 green or red pepper, chopped

1 tablespoon chopped garlic

2 cups raw rice

1 cup diced fresh or canned tomatoes

2 to 3 cups Basic Chicken Stock (see page 162)

1/2 teaspoon dried thyme

2 bay leaves

1/2 teaspoon salt

Tabasco or other hot sauce to taste

2 teaspoons Worcestershire sauce

8 ounces shrimp, peeled and deveined

4 scallions, chopped

1. In a deep skillet or sauté pan, brown the sausage pieces over medium-high heat for 1 to 2 minutes on each side. Remove them to a plate. Drain off the fat, add the peanut oil, and return the pan to medium-high heat. Brown the chicken pieces for 2 to 3 minutes on each side, then remove them to the same plate.

2. Return the pan to medium heat. Cook the onion, celery, and pepper for 5 minutes. Stir in the garlic, rice, and tomatoes. Add the sausage and chicken.

3. Add 2 cups of the stock, the thyme, bay leaves, salt, hot sauce, Worcestershire sauce, and shrimp. Bring to a boil, then lower to a simmer. Cover and cook for 20 minutes. Add more stock if it gets too dry.

4. Adjust the salt, hot sauce, and Worcestershire sauce to taste. Stir in half of the scallions. Remove to a warm platter and garnish with the remaining scallions.

Per Serving: About 527 calories, 153 calories from fat, 30 grams protein, 61 grams carbohydrates, 17 grams total fat, 3 grams fiber, 927 milligrams sodium

Safe Ways with Fish

Safely storing and handling seafood is a basic family health protection. Keeping it fresh means it tastes better, too. If you can, cook it on the same day that you buy it. In any event, do not store for more than a few days.

Here are simple ways to stay safe with seafood:

- Store seafood in a well-chilled refrigerator, between 32° and 40° F. All raw seafood contains some bacteria that can multiply quickly in temperatures above 40° F.

- Place the seafood in a container, or keep it in its store wrapping and then place it in a pan or bowl of ice so that it is chilled really well.

- Before cooking, rinse the fish with cold water and pat dry with a paper towel.

CoNVENiENcE oN HaND

Time management is a popular concept at the office, and it helps enormously in the kitchen as well. When the day's demands pile up and you are faced with a hungry family and little time to prepare dinner, it is great to have a pantry and refrigerator filled with ingredients that allow you to whip together a quick meal.

Use this list for fast meal ideas. It is especially convenient if you have leftovers. Add your own ideas to the list and experience the joy of being prepared.

Cooked Rice	Make quick fried rice by sautéing cooked rice with scallions, cooked and chopped carrots, cooked and diced pork or chicken, and soy sauce.
Cooked Pasta	Add chopped red peppers, zucchini, red onion, chopped basil, and vinaigrette for a tasty cold salad.
Vinaigrette	Steam spinach or arugula in vinaigrette for 1 minute and use to top broiled fish.
Chopped Herbs	Puree chives with olive oil and drizzle over broiled flounder or other fish.
Tomato Sauce	Cook with chopped eggplant, onions, and olives, and spoon over ziti.
Canned Tuna	Sauté with garlic, peas, white beans, and chopped parsley, and toss with pasta and grated Parmesan cheese.
Tortillas	Roll up with chopped lettuce, tomatoes, onions, and cooked meat, and top with low-fat sour cream and salsa.
Pasta or Rice Salad, store-bought	Add sautéed mushrooms and shrimp.

CHAPTER 8

SWEET ENDINGS: FRUIT, FROZEN DESSERTS, AND MORE

Completing a meal with sweets is a food tradition that spans cultural lines. Desserts satisfy a natural desire and can play a role in healthy living. Ripe, luscious fruits, packaged with their vitamins, minerals, and fiber, bring outstanding taste to healthy desserts such as sorbets and poached fruits. Low-fat and nonfat ingredients, especially dairy products, are now available for dessert making. In this chapter you will find recipes that run the continuum from light and fresh to those rich desserts we crave once in a while.

Let the seasons inspire the desserts you prepare. The seasonal fruit guides in chapter 2 can help you plan your creations. When there is a cold wind blowing and snow covers the ground, a warm fruit crisp can be the coziest of endings to dinner. Springtime brings a burst of red strawberries and rhubarb to brighten the table, and then the luscious berries of summer find their way into many sweet sorbets and other cool desserts. When the leaves turn golden and begin to fall and the autumn air turns chilly, it is time to enjoy the warm, rustic tastes of apples and pears.

Dessert making can be fun and a creative experience for children. Some of our favorite family times were spent in the kitchen baking cookies. As young children, Lisa and Jason would pull over a chair to stand on. With a big wooden spoon in hand, they would very seriously mix the batter. Sharing the dessert preparation is a great way for children to learn, and it builds a sense of accomplishment at the same time.

When baking, you'll find the greatest success comes if you stay close to the recipe. Unlike other kinds of cooking in which veering from the recipe often improves the results, baking depends on the particular interaction of ingredients.

DeSsErT wOrKs

It takes a fresh perspective to make desserts that please but that still keep health and nutrition in mind. With just a little bit of time and without any complicated cooking, you can finish family meals in a sensational way. These simple ideas will help you work it all out:

Start with seasonal fruits to bring sweetness to the table.

Desserts offer a pleasing way to add fruit to the menu. When used at their seasonal peak, simple fruit desserts become spectacular (see Chapter 2).

Create light and luscious desserts by using naturally low-fat foods.

Pureeing fruit and using egg whites for meringue or angel food cake are handy methods to keep desserts light and delicious. Take advantage of low-fat dairy products such as frozen yogurt for a great touch.

Serve small portions and create new pairings for real enjoyment.

Try smaller servings of cake paired with fruit sauces and sorbets for a helpful, moderate approach. Different variations of a dessert increase its appeal.

Balance richer desserts with lighter meals.

You may, for example, serve a chocolate cake after a light salad and broiled fish.

ORANGE ON ORANGE

Sometimes the simplest tastes are the most special. This citrus fruit dessert with its intense, tangy flavor makes a delicate ending to a hearty winter meal. The touch of orange peel soaked in the orange syrup and scattered on top of the oranges is also a treat for the eyes.

Serves: 4

Preparation time: 20 minutes

Cooking time: 10 minutes

4 oranges

1/2 cup sugar

1/2 cup water

1. Using a vegetable peeler, remove 4 strips of zest from 1 orange. The strips should not contain any of the white pith. Cut the strips into even thinner strips about 1/8-inch wide. Place the orange zest in a small pot of cold water, bring to a boil, and strain. Do this a total of 3 times to remove the bitterness.

2. In the same pot, bring the sugar, water, and orange zest to a boil. Cook for 5 minutes. Remove from heat and chill.

3. Using a knife with a thin blade, peel the oranges, taking care to remove all the bitter white pith, and separate them into segments (see page 134).

4. Arrange the orange segments on 4 plates. Drizzle the sugar syrup over the segments and sprinkle the candied zest on top.

PER SERVING: ABOUT 183 CALORIES, 0 CALORIES FROM FAT, 2 GRAMS PROTEIN, 47 GRAMS CARBOHYDRATES, 0 GRAMS FAT, 4 GRAMS FIBER, 0 MILLIGRAMS SODIUM.

PEARS POACHED SIMPLY IN SYRUP

Exquisite yet simple to prepare, this dish is especially good when perfectly ripe fruit is hard to find. Try serving it hot or cold with Mixed-Up Fruit Compote (see page 136), nonfat frozen yogurt, or cheese such as Jarlsberg, Fontina, or Havarti.

Serves: 6

Preparation time: 15 minutes

Cooking time: 1 hour

2 cups water

2 cups sugar

3 Bosc pears, peeled

12 peppercorns

1/2 cinnamon stick

2 whole cloves

1. Place all the ingredients in a large saucepan. Cover the pears with a piece of parchment paper or weigh them down with a plate so that they stay immersed in the liquid.

2. Bring to a simmer over medium-low heat. Cook until the pears are tender when pierced with a paring knife, about 20 to 30 minutes.

(Pears can be made ahead and stored in their syrup in the refrigerator for up to 1 week. They will have a more intense flavor.)

3. Remove the pears from the liquid and set aside. Continue to simmer the liquid for about 30 minutes, until it has a syrup-like consistency. Discard the peppercorns, cinnamon stick, and cloves. Keep warm.

4. Cut the pears in half lengthwise. Remove the seeds and core with a melon baller or small spoon. Remove any additional core using a small paring knife.

5. Slice the pears lengthwise and arrange the slices on plates. Spoon the warm syrup on and around the pears.

Twists: A combination of whole cardamom, star anise, and gingerroot to flavor the poaching liquid is a nice substitute for the peppercorns, cinnamon stick, and cloves.

Special occasion twist: Try substituting 1 cup of red or white wine for 1 cup water.

Per Serving: 286 calories, 0 calories from fat, 1 gram protein, 73 grams carbohydrates, 0 grams total fat, 3 grams fiber, 5 milligrams sodium

The Sweet Truth About Sugar

Sugar occurs naturally in foods and is also frequently added in cooking and processing. It comes in many forms, including white sugar, brown sugar, corn syrup, honey, molasses, fructose, glucose, and others. Check food labels; if these ingredients appear first or second, the food is high in sugar.

Sugar contributes to our daily calorie count without adding nutrients, so the Food Guide Pyramid recommends that we limit sugars to 6 teaspoons a day for a 1,600-calorie diet. Remember that sugar can be found in all kinds of foods including candy, soft drinks, cakes, pastries, canned fruits in heavy syrup, sherbet, and sweetened fruit-flavored yogurt. Enjoy the sweetness of sugar but use it sparingly.

AuTuMN aPPLe SoRBeT

This sorbet brings a beautiful fall meal to a light finish. Choose from the many mouth-watering apple varieties at the farmer's market or go apple picking and select your own. Then do taste tests with the children to find everyone's favorite. The subtle, light taste of apple is sublime; pears work equally well.

Serves: 6

Preparation time: 30 minutes

6 apples, such as Golden Delicious, Granny Smith, or Jonagold

2 teaspoons fresh lemon juice

1/2 cup sugar

1/2 cup water

1. Peel, quarter, and core the apples. Quickly sprinkle them with the lemon juice to prevent browning. Set on a cookie sheet and place in the freezer.

2. Bring the sugar and water to a boil in a small saucepan over high heat. Let cool.

3. When the apples have been in the freezer 20 minutes and are about half frozen, place in a blender with the water and sugar mixture. Puree and strain, pressing with a rubber spatula to release the juices.

4. Freeze the strained apple mixture in an ice cream machine according to the manufacturer's instructions.

5. Store in the freezer until ready to use.

For Safekeeping: The texture of sorbet is best if it is eaten within 24 hours. After that it becomes very hard and icy, but it can be melted down and refrozen in an ice cream machine.

Twist: Make pear sorbet by substituting 6 pears for the apples.

PER SERVING: ABOUT 146 CALORIES, 1 CALORIE FROM FAT, 0 GRAMS PROTEIN, 38 GRAMS CARBOHYDRATES, 9 GRAMS TOTAL FAT, 4 GRAMS FIBER, 0 MILLIGRAMS SODIUM

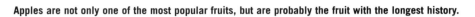
COLD PEACH SOUP WITH FROZEN YOGURT

In this refreshing fruit soup, the golden, jewel-like peaches are a strong contrast to the whiteness of the frozen yogurt. It is a light and delicious finale to any summer dinner.

Serves: 6

Preparation time: 10 minutes

8 to 10 ripe peaches, skinned and pitted

About 1/2 cup sugar

Juice of 1 lemon

Low-fat frozen yogurt (store-bought is fine)

1. Puree the peaches in a blender. Blend in the sugar and lemon until a pleasant balance of sweetness and tartness is reached.

2. Strain, pressing with a rubber spatula to release the juices. Discard the fibrous pulp.

(This can be made ahead and stored in the refrigerator for 1 or 2 days.)

3. Ladle the soup into 6 bowls. Place a scoop of frozen yogurt in each bowl.

Twist: For cold melon soup, substitute 1 large cantaloupe for the peaches.

PER SERVING: ABOUT 281 CALORIES, 18 CALORIES FROM FAT, 6 GRAMS PROTEIN, 65 GRAMS CARBOHYDRATES, 2 GRAMS TOTAL FAT, 5 GRAMS FIBER, 59 MILLIGRAMS SODIUM

EMILY LUCHETTI'S ESPRESSO GRANITA WITH CHANTILLY CREAM

Emily Luchetti, the pastry chef at Farallon restaurant in San Francisco, loves to prepare desserts that are as fresh as a strawberry patch or as light as a cloud. She bubbles with enthusiasm when she speaks about today's desserts: "It's all about moderation. Life is not all or nothing." When planning desserts, she suggests looking at the entire meal. If the main course is simple, then the dessert can be a bit more complicated. She recommends choosing desserts that can be made ahead of time to avoid last-minute preparation.

This granita, with its coffee flavor, is elegantly simple, lusciously light, and takes only minutes to prepare. For an unbelievable texture it is best to stir frequently once you have put it in the freezer.

Serves: 6

Preparation time: 10 minutes plus stirring and freezing overnight

For the Granita:

4 cups cold espresso

1 1/2 cups superfine sugar

1. Pour the espresso into a large bowl. Stir in the sugar.

2. Pour the sweetened espresso into a shallow pan, approximately 9 x 13 inches, and place in the freezer.

3. Every 30 minutes for 2 hours, roughly stir the freezing mixture with a fork. This will give the granita a light, feathery texture.

4. Freeze the granita about 8 hours or overnight, until completely frozen.

For the Chantilly Cream:

3/4 cup heavy whipping cream

1/4 teaspoon vanilla extract

1/2 tablespoon sugar

Small pinch of salt

1. Place all the ingredients in a large stainless-steel bowl. Whisk with an electric mixer until the cream forms soft peaks.

2. Serve the granita in tall glasses or bowls with the Chantilly Cream.

PER SERVING: ABOUT 295 CALORIES, 90 CALORIES FROM FAT, 1 GRAM PROTEIN, 52 GRAMS CARBOHYDRATES, 10 GRAMS TOTAL FAT, 0 GRAMS FIBER, 29 MILLIGRAMS SODIUM

HEAVENLY MERINGUE COOKIES

Float to heavenly places with no fat and only a few calories. Baking these cookies in a low-heat oven produces a light meringue that is crisp on the outside and soft on the inside. This is a classic partner for sorbet. My favorite twist has finely chopped nuts sprinkled on top.

Makes 30 to 36 cookies depending on size

Preparation time: 15 minutes

Baking time: 30 minutes

1/2 cup egg whites (about 4 large egg whites)

Pinch of salt

1 cup sugar

1. Preheat the oven to 300° F. Line 2 cookie sheets with parchment or wax paper.

2. With an electric mixer, beat the egg whites and salt on high speed until soft peaks form.

3. Continue mixing on high speed while adding 1/2 cup of the sugar. Add the remaining sugar by the table-spoonful. Beat for another 1–2 minutes, until the mixture is stiff and shiny.

4. Drop by the spoonful onto the cookie sheets. Flatten each cookie slightly with the back of a spoon.

5. Bake until pale golden, about 30 minutes. Let cool.

For Safekeeping: Cookies last for a few days in an airtight container.

Twist: *Chocolate Meringue:* Add 2 tablespoons Dutch-process cocoa powder to the meringue mixture after adding the sugar in Step 3. Continue beating until the cocoa powder is distributed throughout the meringue, about 1 minute.

Walnut Meringue: Sprinkle the cookies with 1/2 cup finely chopped walnuts just before baking.

Meringue Sandwiches: After baking the cookies, glue the flat sides of two cookies together with your favorite jam or melted chocolate.

PER SERVING: 31 CALORIES, 0 CALORIES FROM FAT, 0 GRAMS PROTEIN, 7 GRAMS CARBOHYDRATES, 0 GRAMS TOTAL FAT, 0 GRAMS FIBER, 19 MILLIGRAMS SODIUM

SHORTBREAD TEA COOKIES

The perfect complement to a luscious bowl of fruit, frozen yogurt, or sorbet. These cookies are wonderful for baking with children. Be creative and try a few twists for fun.

Makes about 48 cookies

Preparation time: 20 minutes, plus time to chill the dough

Baking time: 10 minutes

- 3/4 cup (1 1/2 sticks) unsalted butter at room temperature
- 1 1/4 cups confectioner's sugar
- 4 large egg yolks
- 2 teaspoons vanilla extract
- 1/8 teaspoon salt
- 3 cups flour

---

1. Preheat the oven to 325° F.

2. With an electric mixer, beat the butter until smooth, about 2 to 3 minutes.

3. Gradually add the confectioner's sugar and beat until the mixture is pale and fluffy.

4. Beat in the egg yolks, vanilla, and salt.

5. Stir in the flour.

6. Chill the dough for about 15 minutes, until firm enough to handle, or 1 hour if you want to make cut-out cookies. Shape into 4 logs that are 1 1/2 inches in diameter and cover with plastic wrap. Chill. (This can be done in advance and stored in the refrigerator for up to 3 days or in the freezer for 1 month.)

7. When the logs of dough are very firm, slice them about 1/4-inch thick and place 1 inch apart on an ungreased baking sheet. If making cut-out cookies, roll the dough on a floured surface and cut as desired.

8. Bake until very pale golden brown, about 8 to 10 minutes. Remove from the baking sheet and let cool.

Twist: *Lemon shortbread:* Add 1 teaspoon finely grated lemon zest in Step 4.

Orange shortbread: Add 1 teaspoon finely grated orange zest in Step 4.

Pecan shortbread: Stir in 1/2 cup finely chopped pecans after Step 5.

PER SERVING: ABOUT 83 CALORIES, 27 CALORIES FROM FAT, 1 GRAM PROTEIN, 12 GRAMS CARBOHYDRATES, 3 GRAMS FAT, 0 GRAMS FIBER, 7 MILLIGRAMS SODIUM

Sweet Fractions

Sometimes when it is hard for children to catch on to using fractions, the homework hour can become stressful for everyone. Try baking cookies together. Dr. Ann-Marie Gebhart of the American Society of Clinical Nutrition found that this was the easiest way for her son Jeff to learn what a fraction was. By measuring 1/2 cup of this and 3/4 cup of that, he got to know them all.

Frozen Facts

With an ever-increasing number of choices to bring the meal to a cool conclusion, deciding what frozen dessert to choose can be confusing. Sort out the scoops by checking the label for the fat content. The Food and Drug Administration sets labeling standards for the different types. Most often the different yogurts and ice creams are interchangeable in recipes but deliver different amounts of milk fat. Remember, too, that added ingredients such as chocolate chips, nuts, and crushed cookies increase the total fat and calories. Here are the plain facts about the most popular frozen desserts and their fat standards:

Frozen Dessert	Percent of Milk Fat	Frozen Dessert	Percent of Milk Fat
Ice cream (regular)	Above 20 percent	Nonfat ice cream	Less than 0.5 gram of fat per 1/2 cup serving
Reduced-fat ice cream	Must be at least 25 percent less fat than that brand of regular ice cream	Frozen yogurt	The labeling must meet the same standards as ice cream. Fat range: 11 to 14 percent
Light ice cream	Must be at least 50 percent less fat than that brand of regular ice cream	Sherbet	Fat range: 10 to 15 percent
Low-fat ice cream	3 grams of fat or less per 1/2 cup serving	Sorbet	Fat-free

THE FINEST RASPBERRY DESSERT SAUCE

The vivid ruby-red color and naturally sweet taste of this sauce makes it a wonderful partner for other desserts. Try it over nonfat yogurt, sorbet, angel food cake, or sliced strawberries for a delightful finale.

Makes about 1 cup

Preparation time: 15 minutes

1 cup raspberries, fresh or frozen

1 tablespoon fresh lemon juice

2 to 4 tablespoons sugar

1. Puree the berries in a blender with the lemon juice. Blend in the sugar by the tablespoonful, tasting after each addition, until the desired degree of sweetness is reached.

2. Strain through a fine strainer, pressing with a rubber spatula to release the juices.

For Safekeeping: Store in the refrigerator up to 2 days or freeze up to 2 months.

Twist: *Berry sauce:* Substitute 1 cup any berry or combination of berries for the raspberries.

Peach sauce: Substitute 1 cup peeled, pitted, and sliced peaches for the raspberries.

PER SERVING (ABOUT TWO TABLESPOONS): 28 CALORIES, 0 CALORIES FROM FAT, 0 GRAMS PROTEIN, 7 GRAMS CARBOHYDRATES, 0 GRAMS TOTAL FAT, 1 GRAM FIBER, 0 MILLIGRAMS SODIUM

FOR SAFEKEEPING
Berry Carefully

There may be no delight greater than ripe, sweet summer berries. But be alert that ripe berries are very fragile and do not store well or long. To begin, choose fresh berries that are sweet-smelling, firm, and plump. When you bring them home, it is best to remove the berries from the carton, spread them out in a single layer on a paper towel–lined tray, cover with plastic wrap, and refrigerate. Do not wash them until you are ready to use them. Most berries will not keep more than a couple of days.

Handpicked Berry Harvests

Picking your own berries at a local farm is a great way to spend a late spring or summer afternoon with the kids. The taste of freshly picked berries is wonderful, and the price is great because you do not have to pay for the middleman.

Whether you kneel to pick the reddest, ripest strawberry or stand on your toes to reach the top of the bush and pluck the bluest, plumpest blueberries, you'll find it is an experience the kids will never forget. Pick-your-own farms are also a great place for birthday parties and family gatherings.

Check your newspaper for farm listings or call your county cooperative extension office. Then when you get home, have the kids help create a luscious dessert using your pickings.

CHOCOLATE SAUCE

This satiny-smooth chocolate sauce has a unique lightness about it when poured over frozen yogurt or angel food cake. The flavor twists add a new dimension.

Makes about 1 1/2 cups

Preparation time: 10 minutes

1 cup semisweet chocolate morsels

3/4 cup skim milk

Small pinch of salt

1. Place the chocolate in a heat-resistant bowl.

2. Bring the milk and salt to a boil and pour over the chocolate. Wait about 30 seconds, then stir slowly until the mixture becomes a smooth sauce.

(This can be made in advance and stored in the refrigerator for up to 1 week and reheated in the microwave.)

Twists: Liven up your chocolate sauce by steeping a flavoring in the milk while it comes to a boil. Flavorings could include: a handful of fresh mint leaves for Mint Chocolate Sauce, several strips of orange zest for Chocolate Orange Sauce, 1/4 cup coffee beans for Mocha Sauce. Let the milk stand for 5 minutes, bring back to a boil, strain, and pour over the chocolate.

PER SERVING: 2 TABLESPOONS IS ABOUT 70 CALORIES, 36 CALORIES FROM FAT, 1 GRAM PROTEIN, 9 GRAMS CARBOHYDRATES, 4 GRAMS FAT, 1 GRAM FIBER, 32 MILLIGRAMS SODIUM

SLICED BANANAS WITH BUTTERSCOTCH PUDDING

This dessert features naturally sweet, smooth bananas that pair well with the rich flavor of butterscotch pudding, and you get a health bonus from the bananas' potassium and fiber. The ultimate comfort dessert!

Makes about 1 1/2 cups

Preparation time: 5 minutes

Cooking time: 15 minutes

1 large egg

1 1/2 tablespoons cornstarch

Pinch of salt

1/2 teaspoon vanilla extract

1 1/2 tablespoons butter

1/2 cup dark brown sugar

1 cup low-fat milk

Granulated sugar (optional)

6 ripe bananas

1. In a 1- or 2-quart stainless-steel saucepan, whisk the egg, cornstarch, salt, and vanilla for 2 minutes. Set aside.

2. Melt the butter and brown sugar in another saucepan. Cook over low heat until the butter and sugar blend together. Add the milk and heat until the sugar dissolves. (The sugar will get hard when the milk is added; it will melt again as the milk heats.)

3. Whisk a few tablespoons of the hot milk mixture into the egg mixture. Gradually whisk in the rest of the milk mixture.

4. Over medium heat, whisk the combined mixture constantly until it comes to a boil. Immediately remove from the heat.

5. Pour into a bowl. (If you don't want a skin to form on the top of the pudding, sprinkle it lightly with granulated sugar.) Refrigerate. Cover with plastic wrap when cool.

(This can be done ahead and refrigerated up to 3 days.)

6. Slice 1 banana into each of 6 serving bowls. Top with a few tablespoons of pudding.

PER SERVING: ABOUT 366 CALORIES, 90 CALORIES FROM FAT, 8 GRAMS PROTEIN, 64 GRAMS CARBOHYDRATES, 10 GRAMS TOTAL FAT, 3 GRAMS FIBER, 191 MILLIGRAMS SODIUM

Twist: *Raspberries with Chocolate Pudding:* Replace the brown sugar with granulated sugar and add it to the mixture in Step 1. Omit the butter. Heat the milk by itself in Step 2. At the end of Step 4, stir 2 ounces good-quality bittersweet or semisweet chocolate into the warm pudding mixture until smooth. Follow the recipe from Step 5, using 1/2 cup fresh raspberries per serving.

Lilly's Fruit Faces

Making fruit faces together is a favorite afternoon activity for chef Anne Rosenzweig of the Lobster Club in New York City and her daughter, Lilly. They begin with whatever is in the house, or they go to the farmer's market to pick out the fruit.

Just use the following:

- a slice of melon for the smile
- a small slice of banana for the white part of the eye
- cantaloupe or other melon cut in thin strips for crazy hair.
- a sliced grape for each eyeball
- strawberries for the cheeks

Anne and Lilly always have a great time making the funny face, learning how to cut safely with a knife, and enjoying healthy fruit all at the same time. Before she knows it, Lilly has eaten three plates of fruit.

Better Baking Tips

Baking is a wonderful way to use your creativity, but the approach is different from the way you cook other foods. Because baking recipes are based on strict formulas, they are not the place to experiment unless you are an expert. Follow these steps for best results:

- Read through the entire recipe first so that you are ready for all the steps.
- Preheat the oven before beginning to bake.
- Have all the ingredients at room temperature unless otherwise specified.
- Measure all ingredients carefully.
- Follow the recipe exactly.
- Stir or fold the flour into the batter just enough to combine for cookies, cakes, muffins, and piecrusts.

PATRICK O'CONNELL'S RHUBARB "PIZZA"

There is little question about it: Food is theater for Patrick O'Connell, the chef and owner of The Inn at Little Washington, which is nestled in magnificent Rappahannock County, Virginia. Cooking, Patrick says, "is showing children what life is all about: knowing where food comes from at the most basic level." During his early years at The Inn, he dug up trees on the grounds and replanted them, then built a spectacular garden where dozens of vegetables grow. "The amount of pleasure increases when you grow something, pick it, and use it," he says.

Patrick also loves to resurrect old family recipes and believes it is a way of bringing the family together. His grandmother's recipe is the inspiration for this "pizza," but he has given it a whimsical, modern-day touch. Easy to make ahead and reheat before serving, this dessert brings a spring dinner to a tart and satisfying end.

Serves: 6

Preparation time: 25 minutes

Cooking time: 15 to 20 minutes

Basic piecrust or puff pastry for two 9-inch crusts; store-bought is fine

8 stalks rhubarb, very red in color

1 quart water

1 1/2 cups sugar

2 tablespoons seedless raspberry preserves (optional)

6 small scoops low-fat frozen yogurt or ice cream (optional)

1. Preheat the oven to 375° F.

2. On a floured surface, roll out the dough 1/8-inch thick. Lay a bowl about 5 inches in diameter upside down on the dough, and using it as a pattern, cut out 6 circles with a sharp knife. Prick the circles of dough several times with a fork and refrigerate.

3. Wash the rhubarb and trim off any leaves and brown or bruised spots. Using a sharp knife, slice 6 of the stalks on the bias about 1/8-inch thick and place in a stainless-steel bowl. Roughly chop the remaining 2 stalks and keep separate.

4. In a large saucepan, combine the water, sugar, and raspberry preserves over medium heat. Bring to a boil and remove from the heat.

5. Pour the hot liquid over the slices of rhubarb just to cover them, reserving about 2 cups of liquid in the teaspoon. Keep the rhubarb slices in the liquid until ready to use.

continued >

6. Add the chopped rhubarb to the remaining liquid in the pan and simmer until the rhubarb falls apart and the liquid has the consistency of thick tomato sauce.

(This can be done ahead of time and stored in the refrigerator up to 3 days.)

7. Strain the rhubarb slices and reserve the liquid.

8. Return the liquid to the stove and simmer until reduced to a syrup.

9. Coat several baking sheets with nonstick spray and lay the pastry rounds on them. Spread 1 tablespoon of the thick rhubarb sauce on each round. Arrange the rhubarb slices in a single layer on top of the sauce.

10. Bake the pizzas in the lower half of the oven until the pastry is crisp and golden, about 8 to 10 minutes. Remove from the oven and brush the rhubarb slices with the rhubarb syrup.

11. Top with additional "pizza" toppings or frozen yogurt if desired.

Twists: Optional "pizza" toppings:

strawberry slices as "pepperoni"

pistachios or other nuts as "olives"

grated white chocolate as "Parmesan cheese"

pitted cherries as "sausage"

PER SERVING: ABOUT 397 CALORIES, 72 CALORIES FROM FAT, 5 GRAMS PROTEIN, 79 GRAMS CARBOHYDRATES, 8 GRAMS FAT, 3 GRAMS FIBER, 178 MILLIGRAMS SODIUM

HEALTHY TIMESAVERS
Swift and Sweet

Here are some suggestions for light and lively desserts that require virtually no preparation or cooking:

- a bunch of grapes, sliced apples, or pears with cheddar cheese

- low-fat frozen yogurt with chocolate sauce

- low-fat ice cream with mixed berries

- fruit sorbet or sherbet with biscotti

- fruit salad with mint garnish

- strawberries dipped in a mixture of nonfat sour cream and brown sugar

JASPER WHITE'S PEAR CRISP

Jasper White is a respected consulting chef and a cookbook author. An enthusiast for New England cooking, Jasper loves to cook fish from nearby waters, prepare vegetables from the garden, and make desserts with local fruits. He has a special interest in giving children an understanding about good food; he has even developed a children's menu designed to give them a fun restaurant experience. Jasper enjoys introducing new foods to them and he believes "you can never give up on children."

Everyone enjoys this rustic crisp with its fall colors and the sweet crunch of toasted pecans. This simple dessert has a warm, golden glow and can easily become a family favorite. I love serving it at fall buffet dinners.

Serves: 8

Preparation time: 20 minutes

Baking time: 1 hour

1 cup chopped pecans

1 cup all-purpose flour

1 cup light brown sugar, firmly packed

1/8 teaspoon salt

1/2 teaspoon ground cinnamon

1/2 cup (1 stick) cold unsalted butter, cut into 1/2-inch pieces

8 firm pears such as Anjou, Bosc, or Bartlett

2 tablespoons sugar

1 tablespoon flour

8 scoops vanilla ice cream or low-fat frozen yogurt

1. Preheat the oven to 350° F.

2. Place the pecan pieces on a baking sheet and toast in the oven until golden brown, about 6 minutes.

3. In a mixing bowl, combine the flour, brown sugar, salt, cinnamon, and pecans. Add the butter. Rub the mixture in the palms of your hands, incorporating the butter but still keeping the mixture crumbly. Set aside in a cool place. (This can be made in advance and stored in the freezer up to 2 months.)

4. Peel, core, and slice the pears into 1/2-inch-thick slices. Toss the slices with the sugar and flour. Place in a 6-inch-deep baking dish and cover evenly with the topping.

5. Bake in the oven until the top is brown, bubbly, and crisp, about 1 hour. (This can be made in the morning, kept at room temperature, and reheated when ready to serve.)

6. Divide the warm crisp into 8 bowls and top with ice cream or frozen yogurt.

PER SERVING: ABOUT 377 CALORIES, 198 CALORIES FROM FAT, 3 GRAMS PROTEIN, 45 GRAMS CARBOHYDRATES, 22 GRAMS FAT, 1 GRAM FIBER, 49 MILLIGRAMS SODIUM

MICHAEL LOMONACO'S CLASSIC STRAWBERRY-RHUBARB SHORTCAKE

Michael Lomonaco is very much a big city guy; his New York restaurant, Windows on the World, is 107 floors above the ground. But he has a deep passion about what grows in the ground, and he is eager to share it. I was with him once when he talked to a class of excited New York City fifth graders about how different foods are grown.

Cooking is part of Michael's family heritage, and he works hard to preserve tradition. This classic shortcake has been a spring ritual in American kitchens for hundreds of years. The crumbly shortcakes offer a lovely counterpoint to the vibrant, luscious fruit cascading over them. Make it a part of your spring ritual.

Serves: 4

Preparation time: 40 minutes

Baking time: 35 minutes

For the shortcakes:

1/2 cup flour, sifted

1 1/2 tablespoons sugar

1/2 teaspoon baking powder

1/8 teaspoon salt

1 1/2 tablespoons cold unsalted butter,
   cut into small pieces

2 tablespoons buttermilk

2 tablespoons heavy cream

1 tablespoon butter, melted

1. In a large bowl, combine the flour, sugar, baking powder, and salt. Stir thoroughly with a wooden spoon to combine.

2. Add the pieces of cold butter and stir to coat the small pieces with flour so that they do not stick together.

3. Add the buttermilk and cream. Stir briefly to combine, leaving the mixture as lumpy as possible.

4. Pour the lumpy dough onto a lightly floured surface. Flatten gently with a rolling pin into a squarish shape approximately 1 inch thick.

5. Cut into 4 equal squares. Place the squares on a baking sheet and brush with melted butter. Put the entire baking sheet into the refrigerator for 20 minutes while you preheat the oven to 375° F.

6. Bake the chilled shortcakes until nicely browned, about 20 to 25 minutes.

continued ›

For the topping:

1 cup water

1/2 cup sugar

4 to 5 stalks rhubarb, sliced

3/4 cup heavy cream

2 teaspoons confectioner's sugar

1 teaspoon vanilla extract

1 quart strawberries, washed and sliced

1. In a saucepan, bring the water, sugar, and rhubarb to a low boil. Cook, uncovered, until the rhubarb falls apart and the mixture thickens slightly, to about the consistency of applesauce. Let cool.

2. Place the cream, confectioner's sugar, and vanilla in a bowl and whisk until soft peaks form.

3. Putting it together: Split each biscuit in half. Spread one side with the whipped cream. Top the cream with strawberries. Spoon 1 tablespoon of the rhubarb mixture on top of the strawberries. Top with the other half of the biscuit.

PER SERVING: ABOUT 535 CALORIES, 198 CALORIES FROM FAT, 3 GRAMS PROTEIN, 39 GRAMS CARBOHYDRATES, 22 GRAMS FAT, 3 GRAMS FIBER, 115 MILLIGRAMS SODIUM

NUTRITION POWER POINTS
Strawberry Fields

Irresistibly sweet and remarkably health-promoting, the strawberry is hard to beat. They are fat-free, low in calories, a good source of potassium, vitamin C, and fiber, and higher in folic acid than any other fruit. This water-soluble B vitamin is especially important if you are planning to become pregnant because it helps prevent neural tube birth defects.

When strawberries are in season, from spring through summer, I always have them on hand for easy desserts, toppings for cereal, French toast, and salads. For the sweetest taste, let them reach room temperature before serving. Enjoy!

LISA'S ANGEL CAKE FOR ALL SEASONS

This classic, modern dessert is light, fat-free, and cholesterol-free. It's a specialty of my daughter, Lisa, who has lit up many a festive table with her seasonal renditions of this heavenly dessert.

Serves: about 14

Preparation time: 10 minutes

Baking time: 1 hour

- 1 cup cake flour
- 1 1/2 cups superfine granulated sugar
- 1 1/4 cups egg whites (about 10 large egg whites) at room temperature
- 1 1/4 tablespoons cream of tartar
- 1/4 teaspoon salt
- 1 teaspoon vanilla extract

1. Preheat the oven to 350° F.
2. Sift the flour twice with 1/2 cup of the sugar.
3. With an electric mixer on high speed, beat the egg whites, cream of tartar, and salt until soft peaks form when the mixer is removed from the batter.
4. Add half of the remaining sugar and beat for 1 minute. Add the remaining sugar, 2 tablespoons at a time, beating after each addition.
5. Stir in the vanilla.
6. Fold the flour and sugar mixture into the egg whites, 1/4 cup at a time, just until incorporated.
7. Put the batter in an ungreased 10-inch tube pan and bake until the cake is light golden brown and springy to the touch, about 1 hour. Invert the pan and let the cake cool completely before removing from the pan.

PER SERVING: ABOUT 120 CALORIES, 0 CALORIES FROM FAT, 3 GRAMS PROTEIN, 27 GRAMS CARBOHYDRATES, 0 GRAMS FAT, 0 GRAMS FIBER, 78 MILLIGRAMS SODIUM

SPRING: LEMON ANGEL CAKE WITH STRAWBERRIES

1. Add 1 teaspoon grated lemon zest to the angel cake batter in Step 4.
2. Wash and slice 1 pint strawberries. Sprinkle the sliced strawberries with sugar to desired sweetness. Let stand at room temperature for 30 minutes or refrigerate for several hours.
3. Place 1 slice of cake on each of 6 plates. Spoon the strawberries and their juices on and around the cake.

PER SERVING: ABOUT 140 CALORIES, 0 CALORIES FROM FAT, 3 GRAMS PROTEIN, 32 GRAMS CARBOHYDRATES, 0 GRAMS FAT, 1 GRAM FIBER, 78 MILLIGRAMS SODIUM

SUMMER: ANGEL CAKE WITH SUMMER FRUIT SALAD AND RASPBERRY SAUCE

1. Place 1 slice of angel cake on each of 6 plates. With a slotted spoon, place Summer Fruit Salad (see page 61) on a corner of the cake and let it spill over the side. Drizzle The Finest Raspberry Dessert Sauce (see page 237) around the fruit salad.

PER SERVING: ABOUT 150 CALORIES, 0 CALORIES FROM FAT, 3 GRAMS PROTEIN, 35 GRAMS CARBOHYDRATES, 0 GRAMS FAT, 1 GRAM FIBER, 78 MILLIGRAMS SODIUM

FALL: ALMOND ANGEL CAKE WITH WARM MIXED-UP FRUIT

1. Add ¼ teaspoon almond extract to the angel cake batter in Step 4.
2. Warm Mixed-Up Fruit Compote (see page 136) in the microwave. Place 1 slice of angel cake on each of 6 plates. Spoon the Mixed-Up Fruit Compote on and around the cake.

PER SERVING: ABOUT 203 CALORIES, 0 CALORIES FROM FAT, 3 GRAMS PROTEIN, 48 GRAMS CARBOHYDRATES, 0 GRAMS FAT, 1 GRAM FIBER, 78 MILLIGRAMS SODIUM

WINTER: CHOCOLATE ANGEL CAKE WITH ORANGES AND CHOCOLATE SAUCE

1. Substitute 2 tablespoons of cocoa powder for 2 tablespoons of the cake flour.
2. Peel 2 oranges and cut them into segments (see page 134).
3. Place 1 slice of Chocolate Angel Cake on each of 6 plates. Spoon Chocolate Sauce (see page 238) on the side of the cake. Arrange the orange segments like a fan to the side of the sauce.

PER SERVING: ABOUT 199 CALORIES, 36 CALORIES FROM FAT, 4 GRAMS PROTEIN, 39 GRAMS CARBOHYDRATES, 4 GRAMS FAT, 1 GRAM FIBER, 119 MILLIGRAMS SODIUM

WARM CHOCOLATE FANTASY

Here is a dessert to dream about. Indulge in this fantastic dark chocolate treasure that is somewhere between a soufflé and a small, moist cake. The preparation is easy, and the presentation is personal and memorable. Use it to finish dinners that are very light.

Serves: 8

Preparation time: 15 minutes

Baking time: 8 to 10 minutes

To prepare the ramekins:

2 teaspoons cocoa

2 teaspoons flour

1 tablespoon melted butter

1. Preheat the oven to 350° F.

2. Sift the cocoa and flour together. Brush eight 4-ounce ramekins with melted butter and dust with the cocoa-flour mixture.

For the Warm Chocolate Fantasy:

5 ounces semisweet or bittersweet chocolate

1/2 cup (1 stick) unsalted butter

4 large eggs at room temperature

1/4 cup cake flour

1 cup confectioner's sugar

1. Melt the chocolate and unsalted butter over a double boiler.

2. Whip the eggs with a mixer on high speed until pale yellow and fluffy, about 5 minutes.

3. Fold the chocolate mixture into the eggs.

4. Sift the cake flour and sugar together. Fold the flour-sugar into the chocolate-egg mixture.

5. Fill the ramekins about 3/4 full.

6. Bake for 8 to 10 minutes. The centers should still be runny and the outside edges should be firm. (This can be made ahead and stored in the refrigerator up to 2 days.)

7. Reheat in the microwave on low power for two or three 20-second blasts, until warm. Unmold onto a plate and serve with low-fat ice cream or nonfat frozen yogurt.

PER SERVING: ABOUT 302 CALORIES, 189 CALORIES FROM FAT, 5 GRAMS PROTEIN, 28 GRAMS CARBOHYDRATES, 21 GRAMS TOTAL FAT, 1 GRAM FIBER, 36 MILLIGRAMS SODIUM

TIPS AND TRIVIA
Chocolate Melts

Melt chocolate in a double boiler or on low power in the microwave. It burns at a very low temperature (135° F).

CARROT-WALNUT CAKE

This is really a tea cake, and it's not just for little girls and tea parties. It's so good that the whole family will love it. The carrots and walnuts mixed with the crushed pineapple give the cake supreme texture and taste, and the beta-carotene in the carrots gives a health bonus.

Serves: 8

Preparation time: 20 minutes

Baking time: 25 to 30 minutes

1/2 cup (1 stick) unsalted butter at room temperature

3/4 cup sugar

2 eggs at room temperature

1/4 teaspoon ground cinnamon

1/2 teaspoon finely grated orange zest

3/4 cup finely grated carrot

1/2 cup finely chopped walnuts

1 1/4 cups all-purpose flour

1 1/4 teaspoons baking powder

1/4 teaspoon salt

1/4 cup canned crushed pineapple, drained

1. Preheat the oven to 350° F.
2. Place the butter in a mixing bowl and beat at high speed with an electric mixer for 30 seconds. Gradually add the sugar and continue to beat until the mixture is pale yellow and very fluffy.
3. Add the eggs 1 at a time, mixing on low speed.
4. Stir in the cinnamon, orange zest, carrot, and walnuts.
5. Sift the flour, baking powder, and salt together.
6. Stir in half the flour mixture. Add the pineapple and blend. Stir in the rest of the flour mixture. The batter should be smooth, but do not overmix.
7. Coat a loaf pan (or 9-inch round cake pan) with nonstick spray. Pour the batter into the pan.
8. Bake until golden brown and set in the center, about 25 to 30 minutes.

PER SERVING: ABOUT 296 CALORIES, 162 CALORIES FROM FAT, 5 GRAMS PROTEIN, 31 GRAMS CARBOHYDRATES, 18 GRAMS FAT, 1 GRAM FIBER, 171 MILLIGRAMS SODIUM

TIPS AND TRIVIA
Golden Carrots

Carrots were always sweet, but they were not always orange or golden; carrots of long ago were white, purple, and yellow. This root vegetable originated three thousand years ago in central Asia. In the 1600s the Dutch developed the orange carrots from which all modern-day carrots are descended. It is the beta-carotene in carrots that give them their bright orange coloring.

NANCY SILVERTON'S BANANA AND COCOA SMALL CAKE

Nancy Silverton, chef and owner (with her husband Mark Peele) of Campinile in Los Angeles, shares her passion for food with their three children by making regular trips to the Santa Monica farmer's market and doing all she can to encourage sustainable farming. All of Nancy's children love to make desserts with her and have been baking and cooking with her since they were very little.

The combination of bananas and chocolate in these small cakes has wide appeal, and the bananas offer sweetness along with good nutrition.

Makes about 18 small cakes

Preparation time: 15 minutes

Cooking time: 15 minutes

2 1/2 cups banana puree (from 4 to 5 very ripe bananas)

5 large eggs

1 1/4 cups canola oil

3 1/3 cups sugar

1 teaspoon baking powder

2 teaspoons baking soda

3 3/4 cups flour

1 cup cocoa powder

1 cup chopped pecans

1. Preheat the oven to 350° F. Coat a muffin pan with nonstick spray.

2. In a large mixing bowl, combine the banana puree, eggs, and oil.

3. Sift together the sugar, baking powder, baking soda, flour, and cocoa. Add the dry ingredients to the banana mixture, stirring until just moistened.

4. Fill the muffin cups 2/3 full and sprinkle with chopped pecans.

5. Bake until golden brown, about 15 minutes.

PER SERVING: ONE CAKE IS ABOUT 238 CALORIES, 99 CALORIES FROM FAT, 3 GRAMS PROTEIN, 34 GRAMS CARBOHYDRATES, 11 GRAMS FAT, 2 GRAMS FIBER, 86 MILLIGRAMS SODIUM

APRICOT CAKE WITH APRICOT SAUCE

Sweet-smelling, sweet-tasting ripe apricots are a joy of summer. Enjoy this delicious cake with its intense flavors and benefit from the fruit's rich source of vitamins A and C. Equally good when apples, pears, or peaches are in season. An all-around treat for everyone!

Serves: 10

Preparation time: 20 minutes

Baking time: 25 to 30 minutes

For the Apricot Cake:

1/4 cup (1/2 stick) unsalted butter at room temperature

2/3 cup sugar

2 large eggs at room temperature

1 teaspoon vanilla extract

1 cup flour

1 teaspoon baking powder

1/2 teaspoon salt

2 cups low-fat milk at room temperature

3 ripe apricots, peeled, halved, and pitted

Mint sprigs for garnish

1. Preheat the oven to 350° F.

2. Beat the butter in a mixing bowl with an electric mixer on high speed for 30 seconds. Gradually add the sugar and continue to beat until the mixture is pale yellow and very fluffy.

3. Add the eggs 1 at a time while mixing on low speed. Stir in the vanilla.

4. Sift the flour, baking powder, and salt together.

5. Add half of the flour mixture and blend, then add the milk. Finally, add the rest of the flour mixture. The batter should be smooth. Do not overmix.

6. Coat a 9-inch round cake pan with nonstick spray. Pour the batter into the pan. Arrange the apricot halves on top in a single layer.

7. Bake until golden brown and set in the center, about 25 to 30 minutes.

For the Apricot Sauce:

1/2 cup water

1/4 cup sugar

2 ripe apricots, peeled and pitted

Fresh lemon juice to taste

1. Bring the water and sugar to a boil in a small saucepan over high heat. Remove from the heat.

2. Puree the apricots in a blender with half of the sugar syrup. Adjust the taste by adding a few drops of lemon juice and more sugar syrup until a pleasant balance of sweetness and tartness is reached.

3. Putting it together: Place 1 slice of cake on each plate. Drizzle the sauce around the cake. Garnish with a mint sprig.

Twist: Substitute plums for the apricots.

PER SERVING: ABOUT 191 CALORIES, 54 CALORIES FROM FAT, 3 GRAMS PROTEIN, 31 GRAMS CARBOHYDRATES, 6 GRAMS TOTAL FAT, 1 GRAM FIBER, 308 MILLIGRAMS SODIUM

Fun Fountain Frosties

Bring back the fun of the soda fountain with delicious drinks that refresh while they reinvigorate. Try the different twists for sweet, light endings to a meal, or enjoy as afternoon snacks.

Serves: 1 **Preparation time:** 5 minutes

Citrus Freeze

1 cup orange juice

1/2 cup lemon sherbet or sorbet

1/2 cup ice cubes

1. Place all ingredients in a blender and blend on high speed until the mixture is smooth.

2. Serve in a tall glass.

PER SERVING: ABOUT 248 CALORIES, 1 CALORIE FROM FAT, 3 GRAMS PROTEIN, 56 GRAMS CARBOHYDRATES, 2 GRAMS FAT, 1 GRAM FIBER, 48 MILLIGRAMS SODIUM

Vanilla Float

1 tablespoon low-fat milk

1/2 teaspoon vanilla extract

1 cup seltzer water

1 scoop low-fat vanilla ice cream or ice milk

1. Pour the milk and vanilla into a tall glass and stir together.

2. Add the seltzer water.

3. Place the glass on a saucer to catch any overflow. Add the ice cream.

PER SERVING: ABOUT 113 CALORIES, 18 CALORIES FROM FAT, 4 GRAMS PROTEIN, 19 GRAMS CARBOHYDRATES, 2 GRAMS TOTAL FAT, 1 GRAM FIBER, 60 MILLIGRAMS SODIUM

Cran-Raspberry Fizz

1/2 cup cranberry juice

1/2 cup seltzer water

1/2 cup raspberry sherbet

1. Pour the cranberry juice and seltzer water into a tall glass.

2. Place the glass on a saucer to catch any overflow. Add the sherbet and let it fizz.

PER SERVING: ABOUT 209 CALORIES, 18 CALORIES FROM FAT, 1 GRAM PROTEIN, 48 GRAMS CARBOHYDRATES, 2 GRAMS FAT, 1 GRAM FIBER, 48 MILLIGRAMS SODIUM

Chocolate Frappe

1 cup low-fat milk

1 tablespoon chocolate syrup

1/2 cup low-fat chocolate frozen yogurt

1. Place all the ingredients in a blender and blend on high speed to combine.

2. Serve in a tall glass.

PER SERVING: ABOUT 250 CALORIES, 36 CALORIES FROM FAT, 13 GRAMS PROTEIN, 42 GRAMS CARBOHYDRATES, 4 GRAMS FAT, 0 GRAMS FIBER, 211 MILLIGRAMS SODIUM

Fit for a Cause

Exercising as a family can be good for your heart, and not just physically. Consider registering the whole family for local charity events that involve walking, running, or biking. Your family will spend fun time together and get a good dose of physical activity while raising money for your favorite cause. You may even want to organize a family run or bike ride in your own community to benefit a school or local charity.

CHAPTER 9

AT THE TABLE:

FAMILY SERVINGS

Sitting down at the table to share a meal is a celebration of the oldest rite of humanity. Eating with family and friends is the best way we have to strengthen the social connections that are central to the human community. By coming together for meals, we are both preserving traditions and creating new ones that will provide memories for the future.

Our time at the table enriches our health, too. It is widely accepted by medical and social researchers that eating together as a family influences lifelong health and psychological well-being. Dinnertime family rituals provide powerful and positive influences in our lives because they reinforce the family identity and give everyone "a shared and necessary sense of belonging," says Steven J. Wolin, M.D., a psychiatrist who has studied the effects of family rituals. He says that celebrations and traditions provide an anchor for the family, especially when it is dealing with some trouble, as all families do.

The modern American family has changed dramatically over the past fifty years. Shifts in family structure, the increase in time spent away from home by working parents, the explosion of new food products, and the influence of the media have all contributed to a loss of many of the food traditions that have been passed down for centuries. We've become less linked to family and community.

With all these changes, our mealtimes together take on even more meaning. As we reach the millennium, we are creating new food traditions for the next century that reflect both our new and old values. "Dining together can be a rich experience that has an effect on how you eat for the rest of your life and an impact on other lifetime social behavior," emphasizes Solomon Katz, Ph.D., director of the University Child Development Center. These shared times are a wonderful opportunity to show respect and appreciation for one another and for the freshness and variety of the food that promotes everyone's health.

By preserving many food traditions from our varied backgrounds we are strengthening our connection with the past. For example, many foods with eastern European roots were served at the table when I was growing up in New York and are the basis for many warm food memories. In turn, I have passed these traditions on to my children, who will follow them in their own lives.

The connection of old and new family food traditions is taking place in different ways all across the country. When I visited school lunch programs in Texas, Florida, California, New York, and many other places, I saw firsthand how children were blending their food experiences and their learning experiences. In many schools the foods of Mexico, South America, Japan, Vietnam, Thailand, and other regions are enjoyed along with American favorites such as pizza and chicken nuggets.

There is no doubt it is not always easy to get

FAMILY FUN
Storytimes

Suppertime and storytelling go together in many families. Dr. Linda L. Smith, a nutritionist and story researcher, grew up in eastern Tennessee, a region steeped in the use of story. It all started when her mother said, "Tell your daddy what you did in school today." When either parent said, "That reminds me of..." she was ready to hear the favorites about Great-aunt Zola and other relatives in Appalachia. To get storytelling started at your table, try these questions:

How did the family pet get its name? Get the children involved in telling the story.

What childhood vacations did a relative go on when he or she was young?

Who was the most interesting family member? What did he or she do that was exciting?

" Food bonds the family together and gives everyone wonderful memories that children will keep for a lifetime.

—JOYCE GOLDSTEIN, COOKBOOK AUTHOR AND CONSULTING CHEF "

everyone around the table at the same time. With work, school, sports, and other activities on the family schedule, it can be a huge challenge. Many people skip the family meal and choose to eat on the run, but these time demands and conflicting priorities are challenges that can be met.

Happy Times at the Table

The best family meals occur when everyone actively participates. Involve the children as much as possible and try eating together as often as you can. It is wonderful how the memories of the laughter, the stories, and of course the food linger long after the last bite. Relax, have fun, and find your own way to make your table times work.

Enjoy the pleasure of good food and being together at the table.

Make this a time that everyone looks forward to all day long. Be flexible and responsive to the needs of individual members. If some nights you can't meet at the same time for dinner, meet later on for dessert. Share the day's experiences: what went on at school, work, and play. Keep the mood positive; everyone eats best and healthiest when they are having a good time.

Set a good example for healthy eating, manners, and respect for one another.

Parents are children's most important role models.

Whether children seem to be paying attention or not, they are learning their lifetime habits from their experiences today. This is a wonderful opportunity to pass on important values such as consideration of one another, appreciation, and thoughtfulness.

Encourage learning experiences and positive interactions at the table.

The family table can be a terrific place for children to learn and build their self-esteem. Table talk is best if it is positive and reinforcing. Mealtime is not a time for fighting or berating. Family conversations can focus on building vocabulary, answering geography and science questions, or explaining how food is grown. Give everyone a chance to participate.

Introduce new foods as part of an adventure.

Eating a variety of healthy foods is the basis for healthy living. Celebrate the times you serve a new food or a new recipe. Talk about where the food comes from and add a special touch such as candles or homemade party favors. Even picky eaters will be more adventuresome if they can help pick out the veggies at the store or farmer's market and then help prepare the food.

Tie food experiences to family tales and traditions.

Tell stories about the lives of grandparents, aunts, and

Tell Me More

Begin your meals together with a few words about your day. Have each person talk about one new thing he or she learned that day or that week. Family members can take turns for a month keeping a "Family Mealtime Memory Journal." Decorate the cover of the journal as a family and have each person add his or her own decoration to the front page of the entries for each month.

The International Joy of Eating

The pleasure of food and family is recognized in the dietary guidelines of many foreign countries. In fact, the official nutrition policies of countries such as England, Japan, and Norway clearly state that eating includes the enjoyment of family, traditions, and culture.

The first guideline of the United Kingdom states, "Enjoy your food."

Japan celebrates its culture by saying: "Happy eating makes for happy life; sit down and eat together and talk; treasure family tastes and home cooking."

Thailand's daily food consumption guide encourages: "A family is likely to be happy when family members eat together and enjoy treasured family tastes and good home cooking."

The National Nutrition Council of Norway's message is simple: "Food + Joy = Health."

Celebrate the joy of eating together and the tastes of other countries by preparing an international dinner.

uncles. My mother's family came from Romania, and I still remember the stories she told every time she chopped the roasted eggplant appetizer. She was so proud that her mother's city in Romania had been the first to give women the vote. Every family has wonderful stories that give children a strong sense of identity and security.

Highlight the favorite foods of family members to recognize everyone's individual tastes.

It means so much to children—and to parents—for their personal food preferences to be recognized. In our family, the star of Jason's salads was cucumbers (without tomatoes), and Lisa's salads featured tomatoes (without cucumbers). They've told me that this made them feel special and important. When serving a favorite dinner, encourage everyone to talk about why it is a favorite.

Easy Ways to Celebrate Every Day

A welcoming table helps make mealtime a special experience. Encourage the children to think of new ways to be creative with the table settings. In our house, the children love to add their own personal touches to the table when guests are invited. When they are young, they might need help, but be patient; it's a valuable thing to know.

How the table is set and how we present the food is an expression of our caring. What's more, "the eye eats first," says food historian William Woys Weaver. First impressions count. Here are some good ideas for your table:

Start in the center of the table, with a big bowl of fruit or vase of flowers.

Both flowers and fruit bring vivid colors and warmth to the table. Pick up flowers on the way home from work, gather them from the garden, or fill a basket at the farmer's market.

Do fun things with napkins.

Colorful napkins give visual interest to the table. Try using no-iron cloth napkins that can last all week long and still look good. Pile them in a straw basket to get at them easily. Kids love having their own napkin rings and can even make them for the whole family. Try using old greeting cards or oversized playing cards, and paste the ends together for colorful napkin rings.

Candles bring a glow to everyone and everything.

Create atmosphere with different kinds of candles. Kids can make them easily using one of the many available kits.

Present the food on the plate simply and with style.

Create attractive effects with contrasting colors on the same plate. If you put together odd numbers of foods on the plate, it is more appealing to the eye. Keep the food toward the center of the plate and away from the rim for the best effect. Add a fresh herb sprig or bouquet of herbs such as parsley, sage, and rosemary for a beautiful garnish.

Experiment with different kinds of tableware to add interest.

Using serving bowls and dishes in unusual sizes, shapes, and designs makes the table a visual delight. Vary the table according to the meal, holiday, or season.

Give the table an extra touch inspired by the seasons.

Celebrate with spring forsythia sprigs, summer seashells, fall leaves, or winter pinecones. Encourage the children to think of their own seasonal ideas.

A Shower of Flowers

There is nothing like fresh-cut flowers to brighten the table and brighten everyone's spirits. Here are some tips for easily and inexpensively making flowers a part of your table—and home.

- Buy flowers in season—they will be cheaper and fresher—or, better yet, get them from your garden. Enjoy lilacs and violets in the spring and chrysanthemums in the fall to complement your seasonal menus.
- Keep table centerpieces low so that no one has to peek around the petunias. Arrange the flowers to attract everyone to the table, not distract from the meal and the talk. If you do have a tall centerpiece, place it on a counter or sidebar during the meal.
- Keep a trivet or tray under the centerpiece to prevent water stains on the table.
- Flowers do not need to be in expensive arrangements to look beautiful. Experiment by arranging flowers in different bowls or vases. Or use your imagination and put flowers in watering cans, baskets, spice jars, gravy boats, or teacups.

GoOd-TiME MeNUs

Create fun family mealtimes every day and on special occasions. Celebrate by designing your own menus or trying the twelve seasonal menus that follow. These menus are drawn from the recipes in this book, but you can always substitute dishes, of course.

SpRiNg

Mother's Day Brunch

Start off Mom's special day with this springtime medley. There are all kinds of ways the kids can make this morning memorable. Making cards or decorations, cooking, and cleaning up are all wonderful ways to say, "I love you, Mom."

- *Alice Waters's Orange Juice (page 64)*
- *Roasted Asparagus Salad (page 37)*
- *Italian Frittata with Potatoes, Onions, and Herbs (page 156)*
- *Patrick O'Connell's Rhubarb "Pizza" (page 241)*

Sports and Fitness Dinner

Active families will stay in great shape with this dinner. It's terrific after a family walk or workout. Share the good energy with each other.

- *Minted Cucumber Dip (page 110) with cut-up veggies*
- *Michael Romano's Penne with Asparagus and Red Peppers (page 204)*
- *Mixed Green Salad with Pine Nut Vinaigrette (page 180)*

- *Carrot-Walnut Cake (page 249)*

Good Report Card Dinner

A great way to celebrate great performance. Sprinkle gold stars on the table for fun. This homestyle meal will earn an A+ on all counts.

- *Down-Home Corn Bread (page 148)*
- *Mary Sue Milliken and Susan Feninger's Pork Chili Verde with Posole and Red Rice (page 211)*
- *Greens with Apples, Walnuts, Blue Cheese and Balsamic Vinaigrette (page 181)*
- *Nancy Silverton's Banana and Cocoa Small Cake (page 250)*

SuMmEr

Summer Farmer's Market Dinner

Enjoy the incredible bounty at the farmer's market with this meal. Use market flowers and fresh herbs as well as to create a terrific table. Talk with the farmers about their produce and share their stories around the table.

- *Alice Waters's Rainbow Tomato Pizza (page 184)*
- *Broiled Salmon with Sizzle of Corn and Tomatoes (page 221)*
- *Mixed arugula and spinach leaves with Balsamic Vinaigrette (page 181)*
- *Cold Peach Soup with Frozen Yogurt (page 232)*

Father's Day Barbecue

Get everyone into the act to honor Dad. After the barbecue, try a family relay race or go for a hike.

- *Bob Kinkead's Summer "Salad" Soup (page 168)*
- *Grilled Rosemary Flank Steak (page 205)*

- *Annie Somerville's Summer Beans with Cherry Tomatoes and Tarragon (page 177)*
- *Orzo Salad (page 89)*
- *Shortbread Tea Cookies (page 235) with watermelon wedges*

Seashore Dinner

This is the perfect way to relax after a swim or a walk on the beach. Eat this meal at a table decorated with seashells, and everyone will wish that summer lasted all year long.

- *Goat Hill Farm Tomatoes with Double Basil Vinaigrette (page 179)*
- *Allen Susser's Pan-Roasted Red Snapper with Orange and Mango Salsa (page 217)*
- *Steamed rice*
- *Apricot Cake with Apricot Sauce (page 251)*

HEALTHY TIMESAVERS
Fresh Starts

How do you get kids through those starving moments just before dinner is served? Put some cut-up fresh veggies or sliced fruit on the table to nibble on. They taste even better when they come from the farmer's market or your own garden. Vary the fruits and veggies with the season:

- shelled peas
- celery sticks
- cauliflower florets
- sliced melon
- carrot sticks
- broccoli florets
- cherry tomatoes

FaLl

Soccer Team Party

This meal is a great way to keep the excitement of the game going. Everything can be ready before you leave for the game. Show the team colors proudly in your table decorations.

- *Fiesta Salsa (page 113) and tortilla chips*
- *Rick Bayless's Tomato, Rice, and Beef Casserole (page 206)*
- *Bibb lettuce with Mustard Vinaigrette (page 175)*
- *Ice cream sundaes—make your own for fun*

First Day of School Supper

Make a memorable dinner to kick off the new school year. Take a little extra time to talk about the first day and goals for the year. You can make the meal ahead of time and do the grilling at the last minute.

- *Hummus (page 95) with cut-up veggies*
- *Todd English's Grilled Chicken Marinated in Yogurt and Herbs with Tomato Chutney (page 194)*
- *Steamed Basmati Rice (page 78)*
- *Lisa's Angel Cake for All Seasons (page 246) with Chocolate Sauce (page 238)*

Harvest-Time Farmer's Market Dinner

There are few pleasures greater than a trip to the farmer's market on a crisp fall morning. Fill your basket with the bounty of the harvest.

- *Nora Pouillon's Roasted Butternut Squash Soup (page 170)*
- *Sautéed Sea Bass with Mushroom Ragout (page 219)*
- *Roasted Parslied New Potatoes (page 205)*
- *Jasper White's Pear Crisp (page 243)*

WiNtEr

Fireside Dinner

Put on some music and have a cozy gathering around the fireplace. Great after a winter day of ice skating and sledding. The warm heartiness of the ragout contrasts well with the light dessert.

- *Winter Chicken Stewed Mushrooms and Pearl Onion (page 198)*
- *Puree of Winter Vegetables (page 53)*
- *Multigrain bread*
- *Orange on Orange (page 229)*

Chinese New Year Dinner

Bring in the Chinese New year with this festive meal. Decorate the table with a Chinese theme and read about the different foods that come from China. It is lots of fun to eat the meal with chopsticks.

- *Spinach, Orange, and Almond Salad with Soy-Lime Vinaigrette (page 176)*
- *Shrimp Stir-Fry with Chinese Cabbage, Carrots, and Broccoli (page 222)*
- *Steamed rice*
- *Fresh pineapple spears with Heavenly Meringue Cookies (page 234)*

Cure-All Dinner

When a cold or the flu bug attacks, strike back with this restorative dinner. It is good for whatever ails you—and delicious, too.

- *My Mother's Chicken Soup (page 163)*
- *Joyce Goldstein's Orrechiette with Broccoli Rabe (page 203)*
- *Sliced Bananas with Butterscotch Pudding (page 239)*

GoRdON sINcLAIR'S ToP TEn FAmILy TaBLE TiPs

Knowing about manners and being polite is a part of the whole food experience, says Gordon Sinclair, owner of Gordon's, one of Chicago's most popular restaurants. "Manners are expressions of kindness, originally set up so that people did not offend," he says. A person with tremendous style and with a big heart, Gordon has traveled across the country as a teacher of manners and etiquette, and he says that these kind ways at the table are "as important as knowing how to tie a tie."

1. Be at home at least ten minutes before dinnertime and come to the table when called.
2. Turn off the television and let the answering machine answer calls during mealtime.
3. Say "please" and "thank you."
4. Don't complain about the food at the table.
5. Say something nice. Never, ever argue.
6. Pass to your right with your left hand.
7. Accept what is passed to you, pass it on, or place it in the center of the table.
8. Compliment the person who cooked the meal.
9. Remain at the table until everyone has finished; ask to be excused.
10. Offer to help with the dishes or clear.

Lasting Links: Appreciation and Thanks

When we eat a meal with our family, there is so much to be thankful for. Our appreciation for the food and for one another is very much a part of the total eating experience.

Encouraging expressions of gratefulness in the family sets a warm and supportive tone for each meal. Parents can show a good example by thanking their kids for helping to prepare dinner or set the table. There are different ways of showing our gratitude for the wonderful food on the table. These shared times are a wonderful opportunity to show respect and appreciation for one another and for the freshness and variety of the food that promotes

---

FAMILY FUN

Variations on a Theme

The calendar year offers many opportunities to create meals around a certain theme. For example, you might decide to create several meals on the theme of "Foods of Many Cultures." One evening could feature Thai dishes, and another Italian or Middle Eastern. Have one or two members take the lead in choosing the theme. They can select the menu and shop for the meal. Encourage the family to decorate and dress for the theme as well. Other themes might be:

- Cinco de Mayo Fiesta
- Food Pyramid Picnic
- Valentine's Day Dinner
- Spring Garden Party
- Wild West Barbecue
- Columbus Day Buffet

Breaking Bread

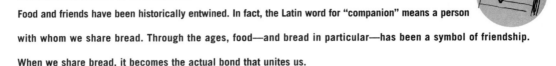

Food and friends have been historically entwined. In fact, the Latin word for "companion" means a person with whom we share bread. Through the ages, food—and bread in particular—has been a symbol of friendship. When we share bread, it becomes the actual bond that unites us.

everyone's health. Some families might say a prayer, while others might toast the person who cooked the dinner. These expressions contribute to a complete and fulfilling experience for everyone.

It is all our hope to be able to provide sustenance

good health, and a happy life for those we care about. By linking food to health and to taste and to family, we are sustaining all that is important and continuing it into the future. As we reach our goals, there is much to be thankful for.

> " The ritual of eating together helps to imbue families
> and societies at large with greater empathy and fellowship. "
> —JOYCE GOLDSTEIN, COOKBOOK AUTHOR AND CONSULTING CHEF

INDEx